NEW CITY UPON A HILL

NEW CITY UPON A HILL

A History of Columbia, Maryland

JOSEPH ROCCO MITCHELL
DAVID L. STEBENNE

THE
History
PRESS

Published by The History Press
Charleston, SC 29403
www.historypress.net

Cover image: The People Tree is Columbia's symbol. It was created by French sculptor Pierre Du Fayet and now graces Columbia's downtown lakefront. It represents Jim Rouse's dream to create a city that would "grow people." *Columbia Archives.*
Back cover: Columbia Town Center Model. This was used to convince Howard Countians that Columbia would not be just another suburban development. It worked. *Columbia Archives.*

First published 2007
Second printing 2007

Manufactured in the United States

ISBN 978.1.59629.067.9

Library of Congress Cataloging-in-Publication Data

Stebenne, David.
New city upon a hill : a history of Columbia, Maryland / David Stebenne
and Joseph Rocco Mitchell.
p. cm.
Includes bibliographical references and index.
ISBN 978-1-59629-067-9 (alk. paper)
1. Columbia (Md.)--History. 2. City
planning--Maryland--Columbia--History. 3. New
towns--Maryland--Columbia--History. I. Mitchell, Joseph R. II. Title.
F189.C68S74 2007
975.2'81--dc22
2007000648

To Helen, who makes everything possible; and to Jason, who makes everything worthwhile.

To Karen, sometime editor and constant partner.

CONTENTS

ACKNOWLEDGEMENTS

Thank you to the staff at The History Press, especially designer Deborah Silliman Wolfe and editors Jenny Kaemmerlen and Deborah Carver.

The following organizations and people played important roles in the making of this book. We acknowledge their contributions and express gratitude for them:

The Columbia Archives, Columbia, Maryland; the Howard County Historical Society, Ellicott City, Maryland; and the Howard County Public Library System for the location and use of materials.

The department of history, Ohio State University, Columbus, Ohio, for a grant that covered the cost of our index compilation.

Sheila Bodell for compiling the index.

William Finley, Daniel Toomey and Jack Bridner, who read a chapter and offered suggestions.

Manse Blackford, Stephen Hall and Jon Rak, who read the entire manuscript and offered suggestions.

The people who consented to be interviewed and provided a human touch to the Columbia story—a complete list of their names can be found on the notes page.

Helen Buss Mitchell and Karen Simonian, who proofread every word and offered valuable suggestions for improvement, and Helen Buss Mitchell, who managed the computer side of the project.

Jason Christopher Mitchell, who offered important technological expertise in the audio-visual and computer arenas.

Thomas Bartholomew and Andrew Nystrom, research assistants at Ohio State University, for locating and copying articles and other materials.

Jeff Bronow at the Howard County Planning and Zoning Office for useful demographic data.

Lawrence Madaras, who offered materials and suggestions.

ACKNOWLEDGEMENTS

The following people and institutions provided the images contained in this volume:
    Barbara Kellner, Robin Emrich and Jeannette Agro at the Columbia Archives
    Jane Usero at Enterprise Community Partners, Inc.
    Barbara Nicklas and Ann Ford at General Growth Properties
    Farida Guzdar and Quent Kardos at Howard Community College
    Randy Clay at the Howard County Office of Planning and Zoning
    Sheila Tolliver at the Howard County Office of the County Council
    Sharon L. Sopp at Howard County General Hospital
    Wylene Burch at Howard County Center of African American Culture
    James Moody at the Maryland Department of Business & Economic Development
    Oakland Mills Community Association
    Maggie Brown and Robert Tennenbaum
    Lloyd Knowles and Liz Bobo
    Betty Caldwell
    Ken Ulman

And finally, special thanks to:
    Barbara Kellner, director; Robin Emrich, archivist; and Jeanette Agro, assistant archivist, of the Columbia Archives, who for more than a year shared their space, materials and most importantly their love of Columbia with us. Without them, this book would not have been possible. Our gratitude is unmeasurable, our respect eternal.

    Robert Tennenbaum, Columbia's chief architect/planner and Columbia pioneer for forty years, who read every word, offered corrections and suggestions and filled us with respect for the city he imbued with so much love and devotion. We and the people of Columbia owe him a great deal.

INTRODUCTION

One may wonder why a city only forty years old needs a history, but Columbia, Maryland, is no ordinary place. When Columbia opened in 1967, it was hailed as a great experiment in urban development that would improve on earlier model city creations in Europe and the United States. Columbia was a city whose developer promised large tracts of public open space, with well-planned communities consisting of nine villages, each with two or more neighborhoods. There would be a Town Center, anchored by a man-made lake and surrounded by residential and commercial properties, with an enclosed shopping mall. Columbia was also to be a racially open city at a time when few places in Maryland were. While it looked to some like a well-organized suburban development, Columbia clearly was much more than that. It was a city built on nearly fifteen thousand acres of farmland located within the Baltimore-Washington corridor, and soon had the look, feel and spirit of a mid-sized American urban center. And Columbia was not created solely for its own sake; it was to be a model for others to learn from and copy—a new "city upon a hill," to use Puritan leader John Winthrop's memorable phrase.

Winthrop used those words to describe the Massachusetts Bay colony, which he and other Puritan settlers from England founded in 1630. To Winthrop, the phrase meant a society that would be pleasing to both God and man. It was a society that also welcomed the accumulation of wealth as a sign of God's bestowing his blessing upon his chosen people.

Columbia possessed those same aspirations from the start. It was intended to be both a model urban center and an experiment in free enterprise capitalism. The parallel extends, too, to both communities' founding fathers. James Rouse, like John Winthrop, was a man whose life was guided by deeply held religious beliefs, although Rouse's were broader and more inclusive than Winthrop's. And so, for all of these reasons, we have appropriated Winthrop's famous phrase as the title for this book.

This book has two major objectives: to present a narrative history of Columbia, Maryland, and to assess Columbia's accomplishments as it approaches its fortieth anniversary in June 2007. We also felt that two ancillary subjects had to be explored:

Howard County's history and James Rouse's life. Without the county's approval, Columbia never would have been born, and so a consideration of Howard County's history as well as Columbia's was needed to explain how each has been shaped by the other. In keeping with that view, the book's first chapter briefly covers the county's history before Rouse changed it. Columbia's story also cannot be separated from James Rouse's life; thus, we include two biographical chapters dealing with the years before he began Columbia. The remaining chapters trace Columbia's development, with Jim Rouse's life and the history of the company that bore his name interwoven throughout. We hope you enjoy this approach we take in telling Columbia's rich and rewarding story.

1.

HOWARD COUNTY BEFORE COLUMBIA

Its location in the mountainous region of Elkridge, and overlooking the Patapsco River, and surrounding country combines in a high degree, the beautiful and picturesque in scenery.
Headmistress Almira Hart Lincoln Phelps, of the Patapsco Female Institute, describing the Ellicott City area, 1854

The Chesapeake Bay region had long been inhabited by various native peoples when European settlement began there in the mid-seventeenth century. The area up to that point had never been a permanent home to any one people, but the founding of the Maryland colony by English settlers in 1634 soon changed that pattern. By the turn of the eighteenth century, pioneering types had migrated from the initial Maryland settlements farther south into what is today Howard County.

Howard County's Colonial History

Howard County did not legally exist until 1851. Prior to then, it was often added to Anne Arundel County or Baltimore County. This is true of most Maryland counties that were created as offshoots of others.

Elkridge (formerly Elk Ridge) holds the distinction of being Howard County's oldest settlement. Because of its location on the Patapsco River, it provided late seventeenth-century tobacco farmers in the area a place from which they could ship their crop to European markets.[1] Tobacco was placed in large barrels called hogsheads and rolled through a system of rolling roads to Elk Ridge Landing.[2]

Maryland's

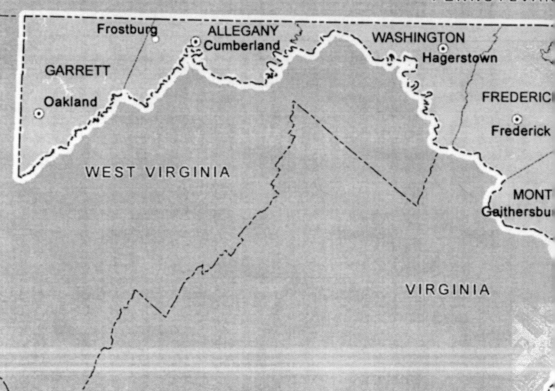

PENNSYLVAN

Frostburg

ALLEGANY
Cumberland

WASHINGTON
Hagerstown

GARRETT

FREDERIC

Oakland

Frederick

WEST VIRGINIA

MONT
Gaithersbu

VIRGINIA

MARYLAND

Department of Business &
Economic Development

217 East Redwood Street
Baltimore, MD 21202
Phone: (888) CHOOSE-MD
http://www.choosemaryland.org

N
W   E
S

0   5   10 15 20 25   Miles

0   8   16 24 32 40   Kilometers

Cities

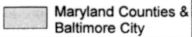

Populated Place

County Seat

State Capital &
County Seat

Maryland Counties &
Baltimore City

urisdictions

Vestminster
CARROLL
HARFORD
Bel Air
Elkton
CECIL
NEW JERSEY
BALTIMORE
Towson
Aberdeen
Ellicott City
Columbia
BALTIMORE CITY
KENT
Chestertown
MERY
HOWARD
QUEEN ANNE'S
ckville
Laurel
ANNE ARUNDEL
Annapolis
Centreville
Denton
shington DC
Upper Marlboro
PRINCE GEORGE'S
Easton
CAROLINE
TALBOT
DELAWARE
Waldorf
Prince Frederick
Plata
CHARLES
CALVERT
Cambridge
DORCHESTER
WICOMICO
Salisbury
Ocean City
Leonardtown
Lexington Park
ST. MARY'S
Princess Anne
WORCESTER
Snow Hill
SOMERSET
Crisfield
BAY
CHESAPEAKE

Labor-intensive tobacco agriculture attracted indentured servants—people both black and white—who sold their labor for a certain time period to pay off a debt. When indentures did not keep pace with demand, laws in Maryland and the rest of the American colonies sanctioned enslavement. Historian Winthrop Jordan has named this shift an "unthinking decision."[3]

The transition from indenture to chattel slavery was gradual. But from the beginning, "before white Maryland settlers associated blacks with lifetime bondage, they placed them in a category far beneath their own."[4] Necessity made slavery possible in America, and prejudice and bigotry were its co-conspirators. The Chesapeake Bay soon became a conduit for the slave trade. One of the slaves brought to Maryland was Kunta Kinte, Alex Haley's African ancestor, who arrived in "Naplis" (Annapolis) on September 29, 1767.[5] The progenitor of *Roots: The Saga of an American Family* was sold to a man from Virginia; two hundred years later, Alex Haley told his story.

In 1699 Thomas Browne, the Patuxent Ranger, was commissioned to explore the area to the farthest limits of the Patuxent River. His work took him as far west as present-day Clarksville, Columbia's westernmost area.[6] Having established a homestead there, he eventually became a neighbor of the Carroll family, who in 1711 received a ten-thousand-acre land grant and began building Doughoregan Manor, the family estate. The area's most noted family, the Carrolls earned special distinction through Charles Carroll, who would be the last living signer of the Declaration of Independence.[7] The Manor house remains Howard County's most noted landmark and is still home to the family's current descendants.

The large Carroll estate drew many, including three brothers from Belfast, Ireland—John, James and David Clark—who in 1799 signed a thirty-year tenure arrangement with the Carrolls in exchange for a house, barn and 150 acres.[8] The stature of the Clark family grew and eventually the area where they lived was named Clarksville. The late Senator James Clark, Howard County's most important political figure in the last fifty years, is descended from John Clark, one of the original brothers.

In 1772 three brothers from a Pennsylvania Quaker family, John, Joseph and Andrew Ellicott, found an ideal location in the area for a flour mill. The town that bore their name—Ellicott Mills (now Ellicott City)—became Howard County's first and only county seat. Because of their religious beliefs, the Ellicotts maintained good relations with the Native Americans and "fought for Indian education."[9] Several members of the family befriended African American Benjamin Banneker of nearby Oella, who shared their interest in mathematics and astronomy. A well-rounded, self-educated man, Banneker would in his lifetime construct a striking clock, publish an almanac and help to survey the boundaries of the nation's new capital on the banks of the Potomac River.[10] A letter he wrote to Thomas Jefferson, challenging his views on black inferiority and imploring him to work for the abolition of slavery, did not convert Jefferson, but at least made him question the assumption of racial inferiority on which slavery was based.[11] The Benjamin Banneker Historical Park and Museum in Oella stands today as a monument to his life and work.

When the American Revolution began, Charles Carroll was one of four Marylanders who were delegates to the Second Continental Congress, the first national governing

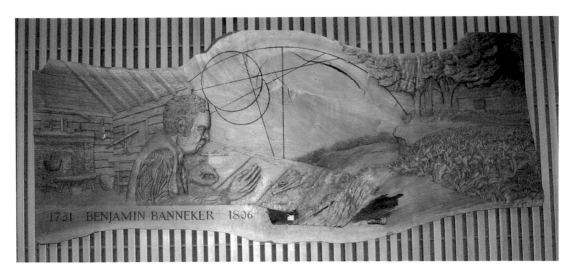

Benjamin Banneker wood sculpture. Commemorates the nation's first African American man of science, who became a friend of the Ellicott brothers. It was created by John Levering, a Columbia Association general manager. *Joseph Mitchell.*

body. During the war, Maryland's troops constituted one-third of the Southern army and fought bravely in such battles as Cowpens, Camden and finally Yorktown. "Nothing could exceed the gallantry of the Maryland Line," declared General Nathanael Greene, the army's commander.[12] This campaign earned Maryland its nickname as the "Old Line State" and greatly enhanced the reputation of one of its commanders, John Eager Howard. Although he never lived in Howard County (Baltimore city was his home), the county would be named in his honor in 1851.

Howard County's colonial period was connected to the city of Columbia when the Rouse Company "out of respect for the land…decided to draw as much as possible from the early names of places in the county."[13] Dr. Caleb Dorsey and his wife Ruth had researched and labeled on a map the properties that were acquired during the colonial period—almost four hundred of them, some owned by the Dorsey family.[14] The colonial family names of Dorsey, Hammond, Snowden, Warfield, Phelps and Talbott were among those that would find their way into the Columbia lexicon. Most of Columbia's village names, in fact, were drawn from Howard County's colonial past.

Howard County and the New American Nation

As the new nation evolved, what would become Howard County was moving along with it. A 1790 census showed the population of Anne Arundel County (of which present-day Howard County was then a part) to be 22,598—10,130 were slaves and 804 were free blacks—together almost half of the county's population.[15] This reflected the agricultural nature of the area and its accompanying system of slave labor.

The Ellicott City Railroad Museum. Located in Ellicott City on the site of the oldest railroad terminal in America, it represents Howard County's significant role in America's transportation history. *Joseph Mitchell.*

Tobacco had been replaced by wheat as the prime crop, attested to by the number of mills established in the area. In order to draw business from farmers outside the area, the Ellicotts built a road connecting their holdings with Doughoregan Manor. In 1806 the Ellicott and Carroll families jointly founded the Baltimore and Frederick Turnpike Company, which enabled them to collect tolls, ranging from two to twelve cents, for goods coming from nearby Frederick County.[16] With the establishment of the toll road, farmers could bring their grain to the mills, where it would be ground and then transported to Baltimore for national and international distribution. The Industrial Revolution was beginning to influence central Maryland.

Iron-making in the area started in the 1760s with the efforts of Caleb Dorsey at Elk Ridge Landing. Soon there were several forges and furnaces along the Patapsco, and their collective production enabled the British North American colonies to become the world's third largest exporters of raw iron.[17] Elkridge became a hub for iron forging, centered on Furnace Avenue, which still offers historical reminders of colonial iron-making. The Ellicott brothers bought the Dorsey business in the early nineteenth century and built a large home by adding on to an existing structure, which dated back to 1744. Today it houses the Elkridge Furnace Inn, where chef and owner Dan Wecker often serves up history lessons with his French fusion cuisine.

These ironworks continued to produce through the Civil War, which helped give the North the industrial edge that was crucial to its success. Paper and textile mills also contributed to the economic diversity of the Patapsco River.

20

A key factor in the valley's continued economic boom was the country's first railroad. Baltimore City, founded in 1729, had replaced Elkridge and Annapolis as the state's leading port. However, some Baltimore businessmen feared that competition from New York's Erie Canal and the about-to-be-built Chesapeake and Ohio Canal might "divert the city's valuable western trade."[18] On February 27, 1827, a group of city businessmen petitioned the state legislature for a charter to build a railroad to the west. It was granted and three years later, on May 24, 1830, the first regular railroad passenger service in the country was established with a thirteen-mile stretch of tracks that connected Baltimore with Ellicott Mills. Within five years, the railroad connected Baltimore with the nation's capital; later it expanded to Harper's Ferry, Virginia, and other points west.

The prestige that Ellicott Mills received as a vital part of the Baltimore and Ohio (B&O) Railroad led to a petition requesting that the Maryland General Assembly separate the Howard District from the remainder of Anne Arundel County. The petition documented that the growth of the area and the poor roads connecting it with the county seat in Annapolis made conducting government business difficult for the people of the Howard District.[19] Recorded in the Acts of 1838, the petition was turned into law by the legislature in the following year. In 1851 another petition and lawmaking process made the Howard District Maryland's twenty-first county, with Ellicott Mills as the county seat. With its own identity at last, the town became a chartered city in 1867, and was renamed Ellicott City."[20]

Slavery in Maryland

Slavery continued throughout Maryland during the antebellum period, especially in the southern and Eastern Shore counties, where large plantations grew labor-intensive crops. Slavery existed in the northern and western counties but was not as prevalent. Howard County, in the center of the state, seemed caught between these two worlds.

In the 1860 national census—Howard County's first—the county had 13,338 people: 9,081 whites, 2,862 slaves and 1,395 free blacks.[21] The large percentage of the latter reflected a trend that had been going on in Maryland since 1790. By 1860 the state's free black population had grown to 83,942, almost on a par with the slave population.[22] Free black residents lived under duress in Maryland—a second-class existence at best—fraught with dangers for those who attempted to break out of that rigidly enforced status.

One of the reasons for the rise in the number of free blacks in Maryland was the growing number of masters who had emancipated their slaves. As a state with divided loyalties, Maryland chronicled both charitable acts of manumission as well as heinous examples of internal slave trading, both intrastate and interstate. Slaves from central Maryland were sometimes sold to Maryland's southern and Eastern Shore counties, where the plantation system was still the order of the day. Frederick Douglass, a native son of the Eastern Shore's Talbot County, spoke of the horrors of plantation slavery. Today the plantation where he toiled is an archaeological site where people are attempting to uncover remnants of the slave culture that existed there.[23] Coincidentally, Talbot County would later become home to James W. Rouse, Columbia's founder.

Between 1830 and 1840, the estimated sales of slaves in the five southern counties—Anne Arundel (including Howard), Prince George's, Charles, Calvert and St. Mary's—amounted to 12 percent of the area's slave population.[24] Thus, Maryland's and Howard County's declining slave population could be attributed to both altruistic and abominable causes.

Wherever slavery existed, there were those who risked life and limb to escape from its bonds, and there were always some brave souls, both black and white, willing to provide assistance during the flight to freedom. A loose network of safe houses developed that came to be called the Underground Railroad. Harriet Tubman, an escaped slave from Dorchester County, Maryland, was the Railroad's most noted conductor. With Maryland's large free black population, a significant number of sympathetic whites and a favorable geographical location, the state became an important link in this freedom route. Evidence that Harriet Tubman led fugitive slaves through the county on their way North has prompted the Howard County Center of African American Culture to begin conducting tours of the sites in the county that were a part of its Underground Railroad experiences.[25]

The Civil War

Maryland's (and Howard County's) divided loyalties in the North-South crisis that would lead to the Civil War were reflected in the presidential election of 1860. John Breckenridge, a Southern Democrat and the most Secessionist of the four candidates, received 45.9 percent of the state's popular vote; John Bell of the Constitutional Union Party, which was created as a Southern-oriented save-the-Union third party, garnered 45.1 percent of the vote; the two major party candidates, Democrat Stephen A. Douglas and Republican Abraham Lincoln, received 6.4 percent and 2.5 percent respectively. When Secession came in 1861, Maryland's reaction would become crucial, given the state's strategic location. In Baltimore, an incident occurred that was interpreted by many as showing the area's Southern leanings: on April 19, a regiment of Federal troops passing through the city on their way to the nation's capital was attacked by a mob, and a riot ensued, resulting in deaths on both sides. Conventional wisdom has viewed this as an example of strong support for the Southern cause, an opinion challenged by Maryland historians Scott Sheads and Daniel Toomey. In their 1997 book *Baltimore During the Civil War*, they state that immigrants from Germany and Ireland entering the city in large numbers since 1840, and having nothing to gain from slavery, gradually diluted the city's support for the South. Northern businessmen coming to the city during this period also had little interest in Secession.[26]

If Maryland had left the Union, the nation's capital would have been entirely surrounded by hostile territory. Preventing this from occurring and keeping the lines of transportation and communication open between North and South were major priorities for Abraham Lincoln and his new administration. Union forces were sent to keep the important transportation lines open, especially the Baltimore and Ohio Railroad; and Confederate forces did their best to keep that from occurring. It was these two forces working against each other that brought the Civil War to Howard County.

Union troops were sent to protect the railroad lines and bivouacked at Relay and Elk Ridge Heights, the former being an important station on the B&O line. On May 11, they had their first victory with the capture of the Winans Steam Gun in Ellicott Mills, preventing it from reaching Southern hands. The gun, made by Ross Winans, a Baltimorean and an ardent Southern sympathizer, was being shipped to the Confederacy disguised as a piece of agricultural equipment. In enemy hands it could have been a formidable weapon, with the ability to throw two hundred balls a minute or launch a single hundred-pound cannonball.[27] According to Howard County historian Daniel Toomey, "it could have been the first weapon of mass destruction or a hoax, as it was never tested."[28] Its capture made it nothing more than an interesting footnote in Civil War history.

When hostilities began, Maryland's border state identity was apparent. Generally, the state's cities favored the Union side while the countryside supported the Confederacy.[29] Fortunately, Howard County remained on the periphery of Maryland's Civil War battles; the only conflict on its soil turned out to be nothing more than an unplanned skirmish. When Robert E. Lee's army was moving though Maryland into Pennsylvania in 1863 (the battle of Gettysburg would be their ultimate destination), J.E.B. Stuart's cavalry was also in Maryland, desperately trying to find them. While attempting to do this, they accidentally ran into a Union force near Cooksville. Shots were exchanged, but nothing of consequence occurred, as Stuart's primary objective was to join Lee and the main army.[30]

In 1864 war came close to Howard County when the battle of Monocacy occurred in nearby Frederick County, resulting in trainloads of wounded being brought into Ellicott Mills on their way to Baltimore.[31] A feared Confederate attack on Ellicott Mills and Baltimore was averted when the Confederate army instead moved toward Washington; again, Howard County was spared.

However, Confederate troops remained in the area and did their best to make life miserable for their Union opponents. Part of a Confederate campaign against Washington resulted in a series of forays, known as the Johnson-Gilmor Raid, which brought the war to the Howard County countryside. Maryland natives General Bradley T. Johnson—a descendant of Thomas Johnson, the state's first governor—and Major Harry Gilmor and his Second Maryland Battalion of Confederate cavalrymen conducted a series of attacks, taking them through Frederick, Carroll, Baltimore, Harford and Howard Counties, disrupting transportation and communication lines. During one of these forays, Johnson stopped for lunch at Doughoregan Manor, the home of John Lee Carroll, a former Maryland governor and a member of Howard County's most noted family.[32]

Howard County's last connection with the Civil War was a sad one. After President Abraham Lincoln's assassination in April 1865, his body was transported from the

Patapsco Female Institute, located on a hill overlooking Ellicott City. In the nineteenth century, it served as a school for Northern and Southern students. *Source unknown.*

nation's capital to its final resting place in Springfield, Illinois. On its way to Baltimore, the train passed through nearby Relay. The man who had led the country through its greatest crisis was carried in a private rail car pulled by a B&O locomotive, the company that did much to ensure the Union victory he had worked so hard to achieve.

Free but not Equal

During the war years, Maryland took steps to deal with the slavery question. Since Lincoln's 1863 Emancipation Proclamation did not affect states that had not seceded, Maryland would have to act. An 1864 Constitutional Convention, controlled by a strong Unionist contingency, enacted a section abolishing slavery in the state. However, the constitution had to be ratified by a popular vote of the citizenry, which proved to be very close. Union soldiers were able to "control" voting on the Eastern Shore.[33] Along with the absentee ballots cast by Union soldiers, this provided the tight margin of victory for the abolitionist side.[34]

By 1867 Democrats had gained political control of the state, and a new constitution made clear that the abolition of slavery was as far as Maryland would go regarding freedmen's rights. It was only through ratification of the Fifteenth Amendment to the federal Constitution in 1870 that black males received the legal right to vote. Numerous attempts by the state's politicos to disenfranchise the freedmen failed, and in many elections "the rate of Negro voter participation was, from the beginning, about equal to that of whites."[35] This was due to the efforts of the state's Republicans.

But the vote alone could not keep discrimination away from Maryland's black residents. A systematic racial segregation eventually referred to as "Jim Crow" came to Maryland in the postwar years, making the state very much like those that had seceded in 1861. The Jim Crow era would last until 1954, when the U.S. Supreme Court's decision in *Brown v. Board of Education of Topeka, Kansas*, marked the beginning of segregation's demise.

During the post–Civil War era, blacks usually depended on their own institutions for support and survival. The black churches in Howard County provided nourishment for the body as well as the soul. And when space for black schools was not available, the churches played an educational role as well. In the 1950s and 1960s, they served as home bases for civil rights rallies.[36] The black churches also provided a leadership platform for its ministers, many of whom became temporal as well as spiritual spokesmen, a tradition followed by Martin Luther King Jr., Ralph Abernathy and Jesse Jackson on the national level, and in Howard County by Reverend John Holland.

The Flood of 1868

The Patapsco River gave the area much of the bounty that attracted people to central Maryland. But like all rivers, in a short time it could take away all that it gave. Such was the case in 1868, when the area experienced what many referred to as the "Great Flood."

Two years earlier, a major flood had occurred in the Patapsco Valley, but it paled in comparison with the one about to devastate the area. On July 24, the skies darkened and the rains began to fall. No one in the valley seemed concerned, but in the river's westernmost region, eighteen inches of rain had fallen and the river was beginning to swell. When it reached the narrow valley near Ellicott City, factories and mills were destroyed, with their equipment carried down toward Baltimore.[37] Homes along the river had no chance, and those who were caught inside were swept away. Some of the victims were found near Baltimore, almost fifteen miles from Ellicott City.[38]

More than fifty people lost their lives in the flood, and beyond this human toll was the destruction of the area's growing industrial plants. Plans were made to rebuild, and by 1878 much had been accomplished. But changes that were taking place west of Maryland doomed the Patapsco Valley's attempted renaissance. The discovery in the Midwest of rich sources of raw materials (oil, iron ore, copper, lead, coal)—and the building of railroads to tie them to eastern markets—sealed the fate of heavy industry in the region.[39] The Industrial Revolution's center moved northward and westward, except for the textile mills, which moved southward.[40] Thus, the Patapsco River Valley would have to be content with its role as progenitor.[41]

Into the New Millennium

Howard County historian Joetta Cramm observed that the county "entered the twentieth century without much fanfare. It remained a rural county with good farmers, hard workers, and a satisfaction with the status quo. The outside world seemed to bypass the county."[42] Population statistics bear this out: in 1910, its white population was 16,106; by 1940 it had increased only to 17,175. The black population reflected the same condition in 1910—3,772; in 1950—3,858.[43]

In 1867 Ellicott Mills had become an incorporated city with a new name: Ellicott City. It also did a thriving business in the liquor trade, since the town was the one "wet" spot in an otherwise "dry" Howard County.[44] When Prohibition became the law of the land in 1920, Ellicott City lost its major source of revenue and began to tax its citizens to make up the shortfall. A taxpayers' revolt led to the revocation of the city's incorporation in 1935.

Howard County felt the pain caused by the Depression, which also brought a migration of people from Appalachia in search of jobs. This new population created problems, which were exacerbated during the World War II years, when clashes between the new locals and army personnel on leave from nearby Fort Meade caused its commander, for a time, to declare Ellicott City off-limits to all military personnel.

During the war, two interesting war-related events came to Howard County. The first was the creation of the first camp for conscientious objectors located at a former Civilian Conservation Corps (CCC) camp in the Patapsco Valley State Park. The work assigned to them was the completion of unfinished CCC projects.[45] The second was the use of German POWs by Howard County farmers during the war. First housed at the Fort Meade brig, and later at the Howard County jail, the POWs would be picked up and brought to a farm, where they would work all day (for twenty-five cents); two meals a day were provided by the farmers. Maryland historian Jack Bridner recounted that Earl and Lydia Sauter, his aunt and uncle, were involved in this program, and when the prisoners who worked for them returned to Germany after the war, the Sauters corresponded with them for more than a decade.[46]

After the Second World War, Howard County began to experience small growing pains, when the national census reported that the county's population had increased from 17,175 in 1940 to 23,119 in 1950, a 25 percent increase. A major cultural event occurred in the 1950s when a movie production company arrived in Ellicott City to film *The Goddess*, starring Kim Stanley, Lloyd Bridges and Patty Duke, with a screenplay by Patty Chayefsky. It told the story of a successful but aging movie star, returning to her somewhat run-down hometown. "Two hundred residents were employed as extras in a movie that ironically reflected the plight of Ellicott City."[47]

Something was clearly needed to give Howard County a jolt and in a short time, a natural disaster would forever change the course of its history. However, in the postwar

Ellicott City today. The county seat has survived floods, fires and a state of decline.
A renewal campaign begun in the 1970s brought it back to life. People come today to
experience its blend of the old and the new. *Joseph Mitchell.*

years, no one in the area would have believed that the county would soon become home
to a city of 100,000 people.

Into the Future

In 1972 Hurricane Agnes created a flood in Ellicott City that rivaled its 1868
predecessor. Some citizens decided to use this as an opportunity not only to repair
the damage, but also to create a new Ellicott City, which would marry its quaintness
to the modern world. In 1976 a campaign entitled "Ellicott City: New Life for an
Old Town" began. Within a few years, the city had been resurrected. This makeover
has succeeded so spectacularly that in its August 2006 issue, *Money* magazine
voted Columbia/Ellicott City the country's fourth best small city in which to live,
describing the area as possessing the "convenience of planned community; charm
of old town."[48]

2.

JAMES ROUSE

MARYLAND SON, 1914–1945

When life gives you lemons, make lemonade.
A favorite Jim Rouse aphorism

The history of Columbia cannot be separated from Jim Rouse's life; they are as connected as child and parent. It was his dream to prove that a city could be both humane and profitable, and Columbia would be his proving ground. A man of many contrasts, he was both an idealistic visionary and a disciple of competitive capitalism, a product of small-town rural life and a national crusader for urban reform. He had the physical appearance and demeanor of a common man, but possessed the mind of a genius as well as uncanny persuasive skills. He was a man of this world, yet possessed a deep, abiding religious faith that guided much of his adult life. To the general public, he was James W. Rouse, businessman extraordinaire; to those who knew him, including many Columbians, he was just plain Jim, a name he clearly preferred.

This man of many contrasts led a life that resembled a twentieth-century odyssey, a long journey with many ports of call, fraught with hardships and full of triumphs, moments of disappointment and extreme elation. His life's journey began on Maryland's Eastern Shore, and his experiences there never left him.

The Easton Experience

In 1914 Easton, Maryland, was a small town of three thousand people located in Talbot County on Maryland's upper Eastern Shore in close proximity to the Chesapeake Bay. It was a place trying to adapt to the new twentieth-century world, a process made difficult because of its strong ties to its traditional rural Southern past. Many of its citizens preferred to look back to the Civil War era instead of forward to the future. This condition, referred to as the "Lost Cause" syndrome, was epitomized by Easton's erection of a statue memorializing the Confederate war dead from Talbot County in 1916.[49] As far as race was concerned, Easton was still living in the past.

With its idyllic small-town environment and racial inequality, it seemed an unlikely hometown for a man whose name would become synonymous with shopping centers, planned cities, urban renewal and civil rights. But it was into this setting that James Wilson Rouse was born on April 26, 1914, the fifth child of Willard Goldsmith Rouse and Lydia Robinson Rouse. A half-brother, John; three sisters, Mary Day, Dia (Lydia) and Margaret; and a four-year-old brother Willard (Bill) were his older siblings. Although Jim's legal birth name was Wilson Richardson Rouse, Bill's exclamation, "I want to name him Dimmy [Jimmy],"[50] assured the world that Jimmy he would be. This act captures the strong bond between the two brothers that would last until Bill's death in 1970. In the 1960s, Jim had his name legally changed to James Wilson Rouse.[51]

Both of Jim's parents had Harford County, Maryland roots, an area in the northern reaches of the Chesapeake Bay. His father was a Spanish-American war veteran who practiced law and dabbled in politics, once unsuccessfully running for Harford County's state's attorney. Rouse once described his father as "the most brilliant man I have ever known…[and] a fantastically well-informed man."[52] He then described his mother as "a very lovely, warm woman, very much a leader in the community, very loved by everyone."[53] Operating in their separate social worlds, the combined personae of this couple molded their youngest son.

When Willard Rouse moved his family to Easton, he eschewed a career in law and entered the volatile world of commodity buying, the products being the Eastern Shore's abundant agricultural produce. This provided his family with a solid, comfortable lifestyle, with inevitable difficult times in a "buy short, sell long" business environment. Bill Rouse recounted that his father "twice tried to corner the tomato market…[but] both times it broke him."[54] These setbacks were temporary and Willard's fortunes managed to rebound. Perhaps his father's risk-taking career inspired Jim to pursue stressful careers as mortgage banker, mall developer and model city creator.

The story of Rouse's childhood in Easton is right out of small-town Norman Rockwell Americana—childhood games, crushes on girls, part-time jobs and a fascination with nature that the Chesapeake Bay encouraged. Later, he would recount to family members his memories of having a black playmate, the son of a family servant. While not able to break down Easton's racial barriers, he was able to understand, even at an early age, the disparity in the future opportunities both would have.[55]

Two personality traits appeared early in his childhood. One was an abundance of nervous energy that made sitting still nearly impossible. The second was a bull-like tenacity that made acceptance of failure difficult. This was best exemplified during a game of "it" when in order to tag childhood friend Porter Matthews, "He dogged him right up the steps in the Matthews's house and caught him at the door of his bedroom."[56] While these two traits may have sometimes exasperated his family and

Young Jimmy Rouse and friends, Easton, Maryland. Rouse is on the far right; the rest of the people are unidentified. *Enterprise Community Partners, Inc.*

friends, his restless energy and strong-willed determination paved the way for the big dreams and successful accomplishments that would mark his professional life.

When the time came for the Rouse children to attend high school, the three girls were sent off to attend private schools in Baltimore, while the boys attended Easton High School. While there, Jim was described by a classmate as being "at the top of his class…very bright…a good speaker and has a lot of confidence coupled with ability and he read and studied a lot."[57] Despite this praise, he earned a C average for his four years at Easton High.[58] "I really wasn't a good student," he later wrote, "I didn't study very well…There have always been more important things to do somehow, so I didn't study."[59] His active imagination and the fact that he was only sixteen years old at graduation could explain his lack of academic achievement.

In extracurricular activities, Jim excelled. His popularity and leadership skills got him elected to several class presidencies. And at Easton High, he continued his lifelong interest and participation in sports by excelling in soccer, basketball and especially track, where he distinguished himself as a fast runner. Even in his later years, he was reputed to play a mean game of tennis.

He was also the founder and editor-in-chief of the school newspaper, *Belfrey Bat*. In the April 1929 edition, he contributed a short story entitled "Soft Money." In it, Joe Godie, an unemployed young man living with his loving mother, robs a bank with his friend Sammie and in the process is shot and killed by the police. As he lies dying, he says: "Tell—Mom—I had to—try something. Tell her not to forget—dad had my life—insured before he died and tell her—to get a coupla' grand—outa' that."[60] The story's content reflects several themes that were to shape Jim's later life—economic problem solving, love for others and willingness to sacrifice for them.

And it presages tragic events in his own life. In 1929 Lydia Robinson Rouse's lifelong weak heart condition forced her to move back to Harford County so that her relations there could care for her. She never returned to Easton and the following February, the family learned through a caretaker that she had died.[61] Jim's father, Willard, developed bladder cancer and was eventually transferred to Union Memorial Hospital in Baltimore for treatment. In June 1930, Jim was graduated from Easton High School; his father died in August. The following month the bank foreclosed on the family home.[62] The idyllic part of James Rouse's life in Easton had come to an abrupt end.

Acquiring an Education

Despite the grief that Jim felt at the loss of his parents, he resolved not to let it alter his plans for the future. In an interview given less than a year before his death, he talked of that trying time: "I felt I was old enough and conditioned enough to handle it, and it would be good for me. I remember feeling guilty at the time thinking, 'How can I feel this way…Why am I not distressed?' And I really wasn't."[63] His attitudes on life and death were reflected in an essay he wrote entitled "Selfishness/Unselfishness." In it he compared a good friend, whose impending death obsessed him, and his father, who continued to plan for the future. Jim contrasted his friend's "selfishness" with his father's deathbed "unselfishness" and found the latter more edifying.[64] Rouse's axiom that optimism is always preferable to pessimism became a cornerstone of his life.

But now there were practical problems to consider. The three Rouse sisters had married and needed no financial assistance. Bill had begun his studies at Johns Hopkins in Baltimore—something he would eventually defer—but Jim's future was in doubt. In his last year at Easton High, he had set his sights on Princeton, but his mediocre high school academic record put an Ivy League school out of reach. Postponing his own college studies, Bill arranged for Jim to attend the Tome School, an upscale private school in Port Deposit, Maryland, where he could improve his study skills and habits—and his grade point average. The Rouse sisters did what they could for Jim, but Bill was his sole means of support; he found employment in investment banking and insurance sales in order to meet his brotherly obligations.

Bill's contribution to Jim's welfare was incalculable. While on breaks from Tome, Jim shared a boardinghouse room in Easton with his brother. The Rouse papers contain memos from Tome requesting payment for tuition and fees, and Bill's apologetic replies accompanying a partial payment.[65] Bill also dispensed some fatherly advice to Jim as his year at Tome was coming to an end: "Best of luck to you…in your studies for this last term, please don't slack up."[66]

At Tome, Jim did "excellent work as Editor of the School paper." He also was a member of the track team. During an invitational track meet in Philadelphia known as the Penn Relays, Jim and three teammates entered a locker room to shower and found it occupied by some African American runners. They promptly turned around and left, assuming their default "Southern" mentality.[67] But that default position was about to change.

Toward the end of Jim's year at the Tome School, Director Murray Busch wrote to Bill, "I certainly wish that it were possible for you to keep Jim here for another year."[68] But economic exigencies and an opportunity for a tuition-free education in a tropical paradise conspired to provide Jim with a chance to enroll at the University of Hawaii in 1931. His sister Mary Day and her husband Bill Pryor, a naval officer, were stationed there. As an orphan, Jim was considered a navy dependent, making him eligible for a free education. A cross-country trip with two of Bill's friends in a Model T Ford preceded a voyage in steerage. Jim later estimated the cost of his trip to Hawaii in the summer of 1931 at eighty-five or ninety dollars.[69]

Jim's first impressions of Hawaii were lyrical—he was overwhelmed by its physical beauty. At the university, themes and essays drew his interest, and he wrote "The Day's Dope," a daily sports column for the school newspaper, covering both island and mainland sports topics. He was also a member of the university track team, good enough to be named "the find of the year" in the school yearbook.[70]

Hawaii's greatest influence on Jim was the gradual transformation it effected on his racial attitudes. In a class essay entitled "Notes on Hawaii," he wrote: "There was first the problem of intermarriage among the races. This crossing of the races led to the rise of a half caste class mentally and morally inferior—a potential criminal element—an offensive caste at best."[71] Yet he also told his sister Margaret: "There is more to Hawaii than its beauty…It's a great thing to go to school with Hawaiians, Orientals, Hindus, (I walked to school every morning with two princes from India) Portugese [sic], and sprinklings of many nationalities, races, and religions. We are becoming closer to the Orient every year and an understanding of its people means a lot."[72]

The first statement mirrors the kind of bigoted attitudes then prevalent in the United States. The nation's immigration policy openly discriminated against people from Southern and Eastern Europe, and Nordic supremacy was considered good science by most citizens. Jim later acknowledged that his experiences in Hawaii forever altered his thinking on race relations. An epiphany-like moment occurred during a track meet, when an exhausted Jim was helped off the track by a teammate. "A glance at the dark skin of his friend made him suddenly aware of the distance his feelings had traveled."[73] As Rouse biographer Joshua Olsen observed, "When Rouse eventually returned to his

Portrait of James Rouse, circa 1932, at eighteen years of age. *Columbia Archives.*

home state, it was with the knowledge that there was nothing natural or morally right about segregation and racial prejudice. When he became involved with shaping the built world, he would refuse to do so along racial lines."[74]

After a year in Hawaii, money problems and his failure to obtain a part-time job made Jim feel like a constant drain on his family's resources. Despite living in a tropical paradise, Jim was homesick for his family and his native soil. "A plaintif [*sic*] wail for the 'Eastern Shore'—Lord how I would love to be back," opened a letter sent to his sister Margaret.[75] He considered dropping out of school for a year in order to earn some money, but once again, a family member came to Jim's rescue.

This time Herbert Balch, Margaret's husband, was able to obtain a scholarship for Jim from the University of Virginia. Jim Rouse must have been joyful when he left Honolulu on the navy transport *Chaumont* on July 18, 1932. The first leg of his journey took him to San Francisco, then on to Norfolk, Virginia, by way of the Panama Canal. Brother Bill had to pull some strings to make the last leg of this journey possible, but after a long trip, Jim was finally home.[76]

At the University of Virginia, Jim majored in political science, taking twenty-one hours of course work (six more than the required load), which included geology, Greek and music, and earning grades that ranged from 95 to 85.[77] In a 1975 interview, Jim recalled living in a boardinghouse and working nights in a restaurant to earn some money. Bill was once again providing some financial assistance to his younger brother,[78] but Jim opted not to return to UVA. With the Depression worsening, he was determined to strike out on his own; Baltimore would become his land of opportunity.

Big City Experiences and Career Opportunities

"I came to Baltimore in the fall of 1933 and that's when the Depression really was seen on the streets," Rouse reminisced. "Every hundred feet there would be a guy selling shoe laces or pencils or apples."[79] He finally found a job parking cars at the St. Paul Garage for $13.50 a week, even though he didn't know how to drive a car. The garage manager, a redheaded Irishman named Johnny Heisman, showed him the basics.[80] Applying for a job parking cars without knowing how to drive is quintessential Jim Rouse: optimism, persuasion and hard work produce results. He never quite lost his reputation as a lousy driver.

In September of '33 Jim applied for and was admitted to the University of Maryland Law School, which was located in downtown Baltimore. He got a night job at the garage, auditing the books, and when the day auditor was fired for stealing, he assumed that job as well. For a seven-month stretch, he worked both the twelve-to-eight graveyard shift and the eight-to-five day shift, seven days a week, sleeping a few hours when he could. For a 116-hour workweek, he was paid the grand sum of twenty dollars.[81] Taking time to eat was a luxury for which he budgeted fifteen cents a day.[82] Attending law school at night after this grueling regimen trained him to function with just a few hours of sleep a day.

In 1935, while still studying law, Jim eagerly sought employment with the Federal Housing Administration, created during the New Deal years to enable more Americans to buy houses and to infuse capital into the home building industry. With the help of state politicos, he was appointed assistant clerk in the FHA's Baltimore office, beginning work on May 15, 1935.[83] A year later, he was promoted to field representative, where he was exposed to all phases of the housing industry.

One of the companies that Rouse dealt with at FHA was Guy T.O. Hollyday's Title Guarantee and Trust Company. Hollyday, who was impressed by Jim's work ethic, suggested that Jim communicate with his firm, "showing how a Title company could profit by specializing in handling FHA loans for home builders."[84] Jim always considered Hollyday a close friend who had a profound influence on his life. Guy and Jim shared Talbot County roots, with Guy's family ties dating back to late seventeenth-century Eastern Shore. The two men shared a strong, faith-based set of activism-oriented moral values, and in the 1950s, they would use them in a battle with the slumlords of Baltimore.[85]

In a detailed four-page letter to Title Guarantee, Jim laid out a program in which "your company can perform a useful and profitable service, and at the same time increase the volume of the business in which you are principally engaged at the present time."[86] A few months later, Rouse accepted an offer from the company to head their new mortgage division. His potential value to the company must have been outstanding because a year later, the company signed a contract to pay Jim a substantial sum of money after five years, in exchange for his services.[87]

During this busy time, Jim finished his degree requirements and was admitted to the Maryland bar. But his fascination with the business world ensured that he would never practice law. Instead, he met Hunter Moss, a Princeton graduate and son of a well-established Philadelphia family, who came to Baltimore to pursue a career in mortgage banking. The two ambitious young men formed a close friendship and entered into a business partnership. They formed the Moss-Rouse Company, a mortgage banking firm, which was made possible by a $20,000 investment from Moss's sister.[88] Because the firm had no capital to lend, they contacted insurance companies who were willing to underwrite the mortgages, with Moss-Rouse receiving a fee for its work. One of these insurance firms was Connecticut General Life Insurance Company (CG), a fortuitous connection for Jim Rouse. Not only did Connecticut General do business with Moss-Rouse, but it also continued this relationship with the James Rouse Company, which was formed in the 1950s when Moss and Rouse amicably parted ways. Connecticut General would later provide much of the upfront money that made Jim's future dream of a model city possible.

Personal Development

In his adult years, Christian precepts and values underlay everything that Jim Rouse did, including all of his business dealings. Reconciling those values with free enterprise capitalism was never a problem for him; when the two clashed, there

James Rouse and Hunter Moss, circa 1940. Business partners for almost twenty years, the Rouse Company was their company's successor. *Columbia Archives*.

was no doubt which one would win out. Surprisingly, these were values he did not develop from his Easton experiences. Despite attending Sunday school regularly, Rouse later wrote, "Religion was never a dominant factor in our [early] lives. It was just something that was expected of people in small town America. Then, by the time I got out of high school and away at college, religion really disappeared and played no part in my life."[89]

Shortly after arriving in Baltimore, Jim attended a service at Brown Memorial Presbyterian Church in Baltimore. Pastor Guthrie Speers delivered a sermon on why people should go to church. Jim seemed transformed: "I didn't miss a Sunday for eighteen months and I wound up joining…and eventually became an Elder in that church and that was where my faith really began to emerge."[90] Countless documents in the Columbia Archives attest to Jim's devotion to and work on behalf of the church in many areas, including fundraising. As late as 1953, he was invited to speak at Brown Memorial on the subject of world federalism.[91]

During his Baltimore years, Jim's political philosophy also took shape. Long interested in political matters, he began to formulate a set of ideals that led him to become a lifetime member of the Democratic Party, inspired perhaps by his FHA work with ordinary people buying their first home. A rejected article, entitled "A Young Man Votes," which he submitted to the *Baltimore Evening Sun* in 1936, expressed the belief that the economic "rugged individualism" of the past had made the country powerful, but its excesses had helped cause the Depression. While he considered economic incentive as "a foundation of our economic life," he believed that it was something that had to be controlled. He concluded with a belief "in the present [F.D. Roosevelt] administration because it has refused to accept as inevitable and irremedial the disastrous results of depression…and has earnestly sought a solution."[92] Membership in the Associated Democratic Clubs of Baltimore further reflected his New Deal liberal leanings.

In his first six years in Baltimore, Jim Rouse had parked cars, audited books, attended law school, worked for the FHA, headed a mortgage department and ultimately co-founded a mortgage banking company—all at a time when economic opportunities were scarce. In 1939 he was only twenty-five years old. But he wasn't finished marking his place in the world, and the best was yet to come.

Banking, Marriage and World War

Jim Rouse's frenetic Baltimore years had left little time for anything but work and law school. But with the establishment of Moss-Rouse, he began to develop a social life with a small group of people, most of whom were friends of his new partner. Among the women who were part of the group was Elizabeth Winstead, whom everyone called Libby. While living in New York, she "had come under the influence of Harry Emerson Fosdick,"[93] who, in a time when fundamentalism dominated Christian thinking, preached a liberal form of Christianity that demanded real personal commitment from its communicants. Using the soon-to-be famous Riverside

Admiral John Towers's staff in the Pacific Theater during World War II. Consisting of business leaders, many would become investors in Jim Rouse's postwar financial projects. Rouse is in the center of the photograph. *Enterprise Community Partners, Inc.*

Church (built by John D. Rockefeller Sr., himself a Fosdick disciple), Fosdick became a nationally known author and speaker.

Libby's strong faith and interest in making the world a better place must have appealed to Jim, as he was undergoing a similar experience with Guthrie Speers at Brown Memorial Church. Jim and Libby eventually began to see each other, and were married on May 3, 1941. Regarding Libby's influence on Jim, Joshua Olsen has written: "Libby's reflections became an integral part of Rouse's own philosophies, especially her musings on social issues, the nature of family life, and the place of religion in all of this."[94] This vision would bear fruit when the city of Columbia was planned and developed in the 1960s.

Jim's marriage and the initial success of Moss-Rouse signaled smooth sailing ahead, but Moss-Rouse was disrupted by World War II, since practically everyone in the company was under thirty-five. In a short time, Hunter Moss joined the marines and Jim Rouse the navy. Harry Batchelor, the company's elder statesman, was put in charge for the duration of the war. The two founders drew up wills in case either of them didn't survive.

Jim's navy preparation began at the U.S. Naval Air Station at Quonset Point, Rhode Island. In a letter written to his siblings, he described the rigorous training as "a mad house of rush, rush, rush," but later in the letter opined that the job that they were doing "makes you have faith in our way of life."[95] After completing training, Jim was deferred from active duty because Libby was pregnant. On July 4, 1942, Lydia Robinson Rouse was born; she would be called Robin. Shortly after her birth, Jim shipped out to the Pacific.

Assigned to the staff of Admiral John Towers, a man at the forefront of naval aviation, Jim quickly rose to the very top echelons of the admiral's staff, where he found himself working with a group of men, like himself, from the world of business. Some of these war buddies eventually found their way into future Rouse enterprises. Jim also became a shark-like poker player, who won a lot more than he lost. Sam Neel, a participant in the games, attributed this to "a dramatic memory" and the fact that "he stayed sober."[96]

While the war went on, Hunter and Jim kept in touch with the company business as best they could, trying to plot Moss-Rouse's future. Jim was discharged first with a Bronze Star, a commendation from Secretary of the Navy James Forrestal and some new friends and future business associates.

3.

JAMES ROUSE

URBAN VISIONARY, 1945–1960

Our cities are in deep trouble. They are worn out, obsolete, ugly and inefficient.
James Rouse in a 1959 speech

The end of the war proved to be Jim Rouse's coming-out party. His war experiences brought him into contact with a group of men who would become some of the nation's future business and financial leaders. Working with them must have given him an aura of confidence that made him think he had the ability to take his hopes and dreams to a higher level. He was not yet sure what they were, but he knew that the local stage would not be a large enough platform. The Maryland son was about to become a national leader.

Working on a National Stage

An ad in the Baltimore papers in 1945—"To those whom we had the pleasure of serving prior to the war and to the many others, whom we may hope we may serve in the future"—declared that the Moss-Rouse Company was "back in business." The war must have energized Rouse, who seems to have spent the years away from the company plotting out a grander future for it.

When Moss was still awaiting discharge from military service, Rouse wrote him a letter on October 25, 1945, outlining his ideas for the company's future growth and development. Admitting that he sometimes gave the impression of recklessly seeking big things for the company and a willingness to sacrifice whatever was necessary to achieve them, Rouse assured Moss that he was only interested in what would be in the company's best interests, and suggested branching out into the fields of commercial and industrial mortgages. Rouse was thinking big, perhaps too big for his partner, who replied, "My only plea is to plan and build the foundation before we move into new fields."[97]

Rouse was ready to act out his postwar business activities on a national stage. A course in public speaking honed his oratorical skills, and he soon became a compelling and persuasive speechmaker. Through mentor and friend Guy Hollyday, who had served as a director of Moss-Rouse since its inception, Rouse also began to take an active role in the affairs of the Mortgage Bankers Association (MBA). He wrote an article, "The Mortgage Man's Role in G.I. Financing," which was published in the July 1946 issue of *Appraisal Journal*. Rouse gave a speech on the same subject at the MBA's Chicago meeting on May 16, 1946. There he admonished his colleagues to deal fairly and honestly with the returning veterans as they became homeowners perhaps for the first time. It was not only the right thing to do; it would be profitable as well. Articles written about the speech appeared in the *Chicago Daily Tribune*, the *Baltimore American* and the *New York Times*, giving Jim the national stage he was seeking and proving to him that his spoken words could be as persuasive as his written ones would be. In the *Appraisal Journal* article, he described the returning veterans as "the most active, vital, and vociferous group in this country," foreseeing "a social, political, and an economic aspect of tremendous potential."[98]

This article also broached a subject that would dominate Rouse's 1950s activities and, indeed, the rest of his life—the plight of American cities: "Mortgage bankers, he said, have not been leaders in attacking such problems as slums, blight, and obsolete building codes. They have not taken the initiative with respect to the improvement of design, livability, or neighborhood planning."[99] Jim Rouse would spend the rest of his life working to change those conditions.

On September 15, 1948, an article in the *Baltimore American* entitled "First Development of a Blighted Area by Private Industry Is Planned Here" mentioned the formation of a committee to study a section of Baltimore known as the "Fifth Regiment Armory Area" to determine how to improve it. The committee used the Federal Redevelopment Act (a precursor of what would become the federal urban renewal program) to purchase the land that would be resold at market value and used for redevelopment purposes. This land was eventually used to construct the Herbert O'Connor Office Building and a State Highway Administration Building.[100] A significant fact about this endeavor is that it was initiated by people in the private sector.[101] James Rouse was cited as chairman of the group, which consisted of some of Baltimore's leading businessmen, including his good friend, Guy Hollyday. This early campaign against urban blight marked the beginning of Jim Rouse's active involvement in improving the quality of life for Baltimore and its citizens.

Next, with Hollyday providing the connection, Rouse joined the Citizen's Planning and Housing Association (CPHA). This group had been formed in 1941 by Frances Morton, a young woman who had dedicated her life to improving Baltimore's blighted areas. As a young girl, she had attended a Sunday school class taught by Hollyday. Rouse brought his knowledge, energy and newly honed public relations skills to the group, which soon gained national attention for what became known as the Baltimore Plan.

Moss-Rouse Headquarters,
1953. Built on Saratoga Street
in Baltimore, it was reputed
to be Baltimore's first office
building built in the modern
style. *Columbia Archives.*

The plan was easy to describe but challenging to implement. A slum area would be identified, inspections would be held by various city departments (housing, sanitation, police, etc.) and violations of existing codes would be enforced, with the housing court as the final step to resolve disputes. Mayor Thomas D'Alessandro Jr. endorsed the plan, and its originality led the National Municipal League to name Baltimore as one of its All-American cities in 1953.[102]

An interesting and successful program that came from the Baltimore Plan was the Fight Blight Fund, set up by Guy Hollyday with the support of some of the city's business leaders, including Jim Rouse. Money was raised to set up a fund that would lend money to poor people who could not pay for necessary repairs to their homes. The fund was revolving in nature because the people who borrowed from it would pay it back with monthly payments they could afford. Then the money would be lent to others in need. The program was not only successful in helping people save their homes, but also instilled in them a strong desire to keep up their home environment and to improve it with further changes.[103]

However, the Baltimore Plan initiators soon learned that their overall approach was too slow and cumbersome, as well as subject to the vagaries of Baltimore political patronage and cronyism. Jim Rouse hit on the approach's major weakness when he stated: "If it took three cops to arrest a motorist…there would be a lot more dangerous cars on the road. Well, it takes five cops [from the various regulatory agencies] to arrest an unsafe house."[104]

The solution was simple: the city must create a single agency with the authority to do the job, and those behind the Baltimore Plan recommended this to the mayor. After some consideration, the mayor refused. He was supported by city bureaucrats, some of whom would lose power if the new consolidation plan was adopted. Some also saw the "possibility that the seldom-seen hand of slum-owning landowners was at work."[105]

When faced with these circumstances, Jim Rouse and Guy Hollyday resigned from the project. Some were critical of their actions, citing the value of an evolutionary—rather than a revolutionary—approach in this matter. Others argued that the program was too small to make the needed changes in the urban landscape.[106] Whatever weaknesses the program contained, it did have some long-term benefits as "the lessons learned in the Pilot Program found expression in a program for the entire country: the program of urban renewal."[107]

Washington Connections

In 1952 lifelong Democrat Jim Rouse decided to support the presidential candidacy of Republican Dwight D. Eisenhower. In a letter to a friend, he expressed admiration for the Democratic candidate Adlai E. Stevenson and claimed to find his international policy statements full of forthrightness and imagination. But Rouse saw the key issue in the campaign as not what the candidates said, but what they would be able to do after they were elected. There, Eisenhower's leadership skills and in particular his ability to create unity out of discord were what the nation seemed to need. Rouse also had harsh words for the Truman administration, and stated that the Democratic Party "needed to be out of power in order that new thinking, new leadership, and new standards may be developed."[108] To these ends, Jim co-chaired a "Democrats for Eisenhower" group in the state of Maryland.

This support for Eisenhower did not extend to the Republican Party in general. Rouse expressed disdain for the more conservative-nationalist wing of the party headed by Robert Taft and had no use for the demagogic rantings of Senator Joseph McCarthy. On the eve of the election, Rouse reacted to one of the latter's more odious speeches by sending a telegram to Eisenhower Campaign Headquarters: "Thousands of your supporters are sickened by McCarthy's outrageous speech. Common justice demands that you disassociate yourself from it…As a strong supporter I implore that you speak out against this demonstration of McCarthy's methods."[109]

Rouse's views on the United States and its role in world affairs were shaped by his strong religious faith, which led him to join the United World Federalists in 1951. The group's policy statement supported the abolition of war through disarmament by all nations under the protection of a world federal government.[110] Among its notable members in the 1950s were Albert Einstein, Supreme Court Justice William O. Douglas, U.S. Senator Alan Cranston and a Hollywood actor by the name of Ronald Reagan, who later in his career distanced himself from the group and its policies. Rouse served for a while as president of the UWF's Maryland chapter.

Eisenhower's election in 1952 provided Jim Rouse a bigger stage on which to shape public opinion on urban affairs. In September 1953, the president sent him a letter asking him to serve on the twenty-person advisory committee of the government's Housing and Home Finance Administration. He was also asked to serve on its five-person executive committee to "work directly…in the task of directing specific investigations and developing concrete recommendations" on housing and finance issues.[111] Rouse gladly accepted the president's offer, but knew making substantive changes in housing policy would be a most difficult task. In a December 12, 1952 letter to a colleague, Rouse had stated that one of Eisenhower's most difficult domestic jobs would be to eradicate slums and create decent housing for low-income families, because "most men in the housing finance industry have very little concern about slums. They are only concerned with getting rid of public housing."[112]

Rouse threw himself into his Washington work with the same intensity and fervor he had expressed in the Baltimore Plan initiative. One interesting outcome was a study and report prepared in 1954 for the Commissioners of the District of Columbia with the highly optimistic title "No Slums in Ten Years." Co-authored with Nathaniel S. Keith, who worked in housing and urban affairs during the Truman years, it stated that "real slum cure requires comprehensive action covering planning and comprehensive action covering the entire city and embracing all the tools required for slum prevention and slum elimination."[113] Rouse's Baltimore experiences apparently taught him the futility of piecemeal approaches to urban renewal.

Much praise followed this report and its vision. An editorial in the *Washington Post*, for example, expressed strong support, but ended somberly with these words: "Now it is up to official, civil and commercial Washington to tackle the menace of blight with all the intelligence, energy and unity of purpose that infuse this report."[114]

Although that kind of response did not materialize, one positive that did come of Rouse's Washington experiences was the formation of a "nationwide, nonprofit, nonpolitical, citizens organization dedicated to improving housing conditions through cooperation with local communities."[115] Named the American Council to Improve Our Neighborhoods (ACTION), it had the support of President Eisenhower and featured Jim Rouse as one of its directors. For a six-year period, Rouse crossed the country delivering countless speeches on the need for urban renewal, all the while honing his own ideas on what makes a city work. In one of his most noted speeches, on May 5, 1959, in Newark, New Jersey (by this time he had been elected ACTION's president), Rouse stressed a theme that he would echo for the rest of his life:

> *We must hold fast to the realization that our cities are for people and unless they work well for people they are not working well at all. We should think and plan and program, not in terms of schools, highways, streets, stores, offices or even dwelling units, but we should*

begin our total plan and program with the first and fundamental purpose of making a city into neighborhoods where a man, his wife and family, can live and work and, above all else, grow—grow in character, in personality, in love of God and neighbor and in the capacity for joyous living. Isn't this the legitimate target of our civilization? Isn't this the only proper target for an effective city?[116]

Within five years, a Work Group would be established to give shape to the future city of Columbia, Maryland. These words would act as its guiding light.

Saving Downtown Baltimore

Despite the time restraints of his national work, Jim Rouse did not lose sight of Baltimore and its problems. In a 1992 interview, he stated that in the early 1950s, the city of Baltimore was in dire straits. It was spending more money than it was taking in. If this trend continued, in ten years, the city would go bankrupt.[117] Something had to be done to prevent this catastrophe. Although his experiences with the pilot Baltimore project frustrated and disappointed him, he joined other city business leaders in forming the Greater Baltimore Committee (GBC). This group would provide the impetus for the revitalization of the city.

Rouse served as chairman of the group's urban renewal subcommittee. With assistance from the city's political establishment, the GBC was able to accomplish a number of projects during the 1950s and 1960s, including construction of the Jones Falls Expressway, development of Friendship Airport (now Thurgood Marshall BWI), construction of the Baltimore Civic Center (now Arena) and creation of both the Maryland Port Authority and the Mass Transit Administration.[118]

Another project that bears examination was the Charles Center Plan, a product of the planning council created by the GBC. Although having no official role in the project, Martin Millspaugh, who co-authored a book on urban renewal in Baltimore, credits Jim Rouse with "generating the thrust that created the Charles Center Plan."[119]

The Charles Street district was located in the heart of downtown Baltimore—and a few blocks from the city's decaying waterfront. The program called for razing the area and replacing it with, as Rouse wrote, "a new heart for Baltimore—a town square, beautiful, lively, human and efficient, with office towers, retail stores, small city parks and underground parking for 4000 cars."[120] When completed, it gave downtown Baltimore a new heartbeat. And what about that decaying waterfront? Ten years later, Jim Rouse and Baltimore's then-mayor William Donald Schaefer would join hands to help create a revitalized Inner Harbor.

Throughout the 1950s, Jim Rouse had become a prominent figure in the city of Baltimore, the state of Maryland and the United States of America. He had served and advised mayors, governors and the president. While this was occurring, changes were also taking place in his mortgage banking career.

The Dealings. Sculpture of Jim and Bill Rouse, completed in 1986 by William Duffy. Located on Columbia's lakeside, it commemorates the close relationship between the brothers. *Joseph Mitchell.*

From Moss-Rouse to James W. Rouse and Company

One of the crucial developments that would make Rouse's vision come to life in Columbia was the creation of his own firm. In the late 1940s, he and Hunter Moss had conducted an introspective evaluation of their company by jotting down their wishes for the company in a "What do we want?" format. Moss stated that he wanted to "be an appraiser" and to "do a commercial mortgage business." He ended his statement with "there is too damn much confusion and agony in the present operation." Rouse stated that he wanted "to get more fun out of work" and admitted he "is seldom doing the work…which interests him the most." He further stated that his interest lay in housing, city development, land planning, architecture, community development and the like.[121] It was clear that the two visions were incompatible.

In June of 1951, Moss and Rouse agreed to form Hunter Moss and Company, as a real estate appraisal business, with Jim as a partner. Moss would still be a partner in their original firm, but his move to a new office building would reduce his activities in the newly renamed James W. Rouse and Company. Moss would no longer solicit commercial mortgages,[122] but did sit on the James W. Rouse Board of Directors.

Later, he would sell his shares in the company, thereby removing himself further from the company business. However, until 1961 James W. Rouse and Company continued to carry Hunter Moss and Company employees on its hospitalization plan. In a gracious letter, Moss thanked Rouse "for letting me delay seven years before snipping the final tie."[123]

When James W. Rouse and Company was formed in 1954, Rouse decided to keep 50 percent of the company and divide 40 percent among the new company's officers. The last 10 percent was temporarily kept in abeyance. Harry Bart, who became Rouse's major partner in the Mondawmin project, told him he was crazy for arranging this because someday "his employees might turn him out of his own business." Rouse replied by saying if he couldn't get one single person in the group to agree with him on any business deal, he didn't deserve to run the company. Despite Rouse's idealism, Harry Bart stated that "I was forced to tell him I still thought he was crazy."[124] Rouse's decision to give the last 10 percent in the company to his brother Bill, who would play a key role in future shopping center developments, helped make the arrangement more secure. Little brother was now looking after big brother.

Shopping Center Mania

These new business arrangements freed Jim Rouse to hop on the shopping center bandwagon that had begun to roll. An outgrowth of the mass migration to suburbia, it would drastically alter the American landscape. To give his company an advantage in this fast-growing business, Rouse formed a separate division dubbed Metropolitan Research. Its purpose was to apply scientific research tools to project feasibility. Originally designed to provide assistance to the company's clients, it was later used to provide the company with information when it entered the development business.

Freedom Shopping Center, located in southeast Baltimore, was Moss-Rouse's first foray into this brave new world, though only as financier. The project involved an eleven-store retail center, anchored by a grocery store, and a 308-unit apartment complex behind it. The latter presented a "captive market of 17,000 persons" for the shopping center. Parking in front provided for drive-in customers who eventually accounted for half of the commercial traffic. The project, completed in 1953, was innovative enough to rate a rave review in *House & Home*, complete with diagrams and pictures.[125]

The next shopping center would be a major project, marking the company's initiation into the world of real estate development. It began in 1949, when the Griswold and Brown families asked Jim Rouse what he could do with a forty-six-acre site several miles from Baltimore's central city. The mansion on it was called Mondawmin, the name suggested by Henry Wadsworth Longfellow, after the legendary Indian spirit who wrestled with Hiawatha.[126] Rouse immediately saw the development potential and formed a partnership with Alexander Brown Griswold to develop it. They were soon joined by Harry Bart, who provided building expertise and investment dollars.

Interior, Mondawmin Shopping Center, Baltimore, 1956. *Source unknown.*

Most people were skeptical of the project. Some feared that its proximity to black neighborhoods might deter white shoppers, but a Rouse research study stated otherwise.[127] Despite six years of naysayers and doomsayers, ground was finally broken in 1955.

Bill Rouse was given the daunting task of selling Mondawmin to retail clients. He had an especially difficult time getting an anchor store (a recognized chain store to

Mondawmin Shopping Center, Baltimore 1956. Rouse's first major shopping project, it was eventually enclosed and became Mondawnin Mall. *General Growth Properties.*

attract large numbers of shoppers) to sign up, but finally persuaded Sears, Roebuck. Mondawmin opened in 1956 with a nearly 100 percent occupation figure, an achievement praised by both the architectural and business communities. Mondawmin's success was so important to Rouse's future that it caused Harry Bart to state: "Let it be abundantly clear that if Mondawmin had failed, it is quite possible that the Rouse Company we know today would not be in existence."[128]

With other prospects coming his way, Jim Rouse had to find the financial means to make them happen. In December 1956, he announced the formation of Community Research and Development (CRD) "to build, own and operate shopping centers in various locations throughout the country."[129] Three million dollars were raised through bond sales, the investors being some of his navy buddies and some heavyweights in the Baltimore construction business. Some of the capital would go to four Rouse projects already under consideration. One of them would occur in his Eastern Shore hometown.

Once he left Easton for more cosmopolitan places, Jim Rouse had often felt nostalgia for its small-town qualities. Attached to his memories of the town as it had been, he initially resisted a proposal from his sister Dia and her husband O'Donnell Pascault to build a shopping center there. Rouse finally agreed, but only on the condition that the new project would be built within walking distance of the center of town.[130] Here was a clue to Rouse's emerging philosophy of commercial development. He wanted to build shopping centers that modernized the town center idea, rather than replacing it altogether. In keeping with this approach, Rouse favored using Baltimore architect

Alexander Smith Cochran, who favored modern architectural styles, rather than the colonial look of the old Easton. Local interests resisted that change so effectively, however, as to defeat it.[131] And so Rouse's project, the neo-colonial Talbottown, emerged as a compromise between new and old in more ways than one. Opened with much fanfare in 1957, the development won the hearts of many residents, who took pride in Easton's new status as the smallest town in America with a shopping center.

Another major shopping center venture was planned for the Glen Burnie area, in Anne Arundel County, just south of Baltimore. Company research showed that the area was growing at a rate four times that of the Baltimore metropolitan area. Furthermore, a major roadway called Ritchie Highway tied Glen Burnie to the state capital at Annapolis. By 1970 it was projected that these two areas would be home to 300,000 people.[132]

In spite of that favorable estimate, Rouse had problems obtaining the necessary financing. The shopping center was to be fully enclosed, with the shops facing each other inside, and no outside advertising permitted. Old partner Connecticut General agreed to finance what became known as the Harundale Mall, and merchants soon began buying in to the Rouse approach to commercial development. The use of the word "mall" is interesting because Harundale was the first enclosed shopping center in the East to be built by a developer.[133] From that time on, a new term was created, and Jim Rouse would be known as a mall builder.

Of all the shopping centers and malls built by Rouse, the one in Delaware Township, New Jersey, known as Cherry Hill and designed by noted urban architect Victor Gruen "was our largest, our finest and our most important center."[134] In this project, Rouse would set forth ideas that would bloom in Columbia a few years later: a heavy dose of nature (his sister Dia was in charge of plants and trees), and a sense of community that could come from a mall. He was so successful in this respect that Delaware Township, New Jersey, later changed its name to Cherry Hill, New Jersey.

By the early 1960s, Jim Rouse's name had become synonymous with mall development. The success of such ventures helped give him the means to begin working on the question that concerned him most: could someone build a better city? Flush with the characteristic optimism of that time, Rouse and his associates would soon decide to try.

4.

COLUMBIA'S GENESIS
1960–1965

Columbia would provide the best possibor environment for the growth of people.
Columbia Plan, 1964

Jim Rouse always stated that there was no single "Road to Damascus" experience that led him directly to Columbia. Rather, it was a lifetime of experiences, beginning with his Easton days, which offered the nurturing environment that small-town America could provide. Later, his work experiences in housing, banking and development taught him how the habitat shaped human beings, for better or worse. To put people in a stable, pleasant setting, he felt, would give them their greatest opportunity for self-fulfillment.

Anchoring these feelings was his deep, abiding religious faith. Since his experiences at Baltimore's Brown Memorial Presbyterian Church in the 1930s, his faith influenced every aspect of his life. "Love thy neighbor should be the first commandment of development" was a phrase he used to argue that religious faith and profitable business endeavors were not incompatible goals. During the 1960s, new religious experiences would strengthen both his faith and his social commitment.

And one must not forget the role that Libby Rouse played in Columbia's creation. Her religious convictions influenced her husband at a time when his own religious values were being shaped. She challenged him to create better environments in his projects; and, as we shall soon see, some of her ideas found their way into Columbia's foundational principles. In the quantum leap from a shopping mall to a model city, two projects—one successful, one not—provided the steppingstones.

Pocantico Hills Plan, 1962. Planned for the development of the Rockefeller family land in upstate New York in 1962, it was eventually rejected by the brothers. Some of its features eventually found their way into Columbia's plans. *Columbia Archives.*

The Pocantico Hills Project

New York's Hudson River Valley is a scenic wonderland whose history dates back to Dutch colonialism. New Amsterdam became New York when the British took over, but the Dutch influence remained. Some of its leading families established large estates along the Hudson, and during the nineteenth century, they were joined by the Rockefellers.

By 1960 three generations of Rockefellers had lived on the family lands in an area known as Pocantico Hills, thirty miles up the Hudson from New York City. Pocantico's translation from Algonquin is "swift, dark stream running between two hills." Straight out of Washington Irving's *Knickerbocker Tales*, its main thoroughfare was named Sleepy Hollow Road. The property included the family estate (a National Trust historic site); two thousand acres of "open space," jointly owned by John D. Rockefeller's five grandsons (John, Nelson, Laurence, Winthrop and David); and separate properties owned by various family members. As the brothers pondered how to manage the "open space,"[135] they asked Jim Rouse to create something they could all live with.

His response was enthusiastic because the outline presented by the Rockefellers "seemed to be broad enough to include the 'ideal community' approach which is most interesting to me."[136] To protect the privacy of the family, plans proceeded without identifying the new Rouse client. A group of experts in various phases of planning and development was hired as consultants, along with social scientists, charged with bringing a human dimension to the process. The most high-profile invitee was noted anthropologist Margaret Mead, who initially expressed great interest in the project, but could never find time to attend the requisite meetings.

Rouse and his staff began by examining "the needs of people and how they might be best fulfilled in a well planned community."[137] Questions were raised regarding size and scale, quality of life, effects on people and the environment and the overriding concern of how to make a successful community. A presentation was made to the brothers in 1962, but the project died when the brothers could not agree; only David supported the Rouse development plan.[138] In 1972 the Rockefellers hired noted landscape architect Hideo Sasaki to advise them on Pocantico's future. Two years later, he reported back: keep it as it is![139] But the process was not a total loss. David Rockefeller's Chase Manhattan Bank would later lend Jim Rouse $10 million to help pay for Columbia's early construction costs. And the vision of an ideal village that Pocantico Hills could have been soon took shape as a nine-village city in Howard County, Maryland.

Cross Keys: From Country Club to Planned Community

During this time period, Jim Rouse made an important hire. Nancy L. Allison was originally employed to do personnel work for the company, but soon became his office manager. She devoted her life to him for more than thirty years, providing a sense of organization to his frantic, creative existence. In later years, she would often answer his mail if he was unavailable. Sometimes when his children, Robin, Jim and Ted, would write to tell their father about an accomplishment, she would immediately write to tell them how proud their father was, and as soon as he returned, she would see that their notes would be the first things he would read. Her loyalty and devotion to her boss were measureless.

Jim Rouse habitually juggled several major projects at the same time. So as Pocantico Hills was running out of steam, another opportunity closer to home moved into prominence. The Baltimore Country Club's golf course was put on the market. According to Ned Daniels, a Rouse executive, "it went on the market on Wednesday, and we bought on Thursday [for $1,700,000], without a clue as to what would come from it…He [Rouse] bought the damn thing and then spent two years figuring it out."[140]

This area interested him because it was near his Roland Park home, an area designed by Frederick Law Olmsted Jr., a noted twentieth-century landscape architect. Rouse's children attended private schools in the area, and he was well known in the community. But there was a major potential stumbling block: if he couldn't obtain the necessary zoning changes, he might have invested a lot of money in a piece of land that would be useless to him.

Always proactive, he conducted a number of neighborhood meetings to explain his intentions and answer any questions people might have. Eye-catching brochures outlining his plans eased public anxieties. And "by presenting no take-it-or-leave-it plan, he adroitly avoided stirring up the neighborhood into hasty opposition."[141] When the time came for the zoning changes to be voted on, no opposition to the Rouse project materialized. Soon, a similar public relations campaign would be used to bring about zoning changes in Howard County that would make Columbia possible.

What eventually came from the planning process was the village of Cross Keys, "a self-contained residential village community consisting of 1000 town houses, garden and high rise apartment units, a tennis club, village shopping center, an inn, office building complex and community facilities."[142] Construction began in 1963 under the leadership of William E. "Bill" Finley, who was hired to manage the as-yet-unannounced Howard County model city project, but was temporarily put in charge of Cross Keys. By 1964, some housing was available for occupancy. As the years slowly passed, other parts of the general plan were completed, with the requisite changes that typically took place in a Rouse project. Many of these alterations were prompted by an attention to detail that bordered on excess. This was Rouse's first planned community and he left nothing to chance. But even before Cross Keys opened its doors, he was planning for a much larger project, which would become the jewel in his crown.

Howard County in the 1960s

Before selecting Howard County as the site for his new city, Jim Rouse had his company explore other potential locations throughout the country. A legal advisor, John Martin "Jack" Jones Jr., and Charles "Chili" Jenkins, a Rouse Company vice-president, explored sites in the areas around Atlanta, Georgia, and Raleigh-Durham, North Carolina. Jenkins himself explored other locations, but none of these showed enough promise to warrant an in-depth feasibility study.[143] There was, however, a location right at the company's back door that was just what they were looking for.

Situated within the Baltimore-Washington corridor, Howard County was a "demographic vacuum" between its two large neighbors, Baltimore and Washington.[144] Before Columbia's genesis, the 1960 county general plan, created by the planning commission, stated that the county's population, currently at 36,152, would reach a 220,000–260,000 level by 2000. It warned that the county "has a great challenge before it to make provisions for such a population increase without destroying the beauty and other values of the County in the process."[145] This alerted the county's residents to the need to control the tide of development that was slowly beginning to change the county. Incidentally, Howard County's population in 2000 was 247,842; long-term demographic predictions are seldom more accurate than that.

The county in 1960 could be described as a mainly rural area with suburbia creeping in not so slowly. Howard County's population increase from 1950 to 1960 (13,033 residents, a 56 percent jump) seemed to reflect this trend. From 1900 to 1950, the county's population had grown more slowly (6,944 residents, or 43 percent) than in the single decade of the 1950s. How much of an increase would the county experience in the future was a question on many citizens' minds, and most wished that it be kept to a minimum. In the election year of 1962, they expressed that view at the ballot box, electing three Republicans—Charles Miller, J. Hubert Black and David Force—who ran on a low-density growth platform. To ensure this program, the county's zoning plan stated that in the rural, western part of the county all parcels of land had to be one acre or more, while the rest of the county was limited to one-half-acre lots. Town houses and apartment complexes were not permitted under existing zoning regulations. Conditions such as these would not be attractive to anyone who wanted to create a city in Howard County.

The three commissioners in Howard County served as both the executive and legislative branches, a system common among rural counties, but one ill-suited for the modern county Howard was soon to become. Much of the legislation affecting the county had to be passed by the state legislature and signed into law by the governor, a most cumbersome process. In the mid-sixties, a move toward charter government proposed a county executive–county council form of government, which would give those two bodies the power to govern in all local matters. Charter government was approved by the voters in 1968.

A visitor to Howard County in 1960 would have found a scattering of small towns—Ellicott City (the county seat), Elkridge, Savage, North Laurel and Lisbon—and a number of suburban housing developments—Normandy Heights, Dunloggin, Beaverbrook, Allview Estates, Dalton, Guilford and Mount Hebron among them. Small shopping centers, anchored by a chain grocery store, were also springing up. Large, non-farm employers were practically nonexistent, with Johns Hopkins Applied Physics Laboratory and W.R. Grace being the exceptions. The rest of the county was rural or moderately suburban in nature, and most Howard Countians wanted it to stay that way.

Despite the Supreme Court *Brown v. Board of Education* decision in 1954, which had declared school segregation unconstitutional, some Howard County public schools were still segregated in the early 1960s. Kenneth Stevens, a political activist, came to Howard County in 1961 and was appalled by the segregated society he found here. He joined the local chapter of the National Association for the Advancement of Colored People (NAACP) with a number of African American leaders in that fight, including Silas Kraft, Elhart Flurry, Leola Dorsey, Reverend John Holland and Roger Carter.[146] By 1966 school segregation in Howard County was a thing of the past. Kraft, a lifetime educator, was a particularly effective leader who led many campaigns to rid the county of all vestiges of discrimination.[147] Recently, Howard Community College recognized his life's work by creating the "Silas Kraft Collegians," a program that attracts students who have not yet realized their full potential, teaching them the skills necessary to maximize their academic capabilities.

But it took time for the general state of black-white relations in the county to improve. Herman Charity, a member of the first class to fully integrate Howard High School, spoke many years later about the segregated nature of the old Howard County. African Americans then could not use area restaurants and motels, and young people could not participate in Howard County Youth League activities and had to have their own separate sports leagues and teams.[148] When Alabama Governor George Wallace carried

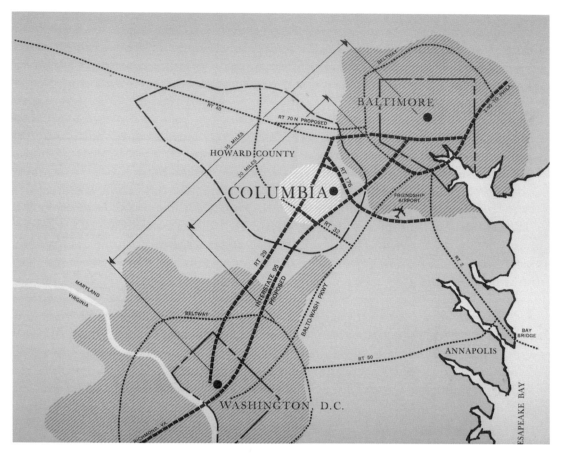

1964 Baltimore-Washington corridor map. Locates Columbia between the two metropolitan areas in a place projected to be the fastest-growing region east of the Mississippi River—a perfect place for a new model city. *Columbia Archives.*

the county in the 1964 Democratic presidential primary, his victory spoke volumes about the county's racial politics. However, the winds of change were stirring, and the county's quiet complacency would soon disappear.

The Great Howard County "Land Grab"

In March 1963, Baltimore city and Howard County newspapers reported large purchases of land in the county...and no one knew the identity of the buyer. "Who was buying this land and what were they going to do with it?" became a hot county topic, and the speculation often bordered on the ridiculous. A Russian diplomatic complex? A West German Volkswagen plant? A United Nations memorial cemetery? Texas oil interests buying for—take a guess? Perhaps the most unusual speculation was that Washington and Baltimore sanitation departments wanted "to use central Howard County as a vast compost heap, utilizing a mythical new chemical process that turned garbage into peat moss."[149] Claude Skinner, a local engineer and surveyor, had a more plausible answer. Because the land was purchased where future sewer interceptors would be located, he was quoted as saying that "it looks to me like a land grab to eat up available real estate for a gigantic housing development."[150] He probably never dreamed how big that development would be.

The road from rural Howard County to model city Columbia was seldom a straight one, and happenstance sometimes affected the process. Mel Berman, a Howard County resident and a member of Rouse's Board of Directors, had long promoted the Baltimore-Washington corridor as a prime development site. He foresaw that a suburban development in Montgomery and Prince George's counties would "jump the Patuxent [River]," and when that occurred, land values in Howard County would rapidly rise.[151] His promotion of the area was so persistent that Jim Rouse and Chili Jenkins took a helicopter tour of the area to assess its development feasibility.[152]

Berman was not thinking model city, but large suburban development. However, in April 1962, he saw a sign on Cedar Lane advertising 1,309 acres for sale. The sign had been placed by Robert Moxley, a partner in a local real estate firm. Berman reported the option to Community Research and Development (CRD) and the decision was made to purchase the land.

Secrecy became an important component in this and all future CRD land dealings. If potential sellers knew who was buying the land and for what purpose, prices would rise prohibitively. Thus, when CRD was ready to buy, E.C. Dukehart, a Baltimore realtor, secretly represented CRD. His attorney was Jack Jones, from Piper and Marbury, a noted Baltimore law firm. No one made the connection that Piper and Marbury was Jim Rouse's law firm and that Jones was representing Rouse and CRD. The first parcels of land were purchased, starting a process that would culminate in Jim Rouse's company owning almost 10 percent of Howard County's land.

"The story of Rouse's negotiations with the land owners over the next months reads like a James Bond novel: secret rooms, plots, strategy, and dummy corporations characterized the process."[153] Because of his experiences as a counterintelligence officer during the Korean War, Jack Jones was the perfect man to carry on such a clandestine operation. Treating his campaign like a military maneuver, he divided the designated area into thirty-five- to forty-square-mile segments and told realtors he would be interested in buying any land within them. In Robert Moxley, a local real estate company owner, Jones had an agent who not only was willing to fill up the grid he was asked to, but requested more to work on. He would put together more tracts of land than the others, thus making him Jack Jones's leading client.[154] Moxley later commented that he didn't know who Jack Jones was buying the land for, but didn't want to be too nosy about it for fear of "killing the goose who laid the golden eggs."[155]

In the meantime, CRD's research department was preparing a research project entitled "Proposed New City." Within the company it was known as the "Green Book," after its cover's color. It reported much useful data, but one section stood out: "The Baltimore-Washington area had the highest growth rate east of the Mississippi, and could be expected to total nearly 6 million by 1980. The proposed new city was right in the middle of this expansion."[156] The road to Columbia had just straightened out. As the secret land purchases continued, Rouse knew he would have to seek additional funds to pay for them. Because of his dealings with the Rockefeller family during the Pocantico Hills project, he contacted David Rockefeller of Chase Manhattan Bank, who "was intrigued by Rouse's ambitious project, but neither he nor his bank could take a lead role in such a risky undertaking."[157]

Rouse then turned to Connecticut General (CG), a firm with which he had been doing business since 1941. A venerable company that was incorporated in 1865, it was beginning to cultivate an interest in the development of office parks. In 1957 CG had moved its headquarters from downtown Hartford, Connecticut, to rural Bloomfield, six miles away. The new complex was like a community without homes; everything that would make it a pleasant—and profitable—work place was included. A 1960s visitor found auditoriums, lounges, shops, cafeteria, libraries, a gymnasium, as well as courtyards and 230 acres of green landscape. Since 25 percent of the interior space was devoted to employee nonworking activities, "the whole building gave the impression of taking the people who work within it into account."[158] A company that provided such an ideal workplace for its employees must have found Jim Rouse's model city plan fascinating.

A proposal was sent to Connecticut General by Jim Rouse in October 1962, asking them to "provide funds required to acquire land for the New City."[159] In face-to-face meetings with its president, Frazar Wilde, Rouse seemed to find that kindred spirit who would be willing to take a chance on his model city. Having risen from office boy to chairman of the board, Wilde, like Rouse, combined the perspective of the school of hard knocks and the shape of the new corporate world. The two men maintained a strong friendship and mutual respect until Wilde retired from CG.

After months of negotiations, a deal was worked out. A new subsidiary, Howard Research and Development (HRD), was created to oversee the model city project. It would be jointly owned by CG and CRD. CG would also be allowed to appoint three of the five members on the new company's board of directors. The silent lending partner that Rouse had originally desired wanted to be a full-fledged partner, able to share in future company profits.[160] This was a risk-taking leap for the insurance company, one that would require it to infuse Columbia with the needed upfront money. Without that kind of backing, the model city could not have survived.[161] If Jim Rouse was Columbia's father, Frazar Wilde could be considered its guardian angel.

The CG funding allowed the land acquisitions to continue under the cloak of secrecy, and while all the deals seemed similar, some stood out. One of the most important—and the most interesting—was one that was scrawled on the back of a real estate plat and signed in a coffee shop in Friendship Airport (now BWI) because Jack Jones was boarding a plane bound for Europe. This deal was important because the land in question included what is today Columbia's Town Center.[162] Its validity was later contested and upheld.[163] Some of the land deals had some interesting twists to them, one being a landowner's insistence that his horse be granted lifetime squatting rights on the property—rights that were granted. By May 13, 1964, Jones had purchased 14,178 acres of Howard County real estate at a price of $19,122,622. The average price per acre was $1,349.

John Shallcross was part of the secret land acquisition team and later became land manager of the acres he helped to buy. Columbia's development was several years away, and with Rouse's company making huge interest payments daily, the undeveloped land had to make money. Shallcross would become Howard County's biggest farmer, overseeing almost six thousand acres of farmland operated by Jim Rouse's 126 new tenant farmers.[164]

On September 23, 1963, Jim Rouse delivered one of his finest speeches at a conference on the "Metropolitan Future" at the University of California, Berkeley. Entitled "It Can Happen Here," the talk was Columbia's engagement party announcement. In it, Rouse argued that a successful city could succeed only if "the Good Environment" was created. Cooperation among architect, planner, designer, social scientist and public official, Rouse insisted, would not only produce new communities, "but will release among the people in them the potential for the noblest civilization the world has ever known."[165] Everyone would soon know that Jim Rouse was going to take a crack at creating such a city.

Selling the Next America to Howard County

On October 29, 1963, Howard County planning chief Tom Harris was attending an American Institute of Planners meeting in Milwaukee. Also attending the meeting was Bill Finley, who worked for Jim Rouse and would later become Columbia's chief developer. Bill had been one of Tom's professors at the University of Pennsylvania, so Tom was not surprised when Bill passed him a note. What shocked him was the note's content: at that very moment, Jim Rouse was informing the Howard County commissioners of his intentions to build a model city in the county.[166] Tom Harris's job was about to get a lot more complicated.

The response to Jim Rouse's announcement was somewhat muted. Considering the strange rumors that had spread across the county during the year of the land grab, some were relieved to see Jim Rouse, a Marylander and a respected businessman with rural, Eastern Shore roots, making the announcement. The local *Central Maryland News* reported that "it was indeed a relief to see they [the landowners] were not greasy-haired, black-suited, limousine-driven mystery men conjured up in so many imaginations."[167]

On the following day, James W. Rouse and Company issued both a press release and a memo to its stockholders. The former hit upon four points that would be made over and over again in the campaign to sell the model city to Howard County: (1) growth will occur; it may be moderated, but it can't be stopped; (2) present planning and zoning cannot preserve real open spaces and new planning and zoning was needed; (3) the important natural resources of the area must be protected; (4) new development should be concentrated into fine, well-balanced communities.[168] Rouse promised his new city would do precisely those things.

The response to the news was cautiously muted; most adopted a "wait-and-see" attitude. William Sanner, the chairman of the planning commission, said that progress couldn't be held back, but "if this adds to the orderly development of our county, that's

James Rouse and Howard County's commissioners, J. Hubert Black, Charles E. Miller and David W. Force (left to right). The commissioners had the power to approve or deny Columbia's creation. Eventually, they said yes. *Columbia Archives.*

what we are all looking for." Robert Marks, president of the Howard County Citizens' Association, a citizens' group with an avid interest in county development, stated that the new community could either be beneficial or detrimental to the county, but hoped that "we won't see people opposing it just for the sake of opposition until the plans are clear." E. Holmes Hawkins, clerk of the county commissioners, was quoted as saying, "Although this exact event is a surprise, we have expected a sudden surge sometime in the future, and I don't feel it will be too much a strain on the county."[169] No ringing endorsements, but no strong denunciations. Considering the magnitude of the plan—and suddenness of its appearance—it was the best that the Rouse Company could hope for.

What followed was a year-and-a-half campaign for the hearts and minds of Howard County's residents and their elected officials. Earlier in the year, M. Scott Ditch, a native Baltimorean, Korean War Marine Corps pilot and managing editor of a weekly Towson newspaper, was hired by Jim Rouse without being told why. After the land purchases had been made public, he was told that he was to serve on the Columbia team, where his newspaper and communications experiences could be put to good use—"communicating Columbia."[170] Bill Finley, who was hired to manage the new city's development, spearheaded the team, and Ditch stated that the "monkey was on his back" to get the plan approved.

Since there was no concrete plan in place, a fact that surprised Tom Harris, the Rouse Company had to develop one to present to the county for its approval. In a community meeting attended by two hundred citizens at a local school, Jim told the audience, "We will plan so well, we will win your support; however, we want you to stay concerned, examine every month what we propose to do."[171] The company had to develop a plan and sell the public on it step by step, which was a formidable task.

To accomplish this, they decided to employ the same tactics that had won over Baltimoreans to their Cross Keys project: good old-fashioned community legwork. For any group, no matter how small, Rouse or someone from the company would come to speak, obtain feedback and go back to the drawing boards. And sometimes plans would be revised as a result. When the residents of the Sebring development objected that the proposed location of a hospital was too close their homes, a more appropriate spot for the hospital was found.[172] Such actions helped to win friends and influence public opinion, something that was not lost on the local politicians. Handsome brochures were prepared for all county politicians and community leaders, and an insert was prepared for local newspapers to be distributed to their subscribers with their weekly newspaper.

Up to this point, the new city did not have a name. The planning group had decided a name that had colonial Howard County significance might be preferable. Using a land grant map created by Caleb Dorsey, an amateur genealogist, they sought possible names for the new city. Names like "The Mistake" and "Poverty Discovered" added some humor to the discussions, but the name Columbia seemed to be the front-runner. When the Howard District separated from Anne Arundel County to become Howard County in 1851, a branch post office had been established at a crossroads known as Columbia, near the present intersection of Routes 29 and 108. This had instant appeal but some were concerned that there were already too many Columbias in the country. However, time was running out without consensus being reached. When the printing had to be sent out, Jim Rouse asked about the name. "We have nothing new to offer" was the response. "We've written in Columbia." "Then Columbia it is," Rouse directed.[173] And in the most serendipitous of ways, the city had a name that seemed to be meant for it.

On November 11, 1964, Rouse unveiled his plan to the county with the word Columbia emboldened on the cover. Its goals were listed on the first page. The new city would: (1) not create an additional tax burden on the residents of the county; (2) respect the land; (3) be a complete and balanced community; (4) set the highest possible standards of beauty, safety and convenience; (5) provide its residents major utilities and services at no additional cost to the county; and (6) provide the best possible environment for the growth of people.[174] People were glad to see that the new city finally had a plan.

The public relations campaign seemed to be working. A CRD-financed opinion survey entitled "Reaction of Howard County Residents to the Columbia Plan" in January 1965 showed that 60 percent of those polled favored the plan, 25 percent were

Columbia Town Center model. This was used to convince Howard Countians that Columbia would not be just another suburban development. It worked. *Columbia Archives.*

neutral and 15 percent opposed it.[175] Another poll taken in February yielded similar results. This public opinion trend was supported by an opinion poll in the March 4, 1965 issue of the *Howard County Times*, in which 75 percent voted for the Columbia Plan.[176] When the Howard County Citizens Association and the local League of Women Voters also endorsed the plan, it was clear that Jim Rouse's group was winning the public relations battle.[177] For the former, the role of Seymour Barondes was significant. His columns in the organization's newsletter, called *Vox Pop*, were instrumental in steering public opinion toward the Columbia side. The latter's support was primarily due to the leadership of Anita Iribe.

While succeeding in winning over the public, Jim Rouse and his staff were having a more difficult time with Howard County's elected officials, especially the three Republican commissioners who held Columbia's fate in their hands. Their ability to pull the plug on the model city at any time caused Jim many sleepless nights.[178] The members of the county's state delegation—State Senator James Clark and Delegates William Hanna and Edwin Warfield—were Democrats who would be responsible for obtaining state funds for roads, water and sewer lines for the new city. Clark and Warfield were large-scale county farmers, and their own interests might not be compatible with those

Richard Hall and Herman Charity (left to right) helped end segregation in Howard County, first as Howard High students and then as members of the county police department, Charity being its first African American policeman and Hall its first African American officer. *Howard County Center of African American Culture.*

of the new city's proponents. But, after initial apprehension, they expressed support for the city with Warfield stating that planned and orderly growth was preferable to "sit[ting] back with your head in the sand and end[ing] up ten years later from now with urban sprawl."[179] Clark concurred by stating that "like a lot of things, we've gotten used to the idea of Columbia. It's important that it succeed."[180]

In December 1964, CRD prepared its recommended zoning regulations, which if approved would be incorporated into the county's regulatory system. County Planning Board Director Tom Harris found these proposed regulations inadequate in two ways: they provided the government with too little control over land usage regulations in the new city, and were weak and unclear on the role of the county's Planning Commission.[181] Lewis Nippard, legal counsel for the commissioners, found the same problems, and also declared the proposal to be "unlawful" because it did not conform to existing county zoning regulations.

What seemed like a life-threatening blow to the model city project actually had the exact opposite effect—the people of Howard County rallied behind the Columbia side. The *Howard County Times* took up the Rouse group's cause, printing results of straw polls that showed the new city's favorable rating at 85 percent. They also printed comments from readers, one of whom said: "I'm a Republican but if those dumb county commissioners can't see that this is the best thing that ever happened, they should be run out of the county on a rail."[182] A comment made to Lewis Nippard by a local politician was more caustic and to the point: "You've just killed Santa Claus!"

"WANTED—LEADERSHIP," screamed Doris Thompson's *Howard County Times* editorial on January 27, 1965. She stated that the future of the county would be determined by the Columbia question, and it was now in the hands of politicians, Republicans and Democrats. "God forbid that they would let this become a partisan political football."[183]

The politicians got the message. New zoning regulations, drawn up by the company, in cooperation with Nippard and the planning commission, were soon completed and submitted to the county in March 1965. The commissioners were noncommittal, but things were looking up for Rouse and his staff. In July the commissioners held a public hearing on the new zoning regulations, expecting a large crowd that didn't materialize. Jim Rouse made a presentation and some citizens gave support to his side. Only two people spoke against the new zoning regulations, but one of them threatened to throw a monkey wrench into the new town plans.

James Hepding was a county landowner who owned a small store and gas station at the intersection of Routes 29 and 32. After the hearing, he filed a lawsuit, claiming that "the new town was damaging the value of his property." While few thought he would win his case, the delay could prove dangerous to a company that was paying huge interest rates on borrowed money.[184] Hepding eventually withdrew his lawsuit and sold his land to Homer Gudelsky, a county landowner and entrepreneur. Jim Rouse had already purchased property from members of the Gudelsky family and had a handshake deal with Homer that he would buy the Hepding land from him if he could acquire it. Gudelsky did so, but decided to keep the land for a while. When Hepding withdrew his lawsuit, Jim was in no hurry to buy Hepding's land, and it was not until 1975 that the "handshake" deal was finally consummated.[185]

In August 1965, news reached Rouse headquarters that the commissioners had approved the new zoning regulations. A party was a fitting end to an almost two-year campaign for county approval. Bill Finley, Scott Ditch and the team could now relax and savor the fruits of victory. The struggle was over; now all they had to do was build their model city and make concrete the high standards they had outlined during the last two years.

5.

COLUMBIA

THE NEXT AMERICA, 1965–1967

We look upon physical planning as the manifestation of social and aesthetic objectives.
Bill Finley and Mort Hoppenfeld to Jim Rouse, October 7, 1963

Even before the county gave final approval to the Columbia project, people were writing about the hopes and dreams it represented. A 1964 *Harper's Magazine* article proclaimed that "it may be the most imaginative attempt yet to capture The Good Life for city dwellers."[186] *Architectural Forum* stated that "it has set out to construct the framework of a society, based on the best information it can find about the wants and needs of people.[187] And in response to Jim Rouse's statement that Columbia "should be a garden for growing people," a 1965 article in the *Washington Star* replied that "the concept could well be called Olympian."[188] To attempt to live up to these high expectations, Jim Rouse had to assemble a staff who shared his dreams and was willing to work hard to make them come true.

Columbia's Triumvirate

It was clear from the beginning that Columbia would be Rouse's baby. He was involved in all of its operations, giving attention to the most minute of details. This was sometimes resented by the shopping mall branch of the company, composed of his old friends and partners, who felt too much attention was given to a part of the company that wasn't making any money; they may also have resented the attention that would be given to Columbia and the newcomers he hired to run it.[189] But the model city was something special, and it continued to get a lot of his attention.

When Rouse began assembling a staff for Columbia, he had to operate under a veil of secrecy to avoid driving up prices in the parts of Howard County that he was buying. Eventually, he was able to find three people who would lead Columbia's development. All had experience, academic and professional, in planned community development.

Bill Finley was the first "planning" hire. Enrolled at the University of California, Berkeley, in the 1950s to study city planning, he discovered the university offered only two courses in that field. A sympathetic professor suggested that he create his own major, which he did by using courses from seven different departments and calling it city and regional planning. Shortly after, Berkeley developed a master's program in the field, and he became one of its first graduates.[190]

Later Finley was hired by Kaiser Aluminum to develop a new community in Ravenswood, West Virginia, on the banks of the Ohio River, where the company was building the largest aluminum plant in the country. This plant would employ 12,000 people, all of whom would need homes with all of the requisite community amenities. He managed this project as Ravenswood's population grew from 1,000 to 25,000. He then taught city planning at the University of Pennsylvania for two semesters, where one of his students was Tom Harris, who would be Howard County's planning director when the plans for Columbia were developed in the early 1960s.

In 1958 Finley was appointed director of the National Capital Planning Commission (NCPC) in Washington, D.C. One of his farsighted accomplishments was the creation of a future plan for the nation's capital and its metropolitan region called the Year 2000 Plan. Part of the plan was a "spoke and wheel" design by which five or six metro and highway corridors would radiate from the city and along their way "nodules" would form in the shape of new town developments. Interestingly, one of them was headed directly to Howard County.[191]

The plan was well received by both politicians and the press, but Finley's tenure at NCPC was about to come to an abrupt end. A political appointment to head the commission wanted to undo all it had accomplished.[192] As a result, Finley planned to leave NCPC and was contacted by Jim Rouse about a planning job related to a new model city project his company was pursuing. After some cryptic correspondence and face-to-face meetings, on October 25, 1962, Rouse announced Finley's hiring in a memo to the company's directors, stating that "it is not our intention to involve Bill Finley in our regular shopping center development work but to concentrate his attention in the large, special projects which I believe are available to us if we are equipped to handle them."[193] Translation: new city.

Finley was hired to be the chief planner for the new city, but told Rouse that he wanted to try his skills as a developer, and he was given the title of vice-president for community development, working directly under Rouse.[194] Finley's tireless work on Columbia made dreams realities. Mort Hoppenfeld would later write that after Rouse, Finley deserved special mention in the Columbia project for his ability to "make the bridge between the corporate world of the private developer and the public-interest world of the community...[and] without his love and devotion, it [Columbia] wouldn't

Bill Finley, Jim Rouse and Mort Hoppenfeld (left to right). Jim Rouse hired Bill Finley to manage and develop the Columbia project. Mort Hoppenfeld was the city's chief planner. *Columbia Archives; photo by Robert de Gast.*

have happened."[195] When Finley was given his job, he promised he would hire the best planner in the country. Mort Hoppenfeld was that person.

Hoppenfeld had spent his life waiting for something like Columbia to come along. As an architecture student at MIT in 1952, he was exploring the relationships between people, cities and planning. In his undergraduate thesis, a potential redevelopment project for a blight-stricken Cambridge, Massachusetts neighborhood, he wrote that his project "is an attempt to rehabilitate and humanize the chaotic scene, and to establish a new setting for the same people according to their social, spiritual, and physical needs."[196] After military service, a master's degree in city planning from Berkeley, some teaching and a stint as chief of downtown planning for the city of Philadelphia, in 1959 he was hired by Bill Finley at the National Capital Planning Commission. When Bill left to take a job with Jim Rouse, Hoppenfeld soon followed. Many Columbians would later remember him for the aesthetic and humanistic touches he brought to the city's planning and development.

Bob Tennenbaum's first Columbia experience occurred when Hoppenfeld, a friend and former colleague at NCPC, asked him to take a drive up Route 29 from Washington. As they reached the Route 32 intersection, Mort asked him to look around and Bob recalled seeing trees, cows, small subdivisions and the like. Four miles later, they reached the Route 108 intersection and Hoppenfeld told Tennenbaum to stop looking and announced, "We're going to plan a new city here. Would you like to join us?"[197] Tennenbaum eventually accepted and came on board in September 1963. With a degree in architecture from the Pratt Institute, a master of city planning degree from Yale—where he had researched and studied new town planning and development—a year's experience at the NCPC and another year working for a planning consultant, he was perfect for the job as chief architect and planner. Speaking later of Tennenbaum's contributions to Columbia, Jim Rouse stated that "he contributed enormously to the Columbia planning process as a talented, sensitive, perceptive, planner/designer."[198]

The major hires had been made and work on Columbia was about to begin. Tennenbaum headed off to begin an analysis of the land, and Finley and Hoppenfeld began to assemble a group of academicians who would advise the planners on how to build a better city.

The Work Group and Columbia's Development

The idea for the Work Group developed from the musings of Jim Rouse, Bill Finley and Mort Hoppenfeld, who wanted to make sure that the behavioral sciences had a role in shaping Columbia's existence. Hoppenfeld and Finley came up with the idea of inviting experts in those fields to act as consultants, but Rouse liked the idea of a "brainstorming group," which would "get all the key disciplines around one table, interacting with each other and formulating new ideas."[199] He never expected that this group would do the actual planning for the company; he wanted them to provide "shafts of light" for his planners to use.[200] The idea was accepted, and work began to compile a list of potential participants. Eventually, Donald M. Michael, a social psychologist, was selected as the group's facilitator.

Bill Finley stated that the first thought was to invite the leading national experts in the various social science fields, but it was dismissed because their ideas were already etched in stone and available in print. "We were anxious for the planning of this town to come from unfrozen minds. So we assembled a rather distinguished group of relatively unknown names in a wide variety of fields."[201] The list of potential candidates was drawn and pared down until fourteen names remained, representing diverse areas of the social sciences, including economics, sociology, psychology, religion, government, education, medicine, housing, recreation and communications. Later, Stanley Hallett, who assisted the Work Group, would describe the group as "represent[ing] the liberal academic tradition and the liberal-social wing of political activists."[202] However, two glaring omissions stood out: there was only one woman and no identifiable minority representatives. Columbia's vision of a diverse and equality-based community was certainly not reflected in the makeup of this group.

Columbia: The Next America, 1965–1967

The Work Group. Jim Rouse hired fourteen social scientists to advise on Columbia's creation. A portion of that group is pictured in a work session, including (left to right) Donald Michael, Herbert Gans, Bob Crawford, Jim Rouse, Bill Rouse and Antonia Chayes. *Columbia Archives.*

Invitations were sent out and accepted, and on November 14, 1963, the Work Group had its first meeting. The night before, Rouse was advised by Finley and Hoppenfeld not to use the word "love" in his presentation. Although the word had been used often in Rouse's speeches and Columbia's planning, they felt that its use might turn off some of the group's academics. Speaking from rough notes that he had scribbled out hurriedly (a common Jim Rouse habit), he laid before the group Columbia's goals: to dignify people; ennoble the landscape and the face of nature; respect and marshal constructively natural forces at work in the area; create a balanced community; create the opportunity for a strong sense of community; provide a wide variety of opportunities in all societal realms; prevent disorders—physical and emotional—to the fullest extent possible; and, be a highly profitable venture.[203] He also encouraged them to be free in all aspects of their work and to let nothing confine them. "Forget feasibility," he encouraged, "it will compromise us soon enough."[204]

Rouse stated later that this session was "the worst day I ever spent, [like] walking through mud."[205] The group seemed directionless, as each participant sought to establish territoriality and began to express negativity regarding Columbia's future. The tenor of the meeting changed when Chester Rapkin, a housing expert, brought up the word

Rouse had been asked to eschew—love! "You know we are all missing the point of these discussions," he said. "We are being asked how in a new community to nourish love." According to Jim Rouse, "the morale and performance of the group was transformed. And from then on, for four months, it was a creative, vigorous, sharing experience."[206]

Looking back on the Work Group's role in Columbia's development, it is difficult to find any facet of the plan that they did not cover. They didn't do the planning but they donated many "shafts of light" for the planners to use. Rouse added that "they gave us more confidence to go forward on every front. We felt there weren't many potholes that we hadn't explored in advance."[207]

A Spiritual Strengthening

During the tenure of the Work Group, Mort Hoppenfeld gave Jim Rouse a copy of a book entitled *Call to Commitment*, written by Reverend Gordon Cosby, the pastor of a small Washington congregation called the Church of the Savior. Cosby had established this ecumenical church in 1947, and its anchor was the concept of mission. Each member was to "combine an inner sense of mission with external applications to 'social uplift'...reinforced by participation in small mission groups," which would become part of the larger church body.[208] Rouse would later describe Cosby as "a perfectly remarkable man," and his church as "the most authentic church of the contemporary world that I know of."[209]

Church of the Savior demanded a strong commitment from its congregants, who were required to take five night courses from its School of Christian Living and commit to a regimen that involved daily prayer and Bible reading, tithing and mission work.[210] Because of his busy schedule, Rouse was never able to gain admission to the congregation, but he and Libby made the trek to Washington once a week for four years to attend classes. Libby was particularly impressed with Gordon Cosby, ranking him with Harry Emerson Fosdick, who influenced her during her young adult years by providing her with spiritual inspiration.[211]

Throughout the rest of his life, Jim Rouse would maintain contact with Church of the Savior, offering advice and expertise on development projects and sometimes donating funds for them. Jim and Libby found this type of commitment-based religion so satisfying that they helped to create a similar community in Columbia during its early days. The Kittamaqundi Community, which emulates the philosophy and program of Church of the Savior, was founded in 1967; forty years later, it is still active.

Planning for the Next America

When he was hired in September 1963, Bob Tennenbaum remembers being led by a secretary to a windowless room in Jack Jones's office building next to Piper and Marbury to study the map of the properties from which Columbia would be made.

70

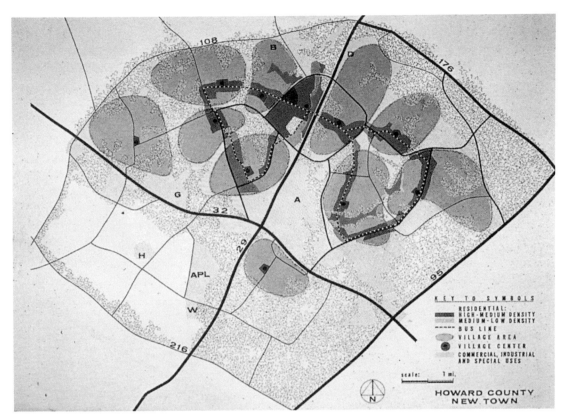

Howard County new town map. It shows the villages located in harmony with the contours of the land. A proposed transportation system ties them together. *Robert Tennenbaum.*

As the secretary was about to lock him in, she told him to call if he needed to leave and she would unlock the room for him.[212] He spent his time shading the properties as Jack Jones acquired them, hence the secrecy. Once the land deals were completed and Jim Rouse's intentions for the land were made public, Bob was moved to the Rouse Company headquarters at Baltimore's Saratoga Street where the planning for Columbia began in earnest.

On October 2, 1963, Hoppenfeld and Tennenbaum sketched out Columbia's first plan. A lake would be built along Route 29, with the Town Center adjacent to its western side, providing the new city with its central core.[213] Later, an elaborate town center was designed, including the lakefront and surrounding area. The name given to this area was Kittamaqundi, meaning "friendly meeting place" in the language of one of the Native American tribes that had inhabited Maryland. The lake is commonly referred to as Lake Kittamaqundi today, although the original intention was to use the name to "apply to both the water and its immediate surroundings, all of which it was hoped would become 'the friendly meeting place' for the new city."[214]

The basic framework of Columbia's plan was the system of villages, designed to replicate the spirit and security of Jim Rouse's Easton childhood. In a June 23, 1963 memo to Bill Finley, he stated "that people grow best in small communities of 5,000

71

Planners and designers at work, 1966. Mort Hoppenfeld, Bob Tennenbaum and Ted Baker (left to right) bringing Columbia to life. *Robert Tennenbaum; photo by Rodney Boyce.*

to 10,000 people, where the institutions that are the dominant forces in their lives are within the scale of their comprehension and sense of responsibility."[215] From this came the plan to create nine core villages, each with surrounding neighborhoods, a decision made easier by the natural contours of the land, which suggested such clustering.[216] Realizing that vision required roads, sidewalks, pathways, an open space system, parks, sewerage and utility connections, a village center, apartments, town houses and single-family dwellings—in short, everything that would be needed to give Columbia's first inhabitants a place to live in comfort and ease.

Expanding the Staff

An expanding project required additional staffing to deal with the many facets of the new town's development. At the beginning, it was clear that something special was being created; "Camelot" became the code word of choice. Donald Michael, the Work Group facilitator, suggested to Jim and Libby Rouse that "because this city should be

different, it should have an historian."[217] When the job was advertised, two applications were received. One applicant had impeccable Ivy League credentials; the other had led a nomadic life, was a budding playwright and had worked for a radical radio station in liberally minded Berkeley, California. After interviewing both candidates, Bill Finley asked his secretary Sandy Price what she thought of the candidates. While she found the first to have the better qualifications, she said the second, Wallace Hamilton, "looks like a lot more fun."[218] Hamilton got the job, and along with ably handling his job as Columbia's first historian, he brought to the company an entertaining, intellectual wit and a prose style seldom seen in corporate America.

Dick Anderson, a certified public accountant, interviewed for a position with the company as a favor for a friend. He became fascinated with the Columbia project and was eventually hired even though he had no experience in the planning and developing arenas. He quickly learned the ropes of the business, and eventually became chief financial officer, followed by stints as Columbia's assistant general manager and ultimately its general manager. At the time, he also was the company's youngest vice-president, an achievement that would later be topped by the even younger Mike Spear.[219]

Jim Wannemacher joined the Columbia staff in June 1965. After receiving a master's degree from the University of Pennsylvania's planning school, he originally signed on with the Levitts, developers responsible for postwar suburban creations in the Long Island and Philadelphia areas. He attended a Mort Hoppenfeld slide show presentation on Columbia in Philadelphia, found it "fascinating" and decided to cast his lot with the new city.[220] For a year, he had no single identifiable job, playing the role of a "gofer." Eventually, he settled in as a project manager and was responsible for projects such as the music pavilion, interfaith center, bus system and the city's first library.

Bill Finley realized that since he was handling 120 different projects within the Columbia plan, someone else needed to actually manage the construction sites and projects. Bob Cameron, originally hired by Bill Rouse to create a construction department within the company, eventually ended up managing both the shopping center and Columbia wings of the company. In Columbia, his job was supervising fifty people who accepted the challenge to bring all the projects in on time and within budget, while also appreciating the company's aesthetic goals and economic needs.[221] After becoming blind, he continued to work at his job, and did so with dignity and efficiency. Bob Tennenbaum wrote that his colleague Bob Cameron "was an amazing guy…[who] had the ability to visualize [plans]. All you had to give him was a verbal description."[222]

Perhaps the most interesting hire by the Rouse Company was Jim Furniss, who read a 1967 *Life* magazine article on Jim Rouse and Columbia and knew immediately that he wanted to be part it. Once he convinced his wife, Betty, that he hadn't lost his mind, he hopped into his topless jeep and drove from northeastern Pennsylvania to Cross Keys for an interview. He met with Jim Rouse, who decided he had no use for someone with a degree in animal science and nutrition who was running a dairy farm. However, when he was about to send him back to Pennsylvania, Furniss told Rouse he wanted to work for him and would to do any job required and learn to do it well. There was a silent pause, then Jim said: "With an attitude like that, you're hired." Jim Furniss worked for Columbia Association (CA) and was involved in many projects, including the landscaping for the new village of Wilde Lake, where he assisted Jim Rouse's sister Dia, who was in charge of that portion of the project. Later, Jim Rouse referred to him as the "Johnny Appleseed of Columbia" for all the trees he personally planted.[223]

These were heady but busy times for the fast-growing Columbia group. Bob Cameron described his colleagues as "the highly talented, energetic, and sometimes crazy, team of people that Jim Rouse had recruited," whose excitement for the project created a "joyous zeal" that sometimes resulted in seven-day work weeks.[224] Bob Morris, a consultant who was brought in to advise on transportation matters, said that "people were doing something they believed in; [to them] it wasn't just an ordinary job."[225] This sense of excitement continued to attract people to the company. In 1970 Bill Finley was trying to convince Mel Levine to join the Camelot crew. When Bill finished his pitch, Levine said, "Give me ten seconds to think about it." He spent almost fifteen years working for the company in a variety of jobs and later worked as a consultant with Jim Rouse on many important projects.[226] Perhaps Jack Jones described the spirit best when he said, "We were out to prove something," that private money could build a model city. "[And] we were young enough and dumb enough to try."[227]

Bill Finley saw the Columbia project as a prototype for new cities that would be needed in the future. He would later state that "what we learn working on Columbia should be carefully scrutinized and passed along in order that the coming generation will gain from our experiences."[228] More seemed to be at stake than a single city; some felt they had a chance to change the course of American urban history.

Economic Feasibility

Jim Rouse had been sincere when he told the Work Group to ignore financial constraints that might interfere with their creative work. However, when the planning actually began, such considerations could not be dismissed. Because he promised that Columbia would make a profit, a goal his major investors shared, economic considerations had to be factored in to all decisions. In late 1963, Robert Gladstone, a Washington economist, was asked by Bill Finley and Mort Hoppenfeld to serve on the Work Group, and also to act as an economic consultant to the company. While on the Work Group, Gladstone wrote a series of position papers on economic matters that became an economic model used to shape the new city's development.

The Columbia Economic Model (CEM) was designed to manage this large-scale development project and determine its economic feasibility for the life of the project. The model assisted the company in the following areas: (1) it required department heads and managers to examine constantly assumptions, needs and prospects for all projects and activities; (2) it put pressure on people to be more efficient in doing their jobs; (3) it ensured that all decisions made were economically viable.[229] The CEM was designed to answer the following questions: How much money will be spent? How much revenue will be taken in? What profits will accrue and when will they be available? To a company that had borrowed $50 million, and had creditors who wanted to make a profit from their investment, the answers to these questions were crucial.

The Green Book, which was created in 1962 to determine the new town's economic viability, came up with a formula that showed that within twelve years after its opening, the profits would total $67 million, a rather hefty sum.[230] However, in mid-1964, Robert Gladstone made his first actual projection—profits for the city's first fifteen years would total only $15 million, due to unexpectedly higher prices for goods, materials and services. This new projection caused the company to increase the residential density rate of the new city to generate more income, and to take steps to ensure that it would have as great a "take-off" period in the early years as was possible to create the momentum necessary to increase the profit margin.[231] These profit-driven compromises with the original vision were sobering reminders of the larger economic constraints Columbia faced as it began to take shape.

Jim Rouse and Frazar Wilde. Wilde's company financed much of Columbia's early construction. Rouse named Columbia's first village and its lake after him. They are pictured with the lake behind them. *Enterprise Community Partners, Inc.*

The Next America Comes to Life

When the planning process began in late 1963, the planners knew little of the nature of the land that was purchased. No on-site survey was possible, due to the secretive nature of the ongoing land purchases. Maps and aerial photographs were ordered, and field surveys—by helicopter, car and on foot by Bob Tennenbaum—were conducted to inspect topographic and land features, to note land forms of particular potential, to identify problem areas and to plot aesthetic features that would be retained or amplified.[232] Locations for schools, industry, low- and high-density housing and lake sites were virtually dictated by the land and the proper usage of it—that is, keeping it in harmony with nature.[233]

The original plan contained a 3,400-acre greenbelt that would ring the new town, in order to define its boundaries and protect it from outside development that was bound to follow. Unfortunately, it took up too much of the land allocated for the city for both open and developed space, and interfered with the natural streambeds that had to be preserved.[234] There was also some thought that the greenbelt might not succeed in separating Columbia from impending development and would be too costly to create.

Connecticut General's original loan for the land purchase project was repaid, and now new funds were needed for the next phase. Negotiations began between Jim Rouse and Frazar Wilde, which resulted in another $25-million loan for Columbia. With that in hand, Teachers Insurance and Annuity Association (TIAA) added $15 million to the fund. Finally, David Rockefeller of Chase Manhattan Bank, who originally deemed Rouse's project too risky and refused to provide financing for the land acquisition, decided that Columbia was viable and contributed $10 million. The document all parties signed in December 1965 became known in the Rouse Company as the "Black Bible" for its significance to Columbia's development. With $50 million in hand, the Rouse group could begin design and construction.

At first, nothing came easily. When construction was about to begin in mid-1966, designers seemed reluctant to hand their projects over to the engineers until they were sure everything seemed perfect, a situation Wallace Hamilton later described as "sitting around there building Saint Augustine's City of God."[235] And the county government did not have enough staff to keep up with the demands that a new city's development placed upon it. When multiple agency approval was needed for projects, the delays seemed interminable. Eventually, many buildings were started before permits were issued.

To the rescue came George Levine, an engineer who, Wallace Hamilton said, "came in like a small volcano." When he announced that construction would begin with or without the plans, the plans soon materialized. When county officials continued to delay projects, George stormed into one of their offices and told one of the consultants that if he didn't speed things up, he would call up his boss and have him fired. In response, the consultant called Jim Rouse and screamed, "Don't let this man back in this room or I will throw him out the window."[236]

Jim Rouse now stepped in and, with his amiable, persuasive manner, was able to smooth feathers and get things going. He also decided that it was time for his staff to get going, exclaiming, "If we we're going to get this town built, somebody's gonna have to make some tyrannical decisions around here."[237] Suddenly, ideas and plans started moving and bulldozers soon followed. Columbia was on its way.

George Levine understood his role in all this. "In this business you have to be an actor," he said.[238] And he was a good one. He also turned out to be a creative engineer. When initial estimates for the dam to create the first village's lake came in at $900,000 and higher—the company had budgeted $500,000 for the project—George stepped in and made some changes in the design. The result: the cost dropped to $250,000 and the lake took two months to build instead of the original estimate of six months.[239]

Construction began in earnest in June 1966 on the Town Center and Wilde Lake Village—a $60-million project—conceived and constructed, as Bob Tennenbaum stated, "with great love and a lot of detail."[240] In the early development years, the Town Center was to have residential units, an exhibit center for the new city and office buildings, which embraced the western side of the lake. Later development was to include restaurants, shops and recreational facilities. Wilde Lake, where 12,000 people would reside in town houses, apartments or single-family dwellings, would require eight miles of streets, two miles of dual-lane landscaped parkway, a minibus route, as well as elementary schools and neighborhood centers complete with "tot lots." Its neighborhoods—Bryant Woods, Faulkner Ridge and Running Brook—were named

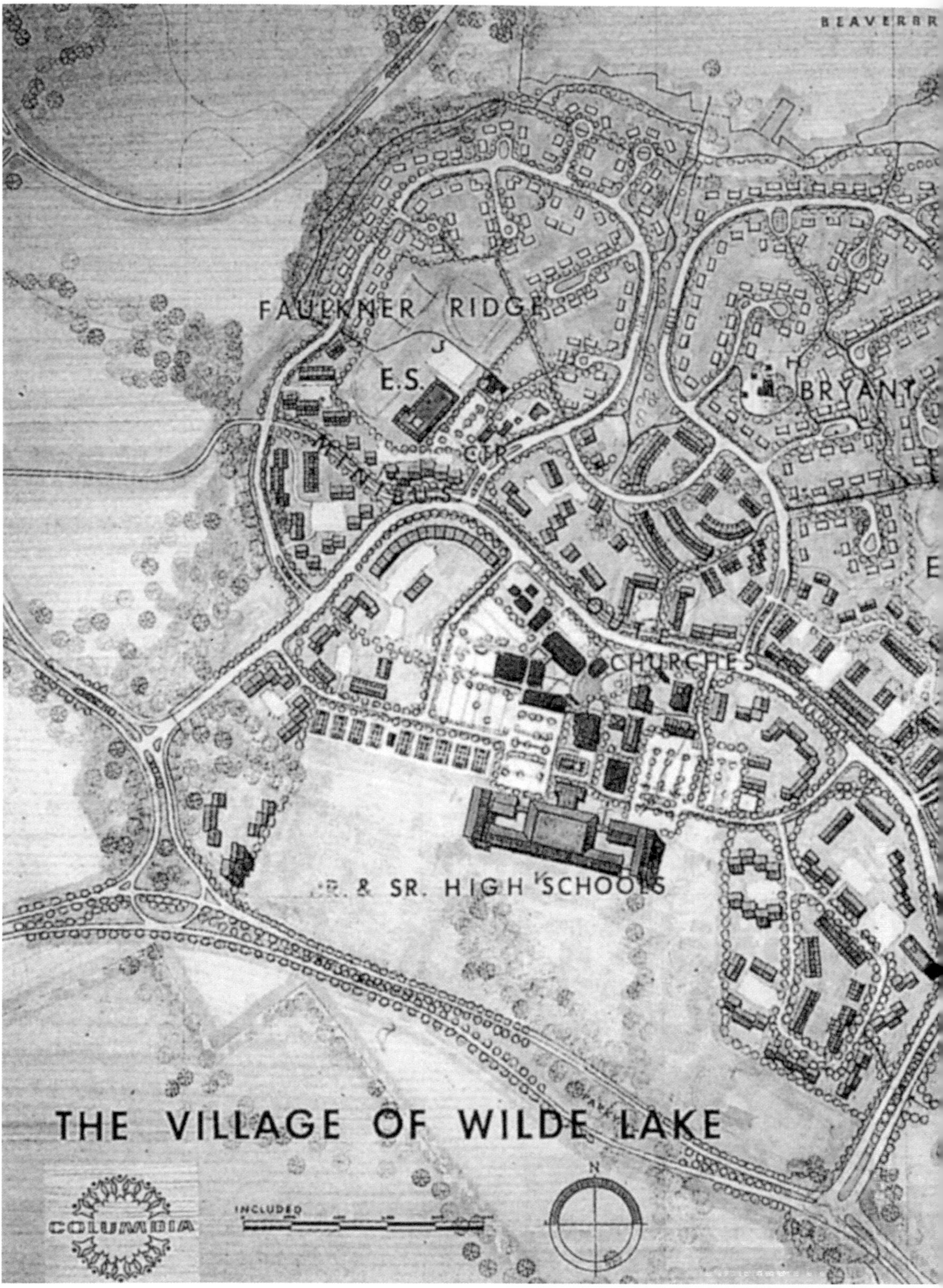

BEAVERBR

FAULKNER RIDGE

E.S.

BRYANT

CHURCHES

JR. & SR. HIGH SCHOOLS

THE VILLAGE OF WILDE LAKE

COLUMBIA

INCLUDED

N

THE BIRCHES

WILDE LAKE

WOODS

TOWN CENTER

The village of
Wilde Lake.
Illustrative
drawing of
the village,
showing its
components,
including
different
types of
housing,
schools,
institutions
and
businesses.
The cluster
of churches
shown was
replaced
by a single
interfaith
center.
*Robert
Tennenbaum.*

respectively for American writers William Cullen Bryant, William Faulkner and a poem written by Robert Frost. Street names also featured lines from their works. The village center would provide space for a village hall and community center, a shopping center, offices and studios, a swimming facility, tennis courts, playing fields and the city's first library and service station. Land was also set aside to accommodate construction of the city's first middle and high schools and its religious facilities center.[241]

Meeting Columbia's opening date, which was set for June 21, 1967, required yeoman work from all involved. Somehow things got done, and the dedication ceremony took place near the dam of the new village's lake. A plaque commemorated the naming for Frazar Wilde of Connecticut General, "whose wisdom, foresight and strong support made Columbia possible." Father John J. Walsh, pastor of the new city's Roman Catholic congregation, stated in his dedication prayer: "Represented here are man's ability to dream dreams of a better world—the faith required to crystallize those dreams—the knowledge and skills of the past to bring the dreams to a present reality." The "new city upon a hill" was officially open for business.

6.

Columbia's First Year
1967

We felt like we came over on the Mayflower, *and there aren't many people who can say that today.*
Helen and Martin Ruther, Columbia Pioneers, Class of 1967

The first families who moved into Columbia in 1967 did so for a variety of reasons. Some came for practical reasons, such as location and affordability. Others were attracted by Jim Rouse's open-door policy regarding race, a rare Maryland occurrence in 1967. Some interracial couples found it to be the only place where they would be accepted by their neighbors. The chance to participate in a new social experiment attracted others. Finally, the pioneering spirit that had fueled American dreams for centuries was being recreated in Columbia. Often, one suspects, more than one of these motives was at work.

Those who came in 1967 found a lakefront with one partially completed office building. Nearby was the exhibit center, designed by the firm of Gehry, Walsh and O'Malley, where people were introduced to Columbia. In the center's first year, 215,000 people passed through its doors. Most came out of curiosity; some quickly decided Columbia would be their next home; for others, Columbia became a possibility sometime down the road, when it was more fully developed.

Those who settled in Columbia quickly realized that it was not going to be a traditional suburban development. Amenities offered to them were coordinated through the Columbia Parks and Recreation Association, which eventually became known as the Columbia Association, or in "Columbspeak" as CA.

Exhibit center interior. For many, this was their first Columbia experience. Thousands flocked to the Frank Gehry–designed building to discover Columbia's hopes and dreams; some decided to make it their home. *Robert Tennenbaum.*

The Columbia Association

A way had to be found to pay for the things that made Columbia special. The county was responsible for the services provided to all of Howard County: schools, police and fire, libraries and welfare. Jim Rouse had promised that Columbia would not be a tax burden to Howard County, and would actually create more tax revenues than it would cost in additional county services. Financing neighborhood centers, swimming pools, golf courses, tennis courts, fitness gyms and generally tending to the community's needs would be the company's responsibility. Plans were conceived in 1965 to pay for these things.

The first idea was to create a separate taxing district, which would permit the company to collect an additional levy on all land in Columbia. This would have required the Maryland State Legislature to pass a law granting such power. At the time, the company was also seeking the legislature's approval for an enabling law, allowing the commissioners to create a new town zoning ordinance, a proviso Rouse badly needed. Concerned about confusion if the zoning and taxing district bills were submitted together, the company opted to separate the bills and request only the more vital zoning measure.[242]

From a series of meetings a plan emerged that called for the creation of a private corporation to manage the facilities and collect taxes from Columbia residents to pay for them. A formula was created by which all city taxpayers would annually pay the new corporation 75 cents for each $100 of assessed valuation of their property. For Columbians who owned a $25,000 home in 1967, their tax bill would have been $112.50. This would be in addition to their county property tax bill, which was assessed at $2.55 per $100 dollars of assessed valuation.

It took more than a year to plan for and then draw up the legal documents to create what became known as the Columbia Association. Jack Jones, who headed Columbia's land acquisition team, guided this process. The governing structure of CA was as unusual as the legal document that made it possible. It was decided that eventually CA should be its own master, free from Rouse Company control. It would be able to operate in an entrepreneurial fashion, by either building its own facilities—such as an ice-skating rink and a health club—or purchase services from outside sources, as it would later do with day-care and early education facilities.[243]

The association's first board of directors consisted of Jim Rouse and six company employees, a membership that would change as Columbia's population grew. For every 11,000 people who moved into the city, a locally elected person would replace one of the Rouse employees. Ultimately, as is the case today, the expanded board of ten people, each representing one of the city's villages and its Town Center, is composed of Columbia residents who are elected to represent each of those constituencies. CA's charter gives it great power and autonomy, causing Jack Jones, who helped write it, to remark wryly that the organization "can do almost anything but wage war and mint money."[244] A national search found Jack Slayton, former city manager of Vancouver, Washington, who became CA's first general manager. Loans totaling $5 million from Connecticut General and Teachers Insurance and Annuity gave the association the funds it needed to get started.[245]

Building Homes

In late 1964, discussions were held about what types of homes would be built in Columbia and who would build them. The enormous task of designing and constructing 36,000 residential units, a combination of single-family homes, town houses and apartments, would clearly require partnerships with outside companies. Decisions regarding how many builders and how many units of each would be built had to be made quickly because the company needed the income from selling land to builders to stabilize its cash flow.

Two alternatives were considered during these discussions. One involved selling the land to large developers, such as the Levitts, and having them build all of the single-family homes. A side proposal would have had one builder do all of the home construction in an entire village. While these master builders were obviously able to meet the new city's construction needs, there was some concern that they might be hard to control, and that their ideas might not conform with those of the city planners.[246] The other alternative—having smaller builders do the bulk of the construction—would give the Rouse Company the control it desired. This was the course that was finally adopted.

In 1966 Jim Rouse made a trip to Pittsburgh on company business and while there decided to look into Ryan Homes, Inc., one of the country's largest builders of single-family dwellings. The company, founded by Edward J. Ryan in 1918, was now run by his three sons, Edward, James and William. An August 20, 1966 *Business Week*

Wilde Lake Village Center, 1967. Features a community center, retail shops with offices above and Columbia's first public library. *Photo by Tadder.*

article entitled "Homebuilder Bucks Ebbing Sales Tide" described the innovative nature of the company, thereby piquing Jim Rouse's interest. He developed a strong bond with the middle son, James P. Ryan, and invited him to come to Columbia and build homes, an offer he accepted. The *Business Week* article concluded with the statement that "the [Ryan] company had been picked to build the first group of one-family homes in James Rouse's new city of Columbia, Maryland, with its targeted population of 100,000."[247] James P. Ryan Company operated under the Ryland logo (Ry for his family name, land for Maryland, his new home). In 1970 the company name officially changed to the Ryland Group. It would eventually build over half of Columbia's single-family homes and would become a large nationwide player in the housing industry. In 1983 Jim Ryan retired at the age of fifty, stating that "the company just out-grew me...and needed someone with more market sense."[248]

Ryland was joined by ten other builders. Some, like Howard Homes, built affordable town houses. Because apartment complexes did not exist in Howard County, no one was eager to take a chance with that market. Jim Rouse hired a builder named Tom Harkins to put up three hundred apartments to test the waters, and they quickly rented out. Rouse later stated that he wished he had built three thousand units to start with, because the demand would have supported such a market.[249] On the whole, the real estate business in Columbia had a great first year.

One thing that soon became crystal clear was that the racial bias permeating the Baltimore area housing market (and had led to all-white neighborhoods and developments) would not be tolerated in Columbia. There were no existing fair housing laws, although one would soon be enacted in Maryland, cosponsored by Baltimore State Senator Verda Welcome and Howard County's State Senator James Clark. When the law was working its way through the state legislature, Jim Rouse went to the General Assembly in Annapolis to testify on its behalf.[250]

Even with the enactment of a fair housing law, there were still tricks and ploys that realtors used to keep neighborhoods segregated. Jim Rouse would not allow any such practices. In a memo sent to all developers and sales associates in Columbia, he declared that "Columbia is a truly open city...we are 'color blind'...and [our policy] is unmistakable to everyone.[251] Mal Sherman, who had a successful real estate business in Baltimore and saw it go "down the drain" due to his support for open housing, came to Columbia to join Rouse's crusade for the same cause.[252] He once reported to Rouse that some salespeople were "steering" white home buyers away from cul-de-sacs with homes that already had been sold to black families. After a brief investigation, a decision was made: the builder would be sold no more lots in Columbia, even though he was president of the Maryland Homebuilders Association.[253]

Sometimes it was difficult to enforce this open-door policy. Once, four black families bought lots in a five-house cul-de-sac and a fifth black family was about to buy the fifth. Jim Rouse agonized over this situation and ultimately asked Sherman to talk the new black home buyers into purchasing a house in another section, which they eventually did. The house was then put into a "housing bank" for a time until it could eventually be sold to a white family.[254]

While some might not have approved of this attempt at social engineering, Jim Rouse never wavered from his belief in racial equality and the role integrated housing could play in making this a reality. Ridiculed or dismissed as foolish for his position on open housing, Rouse stood firm, convinced he was right. Many consider this to be one of his most principled stances. His Hawaiian racial epiphany was beginning to bear fruit.

Searching for a Home

It should come as no surprise that black Americans flocked to Columbia in large numbers to take advantage of its open-door racial policy. After fighting the bigoted real estate community in Maryland for decades, it was refreshing to be told that there was a place that not only accepted you, but also welcomed you with open arms.

Fred and Dorothy Weaver moved to Columbia in 1968 from the District of Columbia. Their friends in D.C. told them they were crazy, and Fred's mother, who had lived in Baltimore, warned the couple that Howard County "was a place where blacks were not allowed to go."[255] Both found new niches in Columbia: Dorothy, with her upbeat personality, lent her rich soprano voice to several church singing groups; Fred, with his strong interest in community affairs and political matters, acted as a gadfly, making sure that Columbia was living up to its ideals. County Executive Omar Jones honored Fred by appointing him to the county personnel board, the first black ever named to a county board.[256]

If black families were eager to move into Columbia, interracial families must have been ecstatic. Neighboring Virginia had an anti-miscegenation law banning interracial marriages, and Maryland, while having no such law, had little tolerance for interracial couples, especially those seeking to acquire a home. Columbia, unique in the region, welcomed multiracial families, and many were happy to accept that welcome. One such couple, Charles and Barbara Russell, happened upon Columbia. After being shown an apartment in Bryant Gardens, they were asked if they would like to rent it, and "thought we'd say yes before they [the sellers] changed their mind."[257] When the Russells moved in and theirs was the first child born in the new city, the event seemed fitting to many residents there. Charles Russell Jr. became, for some time, a Columbia treasure. Jim Rouse was thrilled that Columbia's first child was interracial and constantly used it as a promotion for Columbia's open-door policy, even though some of his own company's officials did not think this was a good marketing ploy.[258]

Michael and Diane Brown were another interracial couple who settled early in Columbia. As Diane succinctly put it, "Anyone who doesn't like the idea of change can't live here." She also looked forward to the time when "there will be no hassle about this: There's no time for that sort of thing here."[259] Those who came and could not live in such a setting eventually moved out. The rest stayed and became part of Columbia's history.

Another human-interest story from Columbia's pioneer phase involves Wes and Rose Yamaka. When Wes was thirteen and living on the West Coast, his family was interned in a Japanese American relocation camp during World War II, where they were all forced to live in a twenty-by-fifteen-foot room. The experience left him feeling like, "You're the enemy, you're a second-class citizen," a self-perception he carried through the years, "like a craw stuck in my throat." After a stint as a minister in California, he had the opportunity to become an educational associate of the Columbia Cooperative Ministry. He and his family moved to Columbia and became a part of the pioneer experience. It was in Columbia that he was finally able to shed the sense of exclusion that had bothered him for so long. He blossomed in the "welcoming aura of Columbia," and discovered "a sense of 'in-ness' that I had never felt before."[260]

No longer feeling like an outsider, Wes was able to follow his life's calling, which eventually included jobs in religious education and public relations work for the Rouse Company, creativity as an artist and co-owner of an art studio and shop and even a stint as a cook in Mrs. Z's, a homey restaurant that quickly became a Columbia institution. Having trained himself as a silk-screen artist, Yamaka's posters hung throughout the restaurant, contributing to the warm ambience of the place. Some said you weren't a true Columbian unless you had a Wes Yamaka poster in your house. When Wes and Rose moved back to the West Coast in 1997, Columbia lost a part of its original family. Back for a recent visit, he said, "Columbia still feels more like home to me than any other place."[261]

Betty Caldwell came to Columbia by way of Senegal, West Africa, after a stint in the Peace Corps, and immediately felt "right at home" with the city's community-based value system. She felt so comfortable with its high ideals and far-reaching vision that

Wes Yamaka silk-screen.
For early Columbians,
Yamaka's art was a prized
possession. This sample was
a cover of a program for the
Kittamaqundi Community.
Betty Caldwell.

Minibus. Columbia's first transportation system was designed to keep automobile traffic to a minimum. Unfortunately, the system never had enough use to warrant its expense, and it was ultimately scrapped. *Columbia Archives.*

she marveled, "I thought Columbia had pretty much been invented just for me."[262] She has held jobs in Washington, D.C., Annapolis, Baltimore and Columbia, but always considered the latter as the anchor of her life. Many other Peace Corps volunteers followed Betty and came to Columbia, finding there an ideal venue for their own caring, sharing community values. By 1985 more than fifty ex-Peace Corps workers had made Columbia their home.[263]

James Medwin's road to Columbia was more circuitous, both figuratively and literally. His family came to Howard County in search of better schools in 1960 and settled into one of the pre-Columbia suburban housing developments, which were rapidly dotting the county landscape. He remembers hunting and fishing in the area that was to become Town Center and Wilde Lake. While a college student, he worked for the Rouse Company as a minibus driver, taking people around the area he knew before Columbia. Impressed with the Columbia plan, after college he returned to Columbia to live, first as an apartment renter, then a homeowner. He and his wife, Claudia, have lived in Columbia since 1971, and have resided in three different Columbia villages.[264]

The physical realities that faced Columbia's first settlers must have tested their mettle—dust, mud and dirt all around, frequent power outages, the busing of their children to outlying schools and noise pollution from all the equipment that was building the city that would soon envelop them. But like many waves of pioneers who had found their way to new lands throughout our nation's history, they persevered and many have made Columbia their lifelong home. If Jim Rouse meant Columbia to be a city to "grow people," its pioneers were the cream of the crop. A special bond developed between these families and, until recent years, reunions were held to commemorate the city's early years and the special role the pioneers played in it.

The Merriweather Post Pavilion

Columbia's Debutante Ball occurred on July 15, 1967. The place was the Merriweather Post Pavilion, located in a tree-filled park named Symphony Woods, with five thousand covered seats and space on the grass for five thousand more. Named for Marjorie Merriweather Post of the Post Cereal family, who was instrumental in getting the National Symphony to adopt it as their summer home, the amphitheater was state-of-the-art in design (created by Frank Gehry and Dave O'Malley after a first attempt proved unsuitable) and sound system (constructed by Chris Jaffe). Projects Manager Jim Wannemacher worked hard in the six months he had to get it ready for opening night, and with the assistance of an industrious group of people, the Post Pavilion was ready to make its debut. The National Symphony Orchestra played; composer Morton Gould created a commissioned piece entitled "Columbia, Broadsides for Orchestra"; and pianist Van Cliburn performed Rachmaninoff's Second Piano Concerto. Vice President Hubert H. Humphrey led a list of distinguished guests that included members of Congress, a cabinet secretary and other influential people. Designed to be a night to remember, the debut concert instead became infamous. The next day's *New York Times* article said it all: "Symphony Gala Ends as Okefenokee of the Arts."[265]

The rains came and never stopped. The concert went on as planned until the orchestra was playing in water up to its members' knees.[266] The newly laid sod could not absorb the deluge and created swamp-like conditions. Newspaper photos showed people slogging to their cars, most of the women barefoot so as not to ruin their shoes. A dinner-dance scheduled at the town plaza had to be postponed as the rains had made the plaza one big puddle and, as the *Times* reported, "The party could not be moved inside because there was no inside."[267] After this inauspicious debut event, the Rouse people repaired the damage and salted away stories they could tell their grandchildren. The Pavilion, in fact, had a successful first season, anchored by the National Symphony Orchestra playing in its new summer home. Also, George Balanchine brought the New York City Ballet to the Pavilion for three seasons of top-notch performances.

Some of these were memorable, but for different reasons. Carolyn Kelemen recounted that a huge downpour threatened to cancel a performance, until Balanchine dismissed the already soaked orchestra. He had a piano rolled out on the stage, and the ballet was performed, accompanied by the single piano. Another performance featured the choreography of Jerome Robbins, a rare treat for local audiences.[268]

Merriweather Post Pavilion Gala. Conductor Howard Mitchell of the Washington National Symphony, Vice President Hubert Humphrey, Marjorie Merriweather Post and James Rouse on stage for the pavilion's first concert. *Columbia Archives; photo by Max Araujo.*

Unfortunately, the National Symphony Orchestra went bankrupt the following year and was only able to pay half of its contracted $50,000 annual fee to the Rouse Company. Money that Mrs. Post was expected to donate never materialized, leaving some people today to wonder why, after all these years, the Pavilion is still named for her.[269]

Columbia: Off and Running

The city's first year was marked by neverending construction and a dizzying number of "firsts": residents, apartments, town houses, single-family dwellings, a gas station and a 7-Eleven store. A transportation system for the city was another first, and after much planning, design and construction, a series of minibuses was ready for opening day events and was used to transport dignitaries and guests to various places. The buses were to operate on a separate road system to avoid traffic snarls and delays. The nineteen- to twenty-three-passenger buses were eighty-one feet long and designed for low-speed and multi-stop-and-start driving.[270] The first route tied the exhibit center to the village of Wilde Lake. This transportation experiment was troublesome from the beginning, mainly for financial reasons, and never developed the way the planners had hoped.

Industrial development was an important part of Columbia's goal to be a self-sufficient city, not only as a revenue stream for the company, but also as the source of employment for many of its residents. The ratio of jobs to city dwellers was a constant source of concern to the planners. Thus, a great deal of effort was spent trying to attract industrial clients to the new city. In 1966 Hittman Associates, a consulting and design firm in such areas as aerospace, energy, metallurgy, medical engineering and nuclear design, was the first to sign up.[271] Only four years old and at the cutting edge of some futuristic technologies, it seemed to be a perfect fit for a city calling itself the Next America. Ground was broken in May 1967, with Maryland Governor Spiro T. Agnew doing the honors; by December, the new plant was up and running. Only one month earlier, Ametek, Inc., manufacturers and distributors of pressure gauges, instruments and testing devices, moved into a distribution center in Columbia. They were joined by Eastern Products Corporation, manufacturers of components used in home construction. This was just the beginning for Columbia's industrial development; bigger enterprises were just around the corner.

Life in the Next America

In Columbia's first village, Wilde Lake, a multipurpose community center was built adjacent to the village green and named Slayton House after Jack Slayton, the Columbia Association's first general manager, who died suddenly in January 1967. His wife, Barbara, decided to stay in Columbia, the place she had grown to love, and became a pillar of the community, serving its citizens as an officer in the Columbia Bank and Trust, the city's first financial institution. Her identification with the community was so strong that upon her death in 1991, an obituary referred to her as the "grandmother of Columbia," a name that some citizens had given to her.[272] Slayton House, owned by CA, met many needs during that first year, serving as a venue for town meetings and religious services.

Right next to Slayton House, construction began on an indoor swim center. With an A-frame shape and built to Amateur Athletic Union specifications, its eight lanes and three diving boards permitted anything from competitive swimming and water ballet to general public use.[273] A mile or so down the road, Hobbit's Glen Golf Course opened for public use. Under the leadership of golf pro Hank Majewski, it grew in stature to become one of the area's best courses. According to Columbia Projects Manager Jim Wannemacher, Hank was not only a consummate pro, but also "became one of Columbia's premier promoters."[274]

The Wilde Lake village center provided the site for another "first"—Columbia's inaugural library. Marvin Thomas was director of the Howard County library system and stood out as a county official eager to meet the challenges that Columbia provided.

Benjamin Banneker Fire Station. Columbia's first fire station opened in 1971. It was designed by noted architect Frank Gehry. *Joseph Mitchell.*

Recognizing that the city might be more demanding regarding library services given the highly educated residents it attracted, he submitted cost estimates well above his budget. Due to Marvin's tenacity and persuasiveness, Bill Finley and Jim Wannemacher generally found a way to keep him happy.[275] Thomas was also a visionary who saw the bright future for the county library system, including a new building in downtown Columbia.

Providing Columbia with fire protection and ambulance service proved to be another example of solid county-city cooperation. The existing system was based on volunteer districts spread throughout the county. However, the closest station was located in nearby Clarksville, several miles from Columbia and quite a distance when dealing with potential life-and-death situations. Clearly, Columbia needed a fire station, but what would it do until one could be built?

Paul Spangler, Clarksville's fire chief, came to the rescue. While his company provided temporary service, he worked tirelessly to see that the new city had everything it needed to provide protection for its residents. Jim Wannemacher remarked that he "could not estimate the hours he [Spangler] devoted to our needs."[276] Jim Furniss, the dairy farmer who Jim Rouse almost didn't hire, proved to be an important liaison between Columbia and the Clarksville Fire Station. Furniss quickly became one of its volunteers, and was instrumental in the planning and development of Columbia's first fire station. He eventually became its first lieutenant. When Benjamin Banneker Company opened, it was manned by two paid county firemen (both from Clarksville) and volunteers recruited from Columbia. According to Jim Furniss, "The relationship between Howard County and Columbia became very strong and I believe that the fire department agreement did a lot to spark the relationship!"[277]

Another positive outcome of this Columbia–Howard County fire accord was the integration of the Howard County Fire Department. Columbian Charles Russell became the Clarksville Fire Department's first African American member. "After a little shakiness at first," things warmed up and Russell eventually was elected the station's secretary. He stayed until Columbia's Banneker fire station opened and remained there until its volunteers were replaced by paid firemen.[278]

Creating a Community

Martin Ruther remembers Columbia's lack of organizations or clubs, and if you wanted one, "you had to start it yourself."[279] An avid chess player, he formed the Columbia Chess Club; forty years later, it still meets, though in a more informal manner. Helen Ruther helped found the Columbia chapter of the League of Women Voters and has devoted forty years to the cause of political education. She also was part of a CA-sponsored welcoming committee that visited newcomers and made them feel at home in Columbia. She developed the habit of matching people with similar interests and many early Columbians owed their first friendships to Helen's matchmaking, one of which resulted in an engagement. When the Columbia Jewish Congregation put on a performance of *Fiddler on the Roof*, Helen played the *yenta*; many considered it perfect typecasting![280]

Fred Weaver recalled Columbia's lack of bars, taverns and restaurants—places where people could socialize and get to know each other. Being politically minded, he craved a forum where the issues of the day could be chewed and digested. He found it in a discussion group on political and social issues organized by county library director Marvin Thomas, himself an early Columbia resident.[281] Much time was also spent attending community meetings, where people could voice their opinions regarding Columbia's growth and development, a process Jim Rouse strongly urged.

These first year's activities exemplified what Columbia would be known for throughout its existence—political activism, social responsibility, charity-based neighborliness—and more clubs, groups and organizations than one could imagine. Much of that spirit still remains today.

On June 21, 1968, Columbia celebrated its first birthday with a lakefront dinner-dance, compliments of the Rouse Company. The city's creators had reason to beam—more than one thousand people lived in a city that had created more than three thousand jobs. There were two lakes, five hundred acres of completed open space and countless physical amenities appropriate for a "city to grow people."[282] It would be hard to conceive of it as a full-blown city yet, but to one journalist, it had "the fresh evening look of a 1968 new town to the Route 29 motorist who passes the lake and brilliantly lighted village around it."[283]

7.

COLUMBIA

MAKING ITS MARK, 1968–1972

It is still very early in the life of the new city, but the development momentum that has been generated is encouraging.
The Rouse Company, 1968 Annual Report

The favorable press that Columbia received before and during its initial period of construction continued beyond its first year. All sorts of magazines and journals were quick to sing its praises and wish for it a bright and productive future. But there were also forces at work that would undermine its efforts and shake the very foundation of its being. Some were internally created; others were external and beyond the control of anyone involved with the new city. The late 1960s and early 1970s were troubling times for the United States. Not even a place like Columbia would be immune.

Jim Rouse's Company in the 1960s

The 1960s were a profitable period for Jim Rouse's companies. In 1960 Community Research and Development reported the opening of its first mall and the promise of more to come.[284] Four years later, the number of malls had grown to five. At the end of the decade, there were twelve, with eight more in the pipeline.[285] The mortgage-banking wing continued to grow, with offices operating in seven major urban centers stretching from coast to coast.

James W. Rouse and Company was the legal name of Jim's company, and because it was cumbersome, people generally referred to it as the Rouse Company. On June 20, 1966, the name was officially changed to the one that everybody already used.

Jim Rouse was the new company's president and chief executive officer, and its stock was traded "over the counter" rather than on one of the major exchanges. Eventually, company stock would be traded on the NASDAQ board.[286] Two years later, it was announced that the Rouse Company was moving its corporate headquarters from the village of Cross Keys to Columbia, on the shore of Lake Kittamaqundi.

In that same year, Rouse announced the formation of the American City Corporation, which was created "to apply the capability gained in planning, developing, and financing new communities to the restructuring of old cities."[287] Leo Molinaro, a friend from Rouse's days with the American Committee to Improve Our Neighborhoods (ACTION), became its president. One of his first acts was to create a symposium where all of Columbia's shapers could share what they had learned with other interested parties. One such person was a Texan named George Mitchell, from a large Greek immigrant family, who had amassed a fortune in the wildcatting environment of the Texas oil fields. He attended, soaked it all in and went back to Houston, to build his own model city named The Woodlands. In the early 1970s, when a lot of Rouse Company employees left the company for a variety of reasons, many found new jobs in George Mitchell's model city.[288]

National Politics Confronts Columbia

One of the most turbulent years in the country's recent history was 1968. The civil rights movement, with the white backlash it engendered, and the antiwar movement, generated by heavy American participation in the Vietnam War, seemed to be tearing the country apart. The assassinations of Martin Luther King Jr. in April and presidential candidate Robert F. Kennedy in June seemed to be harbingers of further tragedies. The political currents would bring Columbians into the national debates and give them an opportunity to tell the world what they and their city were all about.

Senator Eugene McCarthy, whose Democratic presidential candidacy gave the antiwar movement a sense of legitimacy, made a campaign stop in Columbia and was well-received by its strongly liberal-minded, antiwar residents. Another proposed visit would create more of a stir; the request came from Alabama Governor George Wallace's Independent party, with its segregationist, divisive, pro-war stance. When Wallace's supporters asked to use the Merriweather Post Pavilion for their rally, Jim Rouse granted their request.

A subsequent town meeting revealed a divided city: some supported the founder's position and others felt that Wallace was opposed to everything their city stood for, and should not be allowed to speak there. Eventually the developer's opinion carried the day, and people began to make a positive out of this apparently negative experience.[289] A Columbia-led "counter-rally" would be held under the theme of "We have a dream—One America!" These two events would present, in Jim Rouse's words, "an almost historic statement of two very different views of America's future."[290] Fred Weaver emceed the counter-rally, and several people spoke, including State Senator Jim Clark. Columbia resident Charles Russell stirred the crowd when he stated, "You have come to show what brotherhood is and that you believe in true democracy; that all men are truly brothers."[291] When it was time for Jim Rouse to speak, he was brief but eloquent: "One year ago in Howard County, Columbia raised a banner of hope: it was labelled 'the Next America.'" He went on to describe Columbia as a place "where building a community together is a more demanding but rewarding task than by forecasting division— and separation. Where hate is truly overcome by love." Turning this potentially negative incident into a very positive one, he concluded by stating: "We thank you God for the awareness of our strength, our unity, our love that George Wallace generates among us in Columbia tonight."[292] David Barkley of the *Howard County Times* put the exclamation point on the evening when he wrote a few days later: "Fear knocked at the door of Columbia last week. Faith answered. A development disappeared and a community was born."[293]

The new city could not escape the national debate raging in the country regarding the war in Vietnam, and it hit close to home for Columbia's founder. With his active affiliation with the World Federalists and their policy of peace through international cooperation, the policies pursued by the Johnson and Nixon administrations could not have pleased him. However, Rouse did not openly speak out against the war until discussions with his two sons Ted and Jim began to change his mind. Jim ultimately applied for conscientious objector status, and his father eventually testified on his behalf.[294] Furthermore, his daughter Robin's husband, Edward Norton, was a Marine Corps lieutenant stationed in Vietnam, who by 1968 had also begun to question American involvement. In a letter dated February 4, 1968, he expressed that view to his father-in-law, explaining that "sometimes I am not so disturbed by what the United States is actually doing in Vietnam, as I am by what we have convinced ourselves we are doing." He went on to recommend de-escalation as a potentially useful strategy.[295]

Despite his family's feelings, Jim did not speak publicly about the war until May 7, 1970. The invasion of Cambodia, student demonstrations, renewed bombings of North Vietnam and the killing of student protestors at Kent State University in Ohio by national guardsmen finally convinced him to speak out.[296] He and Libby sent a long letter to President Richard Nixon, which appeared the following day in the *Washington Post* as a full-page, paid advertisement. Its headline, in large, bold print, stated **WAGE PEACE, MR. PRESIDENT**. In a clear and passionate manner, Rouse labeled war as "our proven enemy" and urged the president to wage peace "as it has never been waged before."[297] Jim and Libby's actions engendered much support, including contributions to have the piece repeated later in the month in the *New York Times*. It also provoked some pointed criticism and went a long way toward earning Jim Rouse a prominent place on Richard Nixon's "Enemies List." To the people of Columbia, however, who mostly shared the Rouses' view, their stand was received well, with nonviolent demonstrations against the war held throughout the city.

The Interfaith Concept

Another movement that gained ground during the polarizing 1960s was ecumenism, in which religious denominations stress the commonalities they possess while minimizing their differences. Sharing and cooperation would bring congregations together in search of a common good. Columbia provided an ideal place to test the viability of these new religious ideals.

From the beginning, Jim Rouse did not want his new city to have a traditional religious setup, with separate churches dotting the landscape. Land-wise, it was impractical, inefficient and costly. Socially, it would go against the grain of the philosophy of the new city with its emphasis on community-based goals and ideals. Fortunately, there were some like-minded clergy who agreed.

In February 1964, Rouse asked state and national religious leaders to attend a meeting to discuss religious life in the new city. From this session came a memorandum written by Dr. Joseph Merchant of the United Church of Christ in which he urged that "Columbia City be seen as a special opportunity in which the churches could depart from their traditional methods of church development."[298] A month later, the National Council of Churches "designated Columbia as a pilot area in which to explore, experiment, and develop the best new forms of ecumenical ministry which could be cooperatively planned."[299] This brought Dr. Stanley Hallett, executive secretary of the department of church planning of the Church Federation of Chicago, to Columbia to work toward this goal.

Hallett would also advise the 1964 Columbia Work Group on religious matters. He completed a study for the National Council of Churches, which was offered to the group for analysis. Using an economic model, he discovered that carrying charges on individual church properties that were seldom in use "were the extravagance of church life," draining funds that "could be used for an unprecedented range of church-related programs."[300] Besides the usual individual church programs, he saw the potential to create cooperative institutional elements in pastoral counseling, metropolitan and world mission work, church and vocational counseling, a national conference center, retreat centers, an ecumenical institute and a nonprofit religious facilities corporation.[301] To the Columbia planners, Hallett's report must have seemed like manna from heaven.

As Columbia's opening neared, steps were taken to bring some of this work to fruition. In the spring of 1966, a Religious Facilities Corporation, comprising five Protestant denominations, was formed to advance these new religious goals. In its Articles of Incorporation, it stated that one of its aims was "the construction, ownership and operation of facilities for worship and for other religious activities."[302] Reverend Clarence Sinclair, a staff member of the National Council of Churches, stated that the Protestant-oriented group was attempting to broaden the group's base by reaching out to the Roman Catholic and Jewish faiths to join them in this endeavor.[303] Soon after, Cardinal Lawrence Sheen of Baltimore announced the appointment of Father John J. Walsh to be the Catholic coordinator of ecumenism in Columbia.

The groundwork to bring Jews into the interfaith concept began before Columbia opened its doors. The Jewish Council of Howard County was formed in March 1967, and one of its purposes was to participate in the social and religious development of the new city, and "to contribute to the development of policies for interfaith cooperation."[304] The first Jews who came to Columbia created the Columbia Jewish Council and took steps to organize and create a community. Shep Jeffreys, a member, recounted that without sufficient numbers to hire a permanent rabbi, the job of creating worship services mainly fell to the congregation itself.[305] As the number of Jews increased and became large enough to meet different worship needs, three congregations were formed: Temple Beth Shalom, conservative; Howard County Reform Congregation, which changed its name to Temple Solel and eventually became Temple Isaiah; and some congregants from the original council remained together under the name of the Columbia Jewish Congregation, unaffiliated. There was also an attempt to start an Orthodox group but that proved unsuccessful.[306] Eventually, each group was able to attract rabbis and become part of the Columbia interfaith community.

Planning began regarding the construction of an interfaith center in Columbia's Wilde Lake village. Since the Roman Catholics were not officially a part of the Religious Facilities Corporation, steps had to be taken to bring them on board. Although the process was time-consuming and tedious, success finally came when the archdiocese joined and pledged $820,000 in loans for the building, bringing the total raised to more than $2.5 million.

Eventually, the group was asked to select a piece of property they intended to buy, which would then be submitted to the company for design approval. "Father John Walsh suggested simply that the sign say 'This is Godsville.'"[307] On June 22, 1969, ground was broken for Columbia's first interfaith center; two years later "Godsville" opened its doors.

An important creation of the Religious Facilities Corporation was the Interfaith Housing Corporation. In keeping with Jim Rouse's goal of making Columbia affordable to all, the churches decided to devote themselves to that cause. With some seed money donated by the Columbia Cooperative Ministry and the Archdiocese of Baltimore, plans were made to develop low- to middle-income housing. Money from the Federal Housing Authority made possible the building of three hundred units, scattered among several different areas in Columbia.[308] Father John Walsh was the guiding force in the program's development and subsequent success.

Physical and Mental Health in Columbia

Providing medical care for Columbia's first residents was a priority item for Howard Reasearch and Development (HRD). Howard County did not have a hospital, and the two closest ones were St. Agnes in southwest Baltimore and Montgomery County General, to the west in Olney, both about a half-hour drive from Columbia. Furthermore, the County Health Department was seriously understaffed and unable to handle any increased demand for services. Medical services and facilities had to be available, but what shape would they take?

In the speech Jim Rouse had delivered at the University of California, Berkeley, on September 23, 1963, one month before he announced his intentions to build Columbia, he raised many questions that a community developer would have to answer. In the area of healthcare, he asked: "What alternatives are there to discovering and relieving physical and emotional disorders and improving individual and community health? How should these alternatives be fit into physical planning?"[309] Rouse had been thinking a lot about the subject, having hired Dr. Paul Lemkau, professor of mental hygiene at the Johns Hopkins School of Public Health, to advise the Work Group on health-related issues. What finally emerged from those deliberations was shaped by two considerations: first was that people in a city of over 100,000 were going to get sick and need medical care in significant numbers; and second, and more interesting, the community concept "offered an exceptional opportunity to explore new ways not only to care for illness, but to prevent illness."[310] A major part of this would be the establishment of a prepaid, flat fee, comprehensive healthcare program (dubbed simply the Columbia Medical Plan) paid by the insured and offered to all Columbia residents.

The John Hopkins Hospital expressed interest in being involved in the new city's healthcare program and hired Dr. Joseph Sadusk, former medical director of the Food and Drug Administration, to "further develop and implement planning by Johns Hopkins for the establishment of a satellite hospital and Clinics at Columbia."[311] This news was not well received by the Hopkins medical faculty, some of whom feared that this venture might stretch the hospital's resources. Others called it "abhorrent," "a threat to my work" or asserted it was "not going to attract good medical people as residents."[312] Clearly there were problems at Hopkins, as Sadusk resigned after less than a year.

Jim Rouse continued to lobby Hopkins, assisted by Connecticut General, which wanted to become involved in a program they saw as an experiment that could be used as a model for future, more efficient healthcare delivery systems.[313] The plan was finally approved when the parties agreed that Hopkins would be free from any financial risk and would not have to expend any funds for the program. When the fall of 1967 came, the plan was offered to the new city's first residents. Many decided to accept, and by October 1969, the city had its first clinic. Plans were also underway for the construction of a new hospital, which all Howard County residents needed.

Maintaining the community's mental health was also important to Jim Rouse and the planners. According to Libby Rouse, when a good idea was suggested by the Work Group, it was shelved with the comment, "Let the Family Life Institute do it."[314] Such an institution began in 1972, with the creation of a center in Wilde Lake that provided affordable mental health counseling on a sliding fee scale based on the client's ability to pay, making the average cost eight dollars a session.[315] Besides counseling, the center offered educational programs, and in its first six years of operation, fifteen thousand people attended such programs. The center also branched out to include lunchtime parenting programs at various workplaces, including the Columbia Association and the Johns Hopkins Applied Physics Lab.[316] By 1996 the center was averaging six thousand hours of individual and family counseling and fifteen hundred hours of group work. Six hundred families were served by a staff of eleven full-time and part-time staffers and twenty-five mental health professionals on contract.[317] The center's major challenge was to raise sufficient funds to keep the program afloat. In the mid-1990s, the Family Life Center (which the planned Family Life Institute was renamed when it opened) merged with the Family and Children's Services of Central Maryland, a group with branches in Baltimore City and Anne Arundel, Baltimore, Carroll and Harford Counties. Located in what was once Columbia's first public library in the Wilde Lake Village Center, this new organization continues to do the work of Columbia's original Family Life Center.

Public Education, Columbia Style

Public schools in Columbia, by state law, were under the jurisdiction of the Howard County Board of Education, a fact apparently unknown to Christopher Jencks, who prepared a report based on Columbia's operating its own schools.[318] However, his visionary report and those of others set in motion changes that would affect all the Howard County schools. The school system in 1964 had no kindergarten and a six-three-three system of elementary, junior high and senior high education. Due to the suburbanization process that had come to Howard County, many professionals had moved here who had high expectations for their children's schools, which meant that change was imminent. Columbia simply put that process into high gear.

Jencks's report was a reflection of the liberal and experimental educational trend sweeping the country in the 1960s. Some of his recommendations included a kindergarten program, a four-four-four school alignment and innovative alternatives, such as team teaching, ungraded classes, independent study programs and year-round schooling.[319] These were later reinforced by a study commissioned by the board of education, entitled "Toward 1975: A Guide to Schools for 1966–75 in Howard County, Maryland," written by William Alexander and Robert Anderson. Both of these reports were instrumental in bringing about rapid change in the county school system. A kindergarten program and a five-three-four school alignment plan were soon in place. Other changes would come later as a grant from the Ford Foundation, obtained by the Department of Education with the assistance of Mort Hoppenfeld, provided funds to make these innovative ideas possible.

Barbara Rudlin, who came to Columbia in 1968, became actively involved in school matters and was first appointed, then elected, to the school board in the 1970s. She supported the educational changes that Columbia brought to the county, and worked hard to see that Columbia was treated fairly in the school construction process. She expressed disappointment that the demographics "could not justify the original Rouse plan of a middle and high school for each village."[320]

Thus, Columbia was able to influence the future of Howard County's public education system in a meaningful way. The city also proved to be a generous partner when the Rouse Company announced it would donate the land for all Howard County

Howard Community College, 1971. The college opened with six hundred students and this one building. *Columbia Archives.*

schools located in Columbia to the Department of Education. This was yet another way that the new city helped minimize the cost to Howard County.

Columbia seemed destined to have institutions of higher education. The questions were: what kind and how many. In a paper entitled "The University of the City," Wallace Hamilton traced the development of western universities back to medieval European cities when he quoted a Brookings Institution writer who stated, "Universities came into existence to give mind to the city and they continue to exist to provide intelligence for the community."[321] Jim Rouse extended this idea when he stated that a college serves not only as a focus for the intellectual life of the community, "but also as a center for the study of man in his environment."[322] And the first type of college he envisioned was a junior or community college.

A community college (as Howard's would soon be known) was the easiest piece of the higher education puzzle to solve. There were already fourteen of them in the state, but none in Howard County. It was an easy call for the Rouse Company executives; all they had to do was provide the land, and the state and county would do the rest. In June 1969, ground was broken for Howard Community College in the middle of a farm, complete with barn and silo. Under the leadership of Alfred Smith, it opened a year later, with a single building and six hundred students, and has subsequently grown to become a much larger institution of national stature in the community college field.

Providing a four-year college to supplement the new community college would not be as easy a task. But a new city with different ideas of what a city should and could be was bound to attract some interest. One such feeler came from a college that was as new as Columbia itself. It would be called Dag Hammarskjold College, after the late United Nations Secretary General who died in an airplane crash while trying to bring peace to the Central African Congo in 1961. The college, conceived by a Baptist minister named Robert McCan, would provide a polycultural education to students from all parts of the world. Columbia, he felt, would be a perfect place for his college not only because of its proximity to the international communities present in nearby Washington, D.C., but also because "we could participate in all the creative structures of the new city, and we could use it as a teaching mechanism for our students."[323] This seemed to be a match made in heaven. Plans were conceived in the summer of 1966, but Dag Hammarskjold did not open its doors until September 1971. With Jim Rouse's liberal worldview and Columbia's community-based ideals, Dag Hammarskjold College had found a perfect home.

Antioch College, a non-traditional college with a counterculture-oriented study body headquartered in Yellow Springs, Ohio, also expressed interest in creating a branch campus in Columbia. The driving force behind this effort was the college's academic vice-president, Morris Keeton. The process began in November 1967, and for one year plans were discussed for a face-to-face meeting between the leaders of the college and the city. An article in the Antioch school newspaper, while informative and well thought-out, used phrases like "Rouse's Fantasy Corporation" and "Rouseland" and "theoretical oasis" to describe Columbia.[324] When the meeting was held in November 1968, the actions of the Antioch students must have disturbed Rouse. He wrote a personal letter to Morris Keeton, stating that "I am not interested in engaging in a continuing defense of Columbia's purposes against challenge by people who don't believe we say what we mean." He went on to praise Keeton's spirit and good will, but declared he was "not nearly so solicitous of the cynical introspection of the already damaged young people who, to a large extent, represented the Yellow Springs point of view."[325]

Rouse also had a lot of positive things to say about the meeting, but his negative comments presaged conflicts to come. Seven Antioch students were engaged as interns to the Rouse Company for the academic year, and it was hoped that the college would finally find its way to Columbia. A December 8, 1968 statement from Antioch announced the formation of a Field Studies Center in Columbia, which would involve 50 to 150 students who would use "the city of Columbia and the surrounding Washington-Baltimore community as a major learning resource."[326]

This could have been a good match. However, in June 1971, Antioch announced that two-thirds of the Columbia-based students would be moved to the college's Baltimore and Washington campuses because "some programs are uncomfortable in Columbia"; some sources blamed "internal politicking for the move."[327] The Human Ecology Center, primarily studying new town development, remained in Columbia.

Promotion of the arts was always important to Jim Rouse and he took steps to bring art and music schools to Columbia. In 1969 Washington's Corcoran Art Gallery and Baltimore's Peabody Conservatory of Music opened teaching campuses in the new city. But none of this was to last. Within a few years, the only higher education institution left in Columbia was Howard Community College.

Construction! Construction! Construction!

Columbia was one gigantic construction site during its first five years. Buildings multiplied, and every week brought a new "first"—fast food restaurant, movie theater, hotel, etc. The frenetic pace was dizzying at times, but in a city built from scratch, it was a necessary part of life. To Columbia's planners and builders it was a sign of pride and fulfillment—and profits. Rapid growth was necessary to keep pace with the economic model.

On November 11, 1969, Oakland Mills became Columbia's second village with the opening of its village center. Its name evoked old Howard County roots, an early nineteenth-century flour and sawmill. Its neighborhoods of Thunder Hill, Steven's Forest and Talbott Springs also have local history connections; their names are those of old farms and land grants. Its street names were drawn from works by novelist Ernest Hemingway, poet Carl Sandburg and painter Andrew Wyeth. The historical antecedents of the village were acknowledged by the preservation and renovation of the two barns and two silos that were on the property. Twelve shops, an office building, supermarket and bank were open for business, and additional amenities were soon to follow. Eventually, the area would provide space for Columbia's first ice-skating rink and a second interfaith center, named the Meeting House.

Harper's Choice, adjacent to Wilde Lake, became Columbia's third village. It was named for the farmer who sold the land to Jim Rouse during the "land grab." Its three neighborhoods, Longfellow, Hobbit's Glen and Swansfield, were named for poet Henry Wadsworth Longfellow, a work by writer J.R.R. Tolkien and an etching by James McNeill Whistler entitled *The Swan*. The village center opened in August 1971, with the requisite stores and shops, and with a new twist: apartments located directly above them.[328] Kahler Hall, also named for one who had farmed the land on which it sits, is the hub of the village. Later amenities would include the Columbia Athletic Club, the city's first health spa and the Florence Bain Center, Columbia's first center devoted to the needs of the city's senior citizens. Wendy Tzuker, the current village manager, refers to Harper's Choice as the place "where Jim Rouse's vision of community happened," due to its broad mix of both subsidized and expensive housing in the village, as well as the ongoing traditions that developed in its early years. One such event is the Longfellow neighborhood's annual Fourth of July parade and softball game. It claims to be the longest continuously running parade in Howard County, and its spirit "upholds much of what's good about America: children, diversity, community, kindness."[329]

Another part of the construction process had to do with office parks. Industrial development was an important part of Columbia's plan, and the company was constantly searching for occupants for its industrial parks. As always, recruiters set their sights high in hopes of landing recognized corporate giants who would bring revenues and prestige to the new city. In a memo to Bill Finley, Jim Rouse stated that they should simultaneously and aggressively court General Electric (GE) and Westinghouse.[330] Finley followed up on the suggestion and after a lot of difficult negotiations, the company seemed to have succeeded. In January 1968, GE announced that its appliance and

Oakland Mills, then and now. One picture shows the barns on the property Jim Rouse bought in the early 1960s. The second shows part of what was created from those old structures. *Oakland Mills Community Association.*

Harper's Choice Village Center today. The village center was Columbia's third, and one of its unique features was the building of apartments above the shops, a common feature in European town centers. *Joseph Mitchell.*

television division would move to a thousand-acre site in Columbia, starting with a workforce of two thousand, which would eventually reach ten thousand. The Rouse Company conducted a public relations campaign to win the county government and the public over to the proposal. Most of the former already favored GE's coming, and the public was supportive as well, except for a few of its new neighbors who filed a lawsuit to keep GE away from their doorsteps on the grounds that GE's presence would adversely affect their property values. In May 1969, the Maryland Court of Appeals denied the landowners' request for an injunction and plans for the new plant began.

A smaller but equally important addition to Columbia's industrial landscape came when Bendix Field Engineering Corporation decided to move its aerospace division to Columbia. The company was sold on the Columbia site because of "the need to unite Bendix personnel and facilities," which were strewn around seven different locations in the Baltimore region."[331] Bill Rouse spearheaded the campaign to bring Bendix to Columbia, and was lauded for his efforts by T.C. Wolff of the industrial marketing division, when he wrote: "I want you to know that all of us here know that there would be no Bendix sale were it not for you…You're the most valuable marketing resource Columbia owns, and I guess the right word might be 'invaluable.'"[332] Bendix brought additional prestige to Columbia due to its active involvement in the nation's space exploration program, including "getting photographs of the missions into the homes of millions of television viewers around the world."[333]

A Family Tragedy

In 1970 Bill Rouse surprised everyone in the company by announcing his retirement from full-time employment with his brother's firm. Since family circumstances had dictated that he enter the workforce early, he felt that an early retirement was well earned. "I'm one of the few men still in business who has a history of working through the Depression," he said.[334] He stayed on as vice-chairman of the company's board and, with his brother's approval, developed "plans for me to start sailing other seas, but still under the sails of the Rouse Company."[335] He was doing this on October 20, 1970, at one of the company's malls in Ohio. He had excused himself at a meeting because he was not feeling well. When his colleagues went to find him, they discovered that he had suffered a heart attack and collapsed on the restroom floor. An ambulance trip to the hospital confirmed the terrible news—Bill Rouse was dead at fifty-nine years of age.

It was a very sad time for the Rouse Company, and in particular for Bill's family. He had always prided himself on being the good family man that he was. He was also kind to his coworkers and charitable toward his community, willingly giving his time and energy to various causes, including his favorite, the Boy Scouts of America. He was buried in Easton, Maryland, the small town where he had been born.

A year before his death, Bill had to fill in for his younger brother at a large dinner celebrating General Electric's coming to Columbia. He began his speech by describing his brother as "the dreamer whose dreams came true; The doer who gets things done; The deeply religious man who lives his religious concepts every hour, every day…The gay eternal optimist who sincerely believes that things work out for the best if one is working unselfishly. A good citizen, a great man and a magnificent younger brother."[336] Jim Ryan of Ryland Homes attended the dinner and was so moved by Bill's words that he wrote a letter to Jim Rouse, stating that Bill's comments about his younger brother were "the most moving part of the whole evening." He went on to say that Bill "has a tough job, Jim… maybe even in some ways tougher than yours. Take care of that older brother of yours; he will always be there, maybe long after a lot of your present associates have abandoned the ship."[337] Jim responded with a short note, stating, "You are very right about the importance of my brother Bill in my life. He has been a stalwart support at every point and I am deeply grateful for him."[338]

There were company stories regarding open disagreements between the Rouse brothers during meetings, when Jim's unbridled idealism came into conflict with Bill's Depression-shaped realism, especially when it came to economic matters. Some members of the Columbia branch of the company may have resented Bill's admonitions over budgets and spending. He certainly didn't have Jim's vision, but he believed in it, and he would gladly do anything to make it successful. When he was four years old, he gave his younger brother his name; when his parents died, he became Jim's guardian and surrogate parent; he paid the bills and saw to it that Jim got an education, while postponing his own. To the very end of his life, he was still working on his brother's behalf, doing what was good for him and his company. Such love and loyalty is hard to find, and it is fitting that near Kittamaqundi's waters, statues of Bill and Jim Rouse now stand side by side.

Columbia: Making its Mark, 1968–1972

Stability at the Columbia Association

When the Columbia Association was created, Jim Rouse was named its president, and a general manager was hired to run the company. The first such person, Jack Slayton, died suddenly before Columbia opened its doors, and John Levering, an investment executive and close friend of Jim Rouse's, took his place. But John's real passion was in the field of art, and after two years at CA, he left to start an art studio and shop with Wes Yamaka called the Eye of the Camel. Tom Wilson, a parks and recreational director from California, was hired to manage CA, becoming its third general manager in three years.

With CA's rapid growth, replacing Jim Rouse with a full-time president soon became necessary. Padraic "Pat" Kennedy, a native New Yorker, was hired to head the company. His resume contained management experiences with the Peace Corps for four years and Volunteers In Service to America (VISTA) for five years, where he eventually became its director. Kennedy then went to work for Boise-Cascade Corporation, as director of their center for community development and vice-president of their urban housing corporation, which built low-income housing all over the country.[339] Perfect experiences for Columbia—altruistic organizations, community involvement and an urban housing background.

Pat would be CA president for twenty-five years, leading the organization through the highs of expansion and development to the lows of recession and belt-tightening, as well as several direct challenges to CA's existence. His leadership and good will always prevailed, and when he retired in 1998, he had earned the sobriquet from many as "Columbia's Mayor."

Columbia at Five

After five years, Columbia had come a long way. Three villages were up and running, and more were on their way. The city had a community college; Loyola College had opened a branch in the new city and Johns Hopkins University was soon to follow. Columbia had its first high school and middle school, both named Wilde Lake. The downtown lakefront area was rounding into shape with new buildings, featuring its first restaurant and hotel. The sacred and the secular fell into place with the opening of the Wilde Lake Interfaith Center and The Mall in Columbia.

The city's residents had the right to feel proud at the city's fifth birthday party. Their numbers had grown from 1,000 to 21,000. The rains that had dampened guests at the Post Pavilion five years earlier made a return appearance—but could not damage the spirits of the celebrants. A fair at the lakefront was followed by a nighttime "Ball at the Mall." Columbia was feeling good about their communities, and rightfully so. However, storm clouds were beginning to form, as national and local problems combined to create a crisis for the city and its founder.

8.

COLUMBIA IN THE 1970S

Columbia is proceeding on schedule and continues to meet the high expectations that both we and the outside world have placed upon it.
Matt DeVito, Rouse Company Profile, May 1973

As Columbia embarked on its second five-year plan, expectations were still high and prospects of meeting them seemed good. The city had gained much favorable publicity and earned kudos for Jim Rouse and the Rouse Company. However, by the end of the decade, internal and external forces conspired to bring both to the brink of ruin. Those who had praised now criticized, and something occurred in 1979 that no one in 1972 would have thought possible—Jim Rouse retired from active participation in the Rouse Company...and Columbia.

Growing Pains

Many of the planners saw Columbia as a prototype that could be used to reshape the urban landscape. The Rouse Company's ambitious business plan, which Mel Levine embraced in 1970, called for "three shopping centers a year, a Village of Cross Keys every three years, a new city like Columbia every five years, a nationwide chain of Cross Keys Inns."[340] Heady stuff, indeed! Opportunities to make Columbia more than a "one hit wonder" quickly occupied the imaginations of Leo Molinaro and the American City Corporation staff.

Two of the major development projects focused on cities. A plan to revitalize Hartford, Connecticut, envisioned uniting the city with its surrounding suburbs, bringing benefits to both. A second project imagined creating a clone of Columbia (with "slightly taller buildings") on a nine-thousand-acre plot of undeveloped land in Staten Island, New York, called South Richmond.[341] However, the Hartford project struck citizens as too bold, and the Staten Island project died in the quagmire of New York state politics.

Rouse Company Building. Another Frank Gehry creation, its construction began in 1972, and gave the Rouse Company a Columbia base. It is still Columbia's most recognizable building. *Columbia Archives; Photo by Barbara Kellner.*

Rural projects met similar fates. Shelby Farms, ten miles from downtown Memphis, called for the development of two villages and a town center on 5,000 acres. And, on 2,800 acres on Wye Island, Maryland, close to the upper Chesapeake Bay where Jim grew up, Rouse planned "estate residences," from five to twenty acres in size, surrounding Wye Village—706 dwelling units and all the amenities of village life. The proposed population for the entire island was 2,750.[342] Adverse public reaction forced the company to withdraw from both projects.

The growing size of the company (doubled since the mid-sixties), the number of projects being explored and the increased staffing these required produced a huge entity that was sometimes directionless and out of control. When Jim Rouse wanted to send a one-page memo to his vice-presidents, Nancy Allison had to make nineteen copies. And long-term employees were soon earning less than new hires. When Jim ordered a "trim and tighten" reorganization of the company, he hired Matthias J. "Matt" DeVito, a Piper and Marbury lawyer who had spent some time on loan to the company but had little business management experience.

The company began the 1972 fiscal year with a streamlined corporate structure that defined who did what and who was responsible to whom. Ninety employees were pink-slipped, but they represented less than 7 percent of the total workforce.[343] Matt DeVito, named chief operations officer, answerable only to Rouse, described his job as "see[ing] that the whole process of the new organization works on a day-to-day basis, and…that problems are solved and malfunctions corrected."[344] A relief to some and a threat to others, the plan was soon overtaken by national and international circumstances that together brought Jim Rouse's Company and Columbia to near bankruptcy.

A new word had to be coined to describe it—stagflation—a stagnant economy accompanied by rapid price inflation. It created a worldwide economic crisis, the worst since the Great Depression. Among the many factors responsible for stagflation, the most serious was the Arab oil embargo of 1973–74. Its effects were devastating; the Dow Jones Industrial Average fell by almost 50 percent, while the price of gold nearly tripled. The effects on the real estate market were staggering; few dared buy while the economy was spiraling downward and the price of homes continued to rise due to rapidly climbing mortgage rates. Both the country and the Rouse Company's Columbia Plan were in serious trouble.

The economic crisis derailed Columbia's economic model, which required the sale of 2,500 homes a year—a stretch in the best of times—now an impossibility. Home contracts fell by more than two-thirds and Rouse Company stock, following national trends, but more deeply, plummeted from forty dollars to two dollars a share. Jim Rouse's pledge to complete Columbia in fifteen years could not be kept. Negotiating with Connecticut General about the future of Columbia and his role in it, Jim Rouse, the eternal optimist, offered to guarantee personally CG's Columbia loans; fortunately for him, the company refused his generous offer.[345]

CG considered "shutting down the project" for two years and even contemplated bankruptcy, but neither was a viable option. They eventually decided to infuse the Columbia project with more money and hope that things would improve.[346] There were some casualties. In a press release issued on June 25, 1976, CG announced that along with the additional funding, some personnel changes were to take place: Jim Rouse was named Howard Research and Development (HRD) chairman of the board, and James Torrey, a CG executive, became its president.[347] CG had wanted to move HRD out of the Rouse Company building (Mike Spear and Matt DeVito talked them out of that) and, instead of removing Jim Rouse, CG "kicked him upstairs." HRD's share in Columbia was reduced to 20 percent until things got better.[348] Not a great situation, but considering the circumstances, it could have been a lot worse.

Columbia's fortunes improved when CG sent Warren Fuller, a company "troubleshooter," to be the new president and CEO of HRD, a job he would hold for almost ten years. Coming "not as an enemy but a partner in the Columbia project," he quickly established good personal and business relationships with Jim Rouse and Matt DeVito.[349] Together, the three men worked to revitalize HRD and were successful in doing so. The recovery was so complete that when Connecticut General (then CIGNA) was looking to sell its interest in HRD in 1985, Warren Fuller suggested to Matt DeVito that the Rouse Company should be that buyer. Three or four months later, the deal was closed.[350]

It was now up to Matt DeVito to put the Rouse Company's house in order. In a draconian but necessary measure, he reduced its workforce from 1,700 to 500.[351] The number of current company projects was reduced by one-half, and the company bit the bullet, taking inevitable losses early to minimize their effect.[352] The strategy worked and company stability and profitability returned. For these actions, Matt DeVito was referred to by some as an uncaring "hatchet man" and a "bottom line" executive who lacked his former boss's imagination. But others, such as company public relations head Scott Ditch, offer a different opinion. Looking back from today's perspective, he stated simply, "Matt DeVito saved the company."[353]

Columbia: Self-Examination

By 1972 most Columbians seemed to be content with their new city, but criticism was beginning to surface. Some people wondered why all the workers doing the menial tasks around Rouse Company properties were black and practically all the white-collar employees going to work in those buildings were white.[354] This seemed to contradict the racial equality commitment that the Rouse Company preached, and an affirmative action program was put into place to take the first steps in rectifying the situation. Others who came to Columbia assuming that "participatory democracy" flourished there were disappointed to find that, although they could say all they wanted and people would listen, they had no power to affect change. Some complained that Rouse executives "don't take them seriously, and treat them with disrespect."[355]

The attitude of Howard Countians toward Columbia had also changed. Most were still supportive of the new city, but an anti-Columbia minority was beginning to take shape. A 1972 Johns Hopkins Health Care survey of Howard Countians showed that while 44 percent would still have allowed Columbia to be built, 33 percent would not.[356] This weak endorsement was far below the 75–80 percent approval expressed in 1965 when people overwhelmingly thought the county should approve Columbia's plan. Increasing population density, the strain on county resources and Columbia schools that seemed to some to foster racial tension and drug abuse[357] signaled a growing Columbia–Howard County dichotomy.

Columbia Flexes Its Political Muscle

Columbia in its early years attracted people with a commitment to political activism and liberal politics. In the presidential election of 1972, which resulted in a landslide Richard Nixon victory over George McGovern, Columbia's precincts were the only ones in the county the latter carried. Columbians have repeated this pattern, voting for more liberal causes and candidates than those who reside outside the city.

In 1970 Columbia represented almost 15 percent of the county's population. By 1975 that figure would rise to 36 percent, and the county elections of 1974 gave Columbians the opportunity to flex their political muscle. The Columbia Democratic Club, formed in the city's early years, endorsed a slate of four candidates for the five-member Howard County Council and Edward Cochran for county executive. Since the vote was to be county-wide

Howard County Council, 1974. Columbia flexed its political muscle by electing an entire slate of candidates to the county council: (left to right) Tom Yeager, Ruth Keeton, Lloyd Knowles, Ginny Thomas and Dick Anderson. *Howard County Office of the County Council.*

rather than by districts, their prospects for victory seemed slim. Their slate included Ginny Thomas and Lloyd Knowles, both Columbia residents, and Tom Yeager, a southern Howard Countian who came to the ticket by way of a political deal with the Southern Howard County Democratic Club. The results of the election were stunning; these three council nominees and executive candidate Ed Cochran were all elected to office, along with two other candidates with Columbia connections, former city General Manager Richard Anderson and Columbia activist Ruth Keeton, a clean sweep for the new city.

Fearing that this was the beginning of a Columbia-dominated political era, citizens outside the city petitioned for a referendum to change the 1968 County Charter to provide that county council members be elected by districts rather than at large, and draw the district lines to guarantee a non-Columbia dominated council. Some referred to this proposal as the "Balkanization of Columbia," because the city's vote would be spread out, diluted and most likely capable of electing only two council members.[358] A hotly contested campaign ensued in 1976 over "Question C" (the third question on the ballot), with Howard Countians living outside Columbia generally arguing for it and Columbians overwhelmingly opposing it. The election results were close, but the question was defeated. Politically speaking, Columbia had become a voice to be reckoned with.

Acting as a megaphone for this voice, the *Columbia Flier* was a citywide newspaper, created by Zeke Orlinsky, a Columbia pioneer and former assistant state's attorney for Baltimore City. The *Flier* began circulation on June 16, 1969, with its first issue consisting mainly of paid advertising and the "Call of the Wilde," a listing of the week's activities in the new city. The paper, originally created on Orlinsky's dining room table and delivered free of charge to all Columbia homes, caught on and soon changed from an information journal to a community newspaper. Jean Moon joined the paper in 1971, and two years later became its editor. During her tenure, she and Orlinsky shaped the paper into a first-class local newspaper and a powerful voice in Columbia and Howard County politics. Regarding the latter, reporter Tom Graham stated that the *Flier* was first reflecting, then affecting, the vote with its editorials and endorsements.[359] The results in these early elections affirmed a vital role for the paper, which was modeled in terms of format on New York City's *Village Voice*.

Recession and Construction

Although Columbia was not immune to the economic slowdown, 1973 was a banner year, with housing sales of 2,415 units, almost meeting the yearly goal in the company's original economic model. The following year, sales fell to 1,870—disappointing, but not disastrous. However, the 1975 figure of 630 was a disaster, and any repeats could prove to be catastrophic. The 1976 total of 1,384 housing sales represented an increase of 55 percent, and marked the beginning of a upward swing for Columbia's housing market.[360] The future was bright enough to allow Michael Spear, HRD's general manager, to state that "Columbia today is a city with its own economic vitality and momentum… [that] has proven it can weather a recession as deep as the one the nation has just experienced."[361] Columbia and the Rouse Company could breathe a sigh of relief; they had both survived a near-death experience.

Even during the tough times, Columbia had continued to expand. In 1974 Long Reach Village Center, the city's fourth, opened for business, with eighteen stores and 85 percent of its commercial space already leased.[362] The village was named for a colonial land grant, which also contained Phelp's Luck and Locust Park, two of its neighborhoods. The third, Jeffers Hill, was named for noted American poet Robinson Jeffers. The village featured a small interfaith center and an arts and crafts area, which was later named the Visual Arts Center, and Stonehouse, the village association's home base.

Long Reach eventually annexed another village, Kendall Ridge, and would grow to be Columbia's largest village in physical size, population (16,000) and number of households (almost 6,000). This constant growth over the years (different from most villages, which quickly filled to capacity) has drawn a vibrancy from the new residents. Combined with the large number of village veterans from the early years, it has produced a proactive village board and a community not afraid to stand up and be heard.[363]

A year later, Owen Brown would become Columbia's fifth village, named for a postmaster and store owner whose name was given to a road that connects east and

NEW CITY UPON A HILL

west Columbia. Dasher Green, an Owen Brown neighborhood, was named for the Dasher family who operated a farm on the new village's land. Hopewell was named for a colonial land grant, and Elkhorn for an area stream. Elkhorn also names the village's most distinguishing feature, Columbia's third and largest lake, which is two miles in circumference. Owen Brown Village also houses an interfaith center and Columbia's second branch of the Howard County Library. Another village innovation was a connected elementary (Dasher Green) and middle school (Owen Brown), designed to facilitate the development of exchange programs between the two schools.

One unique feature of Owen Brown's shopping center is that it was never owned by the Rouse Company. Giant Foods, whose grocery store still anchors the center, owned it until recently, when it was sold to a management firm. This sometimes caused problems for the village center, which lacked the financial support for some of their projects that other villages received from the Rouse Company.[364] Village Manager Ruth Bohse, who will soon retire after thirty years of service to Owen Brown, speaks of a community that "cares a lot about Columbia, and wants to have a voice in it, and they do."[365] She also speaks of community continuity in that the nursery school, which existed before the village center, still exists, enabling her to have witnessed the growth of some of Columbia's children from nursery school through college and beyond.

Additional notable construction also took place at this time. In 1973 the Columbia Hospital and Clinics Foundations Center, later to be named Howard County General Hospital, opened its doors. It began as a joint venture between Connecticut General Insurance and Johns Hopkins Medicine, the same partnership that created the Columbia Medical Plan. After its beginning as a fifty-nine-bed hospital, a series of active growth campaigns have created a state-of-the-art medical facility. Its purchase by Johns Hopkins Medicine in 1998 gave it the funds and resources to meet the needs of a growing community.[366] Continuous expansion campaigns have only further enhanced the reputation of this excellent medical institution.

In 1975 Columbia attracted another form of healthcare, this one with a strongly Asian influence. The Traditional Acupuncture Institute (TAI), founded by Dianne Connelly and Robert Duggan, brought this ancient form of healing to a new city of people who welcomed it. There were skeptics, however. Some people who visited the building smelled a "funny smoke" emanating from the institute, and reported it to the police. Suspecting marijuana, the police investigated, only to discover the use of herbal moxa, a staple of acupuncture use that is never ingested.[367] The center not only treated but also taught, and many of the acupuncturists currently practicing in the area were trained there.

It took a while for Columbia to develop a stable of restaurants, but eventually they came, and three stood out from the crowd. In 1974 Peg Zabawa opened Mrs. Z's, in the Swansfield neighborhood's vacated Wawa store. This was a self-proclaimed "people place," "where you can feel togetherness. Where creative cooking (bring your own wine), an amusement corner for children, the piano, crafts and artwork invite you to stay longer, to browse, to just 'be together.'"[368] For five years, the restaurant became a "third place," a home away from home for many Columbians. When a fire destroyed Mrs. Z's in May 1979, a valued piece of Columbia was permanently lost.

Howard County General Hospital, 1973. Originally scheduled to be a fifty-nine-bed center to serve members of the Columbia Medical Plan, it quickly became a hospital serving all county residents. *Columbia Archives.*

Clyde's of Columbia opened in 1975 on the Kittamaqundi lakefront. Its cousin, Clyde's of Georgetown, had long been a successful D.C. watering hole and restaurant. With its long, handsome bar and cozy tables, Clyde's was an immediate hit with Columbians, and thirty years later it's still a favorite. Recently, when rumors circulated that the Teacher's Building, above Clyde's, might be torn down, the focus of concern was for Clyde's rather than the entire structure.

In the same year, some businessmen bought the Kings Contrivance Restaurant and because it was then on Rouse Company property, had to lease it from them, a practice that continued until 2002. Set in a large country house, located on a 360-acre farm once owned by the Macgill family, it hearkens back to a time when things moved slowly and good food was to be savored. Its thirty years of fine reviews and thousands of satisfied customers have made it one of Columbia's most sought-after restaurants. Jim Rouse often used the restaurant as a place to close important business deals; the restaurant has a "Columbia Room" where such transactions took place.

Cultural Yearnings

On June 9, 1971, Jim Rouse wrote a memo to Columbia General Manager Dick Anderson stating, "It should also be our posture to cooperate with, nourish, help into

NEW CITY UPON A HILL

being those efforts that emerge in the community with a person or group showing strong initiative to bring off something good."[369] Activist Columbians had already launched some cultural initiatives; one began as a simple conversation among good friends.

In 1968, while attending a fundraiser for presidential candidate Eugene McCarthy, Martin and Helen Ruther and Robert and Marcie Gorrie were lamenting Columbia's lack of a movie house. A follow-up meeting led to the creation of the Columbia Film Society, whose first offering was *Yojimbo*, a film by the celebrated Japanese filmmaker Akira Kurosawa. Two hundred people showed up at Slayton House, but many found the film too violent for their tastes, causing the society's founders to "hide in the bathroom" to avoid the audience.[370] Other films proved more appealing and the group moved to bigger quarters, hiring Tom Brzezinski as resident projectionist during the second season. Tom would also become well known in Columbia for an outdoor film series held every summer at the lakefront. And as an elementary school media specialist, "Mr. B" entertained Columbia's early students with lively and imaginative storytelling sessions.

The group has found a permanent home in Smith Theater at Howard Community College, where it currently offers a subscription series, featuring foreign and indie films that typically don't play at the multiplex. Today, more than seven hundred people see nine films a year. At forty dollars a subscription, it's still quite a bargain.

Three women launched the Howard County Poetry and Literature Society (HoCoPoLitSo). Ellen Conroy Kennedy studied French and literature in graduate school and translated works of the negritude poets and Albert Camus into English.[371] Jean Flanagan Moon also had a graduate degree in literature, and when she came to Columbia in the early 1970s, she began to teach courses on women and literature. Both Ellen and Jean have ancestral roots in Ireland, where the written word is nurtured and cherished. Along with Prudence Barry, a local actress of note, they decided to attract the literary world to Columbia, inviting noted poets and writers to Columbia for readings and book signings. The first program on November 19, 1974, featured two poets, Carolyn Kizer and Lucille Clifton. Since then, many other writers have graced Columbia with their visits, among them Nobel Laureates Saul Bellow, Isaac Bashevis Singer, Derek Walcott and Seamus Heaney. An annual program of the society, its now-famous Irish Evening, was suggested by Ellen's husband Pat in 1979. It blends the words of Irish writers, such as Heaney and Edna O'Brien, with the lilting sounds of traditional Irish music. Visiting writers often speak to students in the county school system through a co-sponsored program. Cable viewers can connect with these writers by tuning into the society's interview series, *The Writing Life*, produced in partnership with Howard Community College. In 1997 Ellen Kennedy was honored for her work by the Maryland Humanities Council, which awarded her their Eisenberg Prize for Excellence in the Humanities.[372] Incidentally, the acronym HoCoPoLitSo was created by Jean Moon's husband, Bob, as a means of shortening a rather cumbersome group name. It has been favored by many of the poets who have graced the society's programs.[373]

Two musical groups debuted in 1977, Columbia Pro Cantare chorus and the Columbia Orchestra. The first, created and led by Frances Motyca Dawson, performs locally, as well as in the Baltimore-Washington area. Its wide repertoire including "fifteen world

Young Columbians. Founded in 1975 by Toby Orenstein, this group brought national attention to its hometown. In 1977, they performed at the Carter White House. *Columbia Archives.*

and sixteen American premieres" as well as "fourteen commissioned works" has reached over 100,000 people.[374] Its annual performances of Handel's *Messiah* are sold-out events. Beginning with a dream and "no music director, no money, very little music, and not many players,"[375] the Columbia Orchestra has grown from performing chamber music to full orchestral works, with members ranging from teenage to middle age. Performing in the James Rouse Theatre in Wilde Lake High School, the Columbia Orchestra offers annually six works from the classical repertory, demonstrating, along with Pro Cantare, Columbia's support for classical music. The Columbia Candlelight Concert annual programs bring outside groups to perform chamber music in Columbia, further enhancing the city as a fine venue for classical music.

Toby's Dinner Theater has also been a long-standing Columbia cultural institution. Since 1972, Toby Orenstein has managed an award-winning dinner theater. Her combination of traditional Broadway fare with more cutting-edge musicals keeps them coming back for more. Countless Helen Hayes Awards (the local equivalent of the Tonys) have come Toby's way. She has taught a generation of Columbians how to act;

some of her students have made their way to Broadway stages. In 1975, she also put together The Young Columbians, a traveling troupe who brought their city's message to many audiences, including the Carter White House.

Race in the Next America

The 1960s were one of the most turbulent decades in the century, with the civil rights and antiwar movements, as well as the violence caused by those who opposed them. In America, this was the decade of Selma and Birmingham; Schwerner, Goodman and Chaney; "I Have a Dream" and the assassination of two of the movement's most notable leaders, Martin Luther King Jr. and Robert F. Kennedy. Columbia began during these troubling times, and some dared hope that things would be different in a model city, open to all. Columbia was the city that had stood up to George Wallace. Perhaps it would be a place where blacks and whites would live together in peace and harmony. While the surface was tranquil, the Rouse Company's open city marketing campaign had raised expectations. Jean Toomer, a social scientist and Columbia resident, found anomalies regarding the company's campaign and the lack of black salespeople in the company.[376] While Toomer sought to right that wrong, some people took a more direct approach to solving the problem.

In 1971 Douglas B. Sands, the president of the Howard County Branch of the National Association for the Advancement of Colored People (NAACP), wrote a letter criticizing the Rouse Company for its lack of attention to issues of race, including the absence of blacks at the management level of the Rouse Company, the small number of black-owned businesses in Columbia (there were two) and the lack of much low-income housing in the city. "We find his [Jim Rouse's] efforts short of any significant accomplishments for minority people and disadvantaged people generally and significantly barren for blacks in Howard County."[377]

Rouse must have been stung by this criticism, and immediately took steps to act on Sands's complaints. He hired Edward Scarborough, a sociologist and Columbia resident, to be the company's manager of race relations; his first job was to develop a minority hiring policy.[378] Within a week, the company hired three black mortgage bankers, one black lawyer and one black leasing salesman. In announcing these hirings, Jim Rouse admitted that "a lot exists still to be done."[379] Addressing the lack of black-owned businesses in Columbia, the company set up a department for small business development, to offer all small businesses, including black-owned ones, "expertise and assistance…in merchandising, management, financing, marketing, research, and market analysis."[380] This resulted in a moderate increase of black-owned businesses. As far as low-income housing was concerned, only the efforts of the Interfaith Housing Corporation made a dent in the lack of low-income housing in Columbia. The Nixon administration's decision to cut back funds to subsidize the construction of such housing undermined more ambitious goals in this area. Jim Rouse would always consider this problem to be his biggest Columbia disappointment.[381]

Groups of teens began gathering at the lakefront at night, sometimes engaging in violence and crimes. Herman Charity, an African American police officer who worked in the downtown area, recalled that most of those who engaged in such crimes did not live in Columbia or Howard County, but came from Baltimore or Washington in search of wealthier targets.[382] Although there were white/black confrontations, the charge of "antagonistic racism" remained unproved.[383]

But reports that African American teens had taken de facto control of the Wilde Lake and Oakland Mills Teen Centers and discouraged white teens from using the facilities raised anxieties and caused some Columbians to call for a reexamination of black/white relations in their city. Incidentally, some of the problems at the teen centers were also attributed to those who did not live in Columbia.[384]

The self-examination of race relations in the county took many forms. A 1975 article in the *Columbia Flier* entitled "Black Groups: A Chance for Leadership and an Opportunity to Meet Minority Needs" explored the presence of all-black groups and clubs in Columbia, and justified their role in providing avenues for leadership, black pride and advancement.[385] A 1976 study on Black Family Life, commissioned by the city's Family Life Center and chaired by Jean Toomer, pointed out the need for people and institutions to be on the same page in providing mental health services for all citizens. The study brought together thirty different groups and agencies; many met for the first time "and discovered there were ways they could work together."[386]

A very ambitious undertaking was a project entitled "Survival of Black and White in the Next America," sponsored by the Harper's Choice Community Association. It featured a village-wide survey, followed by three seminars, the purpose of which was to "raise people's consciousness about cultural differences between blacks and whites."[387] The survey's results showed that a large percentage of both blacks and whites felt they got along well with the other group in Columbia, but also felt that cultural differences continued to divide Columbians along racial lines. One follow-up from this point was the formation of a discussion group to study race relations and culture.

During this difficult national conversation about race relations, there is no way to assess how much of an effect these efforts might have had in promoting better race relations. But, unlike some other corners of America, Columbians were at least talking to and not shouting past one another.

A Gender Revolution

During the same ten-year period, feminism revived, which eventually affected Columbia as much, if not more, than the civil rights revolution. Betty Friedan's *The Feminine Mystique* was published in 1963. In it, she described the general malaise many post–World War II American women felt, but could not identify; they were unhappy, but knew not why. She labeled this condition "the problem that has no name," and identified it as caused by women who "want something more than my husband and my children and my home."[388] In the following year, Antonia Chayes, the only woman on Jim Rouse's

Work Group, delivered a paper to the group concerning what women's needs might be in the new city. Her paper concentrated on three areas: (1) an institution for continuing education; (2) child and family care centers; and (3) family life education, and ended with a comment about the needs of the "frail sex."[389]

Jim Rouse did not have any openly negative views about women and women's rights; neither was he at the forefront of the feminist revolution. His views on women seem to have been shaped by the family values inculcated in his Easton childhood: men and women; husbands and wives; mothers and fathers—two different spheres of influence. This was reflected in his company practices; the sexes were categorized as "men and girls,"[390] with stereotyping reflected in both jobs and status. And it would be a while before any women made the Rouse Company's list of vice-presidents. Early advertisements for Columbia were full of pictures that seemed right out of a 1950s sitcom.

Fortunately, some of the women who came to Columbia did not accept this limiting set of roles. Louise Eberhardt, who came to the city in 1969 as an urban associate for the Columbia Cooperative Ministry, soon began meeting women who were "under great personal stress." Unhappy, lonely and suffering from depression, "these women in Columbia were left with the feeling that there must be more in life than what they were experiencing."[391] Small group meetings of ten to fifteen women, with Louise Eberhardt acting as facilitator, provided a forum for expressing and dealing with these feelings.

When Eberhardt was asked by Reverend Gerald Goethe to work with women from the congregations of the Wilde Lake Interfaith Center, two weekly programs called "It's Open" were held at the Other Barn in Oakland Mills. One program featured a speaker; the other an experiential education program, facilitated by Eberhardt.[392] On March 2, 1973, the Women's Resource Center was created to coordinate activities and reach out to more women. Impetus for the center came from the Columbia Association and the Family Life Center, both of which were supportive of its goals.[393]

A number of programs were developed to meet the varying needs of Columbia's women. According to participant Mary Margaret Kamerman, family role questions were important to some, gender and sexuality for others. Consciousness-raising groups were popular, and leadership for women was always stressed in all the programs. Available day care made it all possible.[394]

In May 1973, the center printed a document entitled "Women's Needs in Howard County," listing education, employment, health and medical aspects, mental health, child care, parental guidance and divorce as its focuses. In 1974 these needs were confirmed by a study funded by the Columbia Association entitled "Women's Needs in Columbia." In the following year, the Columbia Association (CA) awarded the center two grants for program expansion.[395] In 1976 a conference entitled "A Day for All Women," co-sponsored by the Women's Center and the Howard County Poetry and Literature Society, was held, featuring workshops and an appearance by noted writer Judith Viorst.

The Women's Center closed in 1981, due to a decrease in clientele for its programs, lack of funding and staff burnout.[396] In its brief history, however, the center inspired women and helped many find a meaningful life in the new city and beyond. In 1990 a

Women's Center reunion was held and each participant was asked to write about what they were doing with their lives since the center closed and what the center had meant to them. Many stressed not only the continuing importance of family and children in their lives, but also mentioned new careers, educational experiences and a new outlook on life. While some looked back nostalgically to the Women's Center and the nurturing environment it provided, most were confidently looking forward to a new future, using what the center had helped inspire within them.[397]

Revolt from Within

Columbia's early residents spent a lot of time attending meetings dealing with village, neighborhood and citywide matters. Some found to their chagrin that their input was sought, but not always taken seriously. As a 1972 researcher studying citizen participation in Columbia observed: "The positions held by the residents…seem to be empty, powerless positions…One cannot expect people to participate unless they have some kind of decision-making [role] or at least a visible partnership in decision-making."[398]

Motivated by the economic effects on CA and strained relations between the Columbia Council and HRD, a grass-roots movement began to reform Columbia's governance model.[399] A committee was formed to explore alternatives, and members reported to a citywide meeting their concern about "the manner in which governing boards are elected, and the way Columbia Association and Howard Research and Development are operated."[400] In September 1972, their report included a call for community leadership, incentives for citizen participation and recommendations regarding how HRD and CA should relate to the community.[401] Included in the report were letters by CA president Pat Kennedy and Mike Spear, HRD vice-president and Columbia general manager, outlining the steps each group was taking to address some of the Roles Study Committee's concerns.

There was nothing radical in either the committee's report or the institutions' responses. However, remembering that the recession of 1974–75 had brought CA to the brink of bankruptcy, and only an $11-million loan from HRD had saved the organization, some residents began to explore alternatives to the CA covenant. Two possibilities were offered—special tax district status and incorporation. The first would replace CA with a special state tax district; the second would result in home rule. Even those who favored some kind of change couldn't agree about the appropriate choice.

The special tax district advocates acted first. The Columbia Council approved the plan and petitioned the state legislature for such status in January 1978. However, as the bill slowly worked its way through the legislature, it arrived too late in the session for approval, and petitioners were asked to resubmit the proposal during the next legislative session in January 1979. In the same year, the incorporation issue was brought before the Columbia Council and received little support.[402] For the time being, a majority of Columbians were either satisfied with CA's governance of Columbia or did not like any of the options offered by its opponents enough to make a change happen.

Columbia Turns Ten

In June 1977, Columbia celebrated its tenth birthday, with a lot for which to be grateful. The recession was fading away, and better days seemed to lie ahead for the parent company. The city's growth had been phenomenal, from 1,000 inhabitants on the first anniversary to 45,000 nine years later. Columbia could now boast of having 14,000 dwelling units, 750 stores and businesses and 1,900 acres of open space connected by twenty-eight miles of pathways. It also counted seventeen public schools and an equal number of swimming pools within the city's five villages. It had an athletic club and countless recreational facilities. For Howard County, Columbia provided $736 million of assessable property.[403]

Of all the festivities, the most meaningful was the one the "pioneers" threw for themselves. Besides exchanging old war stories, they celebrated the fact that the second generation of some pioneer families had decided to live in Columbia, extending a sense of continuity to the community. Several Rouse Company employees who were also pioneers—Bob Tennenbaum, Jim Wannemacher and Mal Sherman—were recognized for their contributions to the city, and a special Wes Yamaka silk-screen print was given to each pioneer family.[404] The city had a bright future ahead of it, but it would have to navigate that future without the captain who had brought them to this point.

Jim Rouse Retires

The seventies were challenging times for Jim Rouse. In 1973 he separated from his wife Libby, and four months later a divorce decree ended their thirty-two years of marriage. Jim had initiated the separation, claiming "deep personal incompatibility."[405] Libby stated that "we had some not unusual interpersonal difficulties, but we needed a kind of help we were unable to get."[406] Later, she claimed that "we had a wonderful marriage that fell apart basically over a misunderstanding."[407]

While the divorce was being finalized, Jim visited friends in Norfolk, Virginia, and during his visit the group decided to play some tennis. Needing a fourth, they invited a friend, Myrtle Patricia "Patty" Traugott to join them, in what Jim later described as a "divine accident meeting."[408] Jim and Patty discovered that they had much in common, including active and lively personalities, similar religious beliefs, a strong interest in urban affairs and a commitment to helping people.[409] They continued to see each other, and their feelings deepened. In November 1974, they were married in Washington at the Church of the Savior, the faith community that meant so much to Jim.

In April 1978, Columbians and others were shocked to read that Jim Rouse was retiring as chairman of the board of the Rouse Company. Matt DeVito would replace him. Jim's final appearance would be at the company shareholders' meeting on May 24, 1979. He bowed out there with a flourish, using "There is a way of thinking in this Company" as his theme, and giving all the credit for its success to its employees. But in the last paragraph, he delivered a warning that still resonates: "It is when the bottom line becomes the top line—the object of the enterprise—that business gets mixed up,

Jim and Patty Rouse. The couple were married in 1974, the second marriage for each. They became an inseparable pair, sharing both their private and public lives. *Enterprise Community Partners, Inc.*

off the track, loses its way. The way to find new opportunities is to discover needs or yearnings of people that are not being satisfactorily met. The way to prosper is to do that well."[410]

Jim Rouse's career was not over. He would now devote his time and energy to revitalizing urban neighborhoods and communities, and make them better places "to grow people." And while Columbians wished him well and thanked him profusely for what he had done for them, they wondered what the future would bring to a city that lost its father, and a company that some feared might have lost its soul.

9.

COLUMBIA IN THE 1980s

A very special dynamic is moving Columbia forward, independent of regional and national factors.
Chuck Tuchfarber, HRD marketing director

By the mid-1980s, there were few vestiges of the economic recession of the previous decade in the Rouse Company. A new, streamlined organization and strong leadership from Matt DeVito brought the company back to prominence. In Columbia, a new set of leaders was installed; the only holdover from the formative years was Mike Spear. Jim Rouse was deeply involved with his new project, strategies for making better environments out of urban landscapes. And the residents of Columbia were working hard to keep their city's ideals alive.

Rouse Company Revival

Despite a sluggish national economy in the early 1980s, the Rouse Company continued to grow and prosper. Finding interest rates too high to borrow money to develop new shopping centers, the company decided to switch its focus from suburban mall development to downtown city sites, and to buying and restructuring existing shopping centers.[411] In 1981 the company was operating fifty-two shopping centers, thirty-four of which it owned. And the success of its Faneuil Hall "festival marketplace" in Boston led to the development of others, including a waterfront project in Baltimore called Harborplace.

Plans to develop the area had been in the planning stage for almost fifteen years. Journalist Martin Millspaugh was chosen to head Charles Center–Inner Harbor Management, Inc., a nonprofit firm that represented the city in its development plans. It was Millspaugh who interested Jim Rouse in the project, stating that a Faneuil Hall marketplace was just what Baltimore needed. Ultimately, Rouse agreed and he and

Mayor William Donald Schaefer became the catalysts for the project.[412] A campaign to win public support for the project began, and ultimately the voters approved the project in a citywide referendum.

The opening on July 2, 1980, was a festive occasion, and Rouse's role in it was commemorated the following month, when *Time* magazine featured a picture of him on the cover, with the title of the lead article, "Cities Are Fun!" The article turned out to be more about Jim Rouse and his life's work than Baltimore and Harborplace; but for a moment, he shared the national stage with the city for which he had done so much. The state of the Baltimore Inner Harbor today, with its sports stadiums for the hometown Orioles and Ravens, the National Aquarium, Maryland Science Center and the American Visionary Arts Museum, attests to the wisdom of the Rouse-Schaefer partnership that Harborplace helped to create. Coincidentally, Jim Rouse's son Ted served as the latter's board chairman and led a campaign to expand the museum to include the Jim Rouse Center for Visionary Thought, which explores ways in which the urban landscape can be improved through thought and action.[413]

Within a year, 21 million people had visited the Inner Harbor; 14 million of those were Baltimore area people who made multiple visits; the remaining 7 million were tourists.[414] Today, the Inner Harbor continues to be Baltimore's center of activity, with Harborplace as its anchor.

An ominous cloud hanging over the Rouse Company at this time was the threat of a takeover by a corporate raider. One such attempt was made in 1981, when the Sheuer investment group bought 7 percent of Rouse Company stock and announced its intention to acquire majority ownership of the company. However, the untimely death of the Sheuer group's head caused the project to be abandoned.[415] Later, a Canadian real estate investment firm called Trizec bought 20 percent of Rouse stock. What was intriguing was that both Rouse and Trizec were in the same line of work and had similarly sized companies.[416] No intent to purchase more Rouse stock was announced, so Matt DeVito confidently told Rouse stockholders that Trizec was a "high type firm and very responsible," and "we have no reason to alter any plans we have made for the future operation of the company because of this situation."[417]

Becoming stronger is a good strategy for averting a takeover, and the Rouse Company began churning out some very strong numbers. In 1980 its earnings were $13,410,000; by 1985 the figure had risen to $36,620,000; and in 1989 topped off at $60,205,000. In that ten-year period, the firm annually averaged between three and four new downtown development projects. The list included Harborplace in Baltimore (1980), South Street Seaport in New York (1983), New Orleans Riverwalk (1986), The Gallery at Harborplace (1987) and Underground Atlanta (1989).[418] As corporate takeovers failed to materialize, the Rouse Company was prospering; and across the parking lot from company headquarters, its founder was beginning some projects of his own.

This solid financial growth enabled the company to take a bold step: buying Connecticut General's 80 percent share of Howard Research and Development (HRD). The insurance company had merged with Insurance Company of North America to form CIGNA, and announced its desire in 1985 to sell its share of Columbia. Before anyone else could make an offer, the Rouse Company made a preemptive bid. Its $120-million offer was accepted, bringing an amicable end to the partnership with Connecticut General that had meant so much to Columbia in its early years. This proved to be a financial boon to the Rouse Company; within two years, Columbia was making a lot of money, and continued to do so.[419] If CIGNA had waited a bit longer, it could have shared in these long-awaited profits.

Columbia Neglected

Once Jim Rouse retired, there seemed to be a change in the company's attitude toward Columbia. The city was no longer the company's primary focus; instead the Rouse Company chose to concentrate on its other real estate projects. A local newspaper observed, "Because the company wants to diversify, officials said that it's time to devote its energies elsewhere and let Columbia mature on its own."[420] Some who worked for the company also noticed increased interest in the accumulation of personal wealth by the new management team, some of whom had stock options built into their contracts. The higher the price of Rouse Company stock, the more money they made.[421] The arrival of the Reagan era had helped create a social context in which greater profitability soon became the top priority, even at a socially concerned firm like the Rouse Company.

Similar criticisms were aimed at the company's subsidiary, HRD. The word most commonly used to describe HRD's attitude in dealing with Columbia's people and businesses during this time was arrogance, a condition confirmed recently by Matt DeVito.[422] In 1989 Clairborn Carr, a former HRD employee and rival developer, said of HRD: "If I were God, I'd try to give the organization a greater sense of humility."[423] HRD's General Manager Douglas McGregor stated, "The perception of arrogance is something I've heard before and something we try to overcome." He went on to say that a major reason for it is that HRD "is a big fish in a small pond, and the smaller fish don't always like it."[424]

In dealing with tenants, the company was inflexible regarding rents; a market price was set, and those businesses that were unable to meet it were forced out. It happened in the Mall in Columbia, where Jim Rouse had earlier decreed that some locally owned businesses ought to be present and not just the large chain stores that were its major tenants. When these small stores could not meet the rising rents, they were evicted and soon replaced by chain stores.

This also happened to longtime shopkeepers in the village centers. Ron Lachman was a butcher who established a shop in the city's Wilde Lake Village Center in 1967. When he couldn't meet the rising rental rates, he was moved to another, less desirable location, and eventually went out of business. Lachman was quoted as saying that the Rouse Company is "no longer interested in the people or merchants who helped them establish the place. They're only interested in who can pay the high rent."[425]

A similar situation occurred with Robert Harper, who operated a dry cleaning establishment in one of the city's village centers, and he responded by filing a $28-million antitrust lawsuit against the company, accusing it of refusing to renew his lease or allow him to retire by selling his store.[426] Although Harper lost the lawsuit, the case brought unfavorable publicity to the company, a situation compounded by the fact that Harper was a minority entrepreneur, someone the Jim Rouse–run company would have tried to help.

Some disagreed with the negative perceptions of the Rouse Company that surfaced. Earl Arminger, a builder who was developing an outparcel that abutted Columbia, stated that "I have not found that they're arrogant…[and] they've always been fair with me."[427] Even Claiborn Carr, previously critical of the firm, could say that "a company with less integrity would make it difficult" for his firm and others to compete with HRD.[428] Joan Lancos, a CA representative, said that some of the negativity toward the Rouse Company may have been nostalgia for the Jim Rouse years, when things were done differently: "They miss those early days, when Rouse was a friendly kind of guy. Now, he's been replaced by guys in $800 suits."[429]

Inner City Housing

The plight of the urban poor that Jim Rouse witnessed in Baltimore in the 1950s and 1960s never left him. And the fact that he wasn't successful in doing much about it then motivated him to make that issue his last crusade. In Rouse's mind also was the example of Jubilee Housing, a Church of the Savior mission project, in which two women were responsible for renovating two tenement buildings in the Adams-Morgan neighborhood in the nation's capital. He had made that possible by guaranteeing the $625,000 loan that funded the project. It later grew into a five-building project, which also provided a health clinic and day-care facilities for its residents.[430]

If two women could accomplish so much with so little, Rouse wondered what could happen if corporate America got behind more such projects? Mel Levine, who had worked for and with Jim on many projects, was invited to Jim's new office in the American City Building in 1981. "The name on the door was ROBIN HOOD, INC. I joined Jim, his wife Patty, Nancy Allison, and Matt DeVito as Jim raised a glass of sherry and said: 'Here's to revolutionizing the capitalist system.'"[431] The Robin Hood name was eventually changed to the Enterprise Foundation at the suggestion of former cabinet secretary John W. Gardner, who thought the initial moniker might make corporate fundraising difficult.[432]

The organization had two major arms. The Enterprise Foundation itself was a nonprofit organization designed to provide adequate housing for the urban poor. A subsidiary, Enterprise Development, was a bona fide for-profit organization involved in urban projects similar to those of his former company, but on a much smaller scale. The profits from such projects would flow to the foundation and its city housing projects. As with all Jim Rouse projects, lofty goals and unbounded optimism were ever-present features.

Although Matt DeVito was on Enterprise's board of directors and the Rouse Company was giving the Foundation rent-free quarters, a rift soon developed between the founder and his former company. When Jim Rouse retired from an active role in the Rouse Company in 1979, he was given the ceremonial title of chairman of the board. When he solicited business for Enterprise Development, some people wondered which hat he was wearing, the Rouse Company's or Enterprise's. In 1984 members of the Rouse Company board of directors approached Matt DeVito about this problem and how it might affect company business. When he raised this issue with his former boss, DeVito first asked Rouse to leave Enterprise Development, and when he refused, Matt asked him to give up his Rouse Company chairmanship and stay on as a director. Rouse refused that idea as well and decided to sever his ties with the company he had created.[433] The final link between the creator and his creation was broken.

It was a very emotional moment when Jim Rouse bid farewell to his company at the 1984 stockholders' meeting. Quoting from Ecclesiastes, he said, "There is a time to plant, a time to harvest. I'm going to harvest what you have put in me." He went on to call Enterprise "a child of the Rouse Company" and wished he could still be a part of it, "but that's not possible."[434] He expressed gratitude to Matt DeVito, and Matt returned the gesture by presenting his former boss with some gifts. But beneath the surface, bonds had been broken and were never repaired. Today, DeVito says that he often thinks about this and expresses deep regret for it, without knowing what could have been done to prevent it.[435]

A Death in the Family

On March 26, 1985, Mort Hoppenfeld died of a heart attack while jogging in the city whose plans he filled with love and care. Mort had left the Rouse Company in 1975 to become dean of the University of New Mexico's School of Architecture and Planning, taking a sabbatical during his tenure there to work on a plan for a proposed new capital city for Alaska. He returned to the Columbia area, and had his own consulting firm, before joining Jim Rouse's Enterprise team in 1982, where he "oversaw the design and planning of all projects."[436] In 1983 he wrote a letter to his boss that began with the words, "It's time we wrote a book—" and proceeded to sketch an outline of a book entitled *The Design and Development of Better American Cities*.[437] The book was never written.

In Hoppenfeld's obituary, Jim Rouse was quoted as saying that Mort "had no peer in the field of urban design. He gave his talent, wisdom, and energy to producing the best possible places for people to live and work, without concern for personal credit or applause."[438] After his death, a memorial sculpture was commissioned and the artist Jimilu Mason responded with *The Hug*, showing two lovers in a warm, passionate embrace. A nearby plaque simply states: "Mort Hoppenfeld: Whose plans and designs for Columbia embrace all people." The statue is placed on a spot that affords a magnificent view of the lakefront, a place he said he designed with lovers in mind. Through the tree branches above one can glimpse the golden arms of the People Tree shining through, as if to affirm the importance of a man to whom Columbia owed so much.

Columbia Matures

The 1980s were a strong, steady growth period for Columbia. In 1980 the city had a population of 54,100 living in nearly 17,000 homes and served by 930 businesses, which employed 26,000 people. By 1985, those figures had grown to 63,000 people in 21,228 homes, and 1,700 businesses employing 38,000 people. And in 1989, the data showed a population of 71,000 in 26,621 homes, with 2,000 businesses and 49,600 jobs.[439] The year 1984 was particularly good, with Columbia's land sales for homes totaling $36.8 million, a new record for the city. Commercial properties increased by 28 percent from the previous year."[440]

The company restructuring in the late 1970s brought a change in Columbia's management. Mike Spear, who held the general manager's job for most of that decade, was promoted to executive vice-president in charge of development for the Rouse Company. His place as Columbia's general manager was filled by Douglas McGregor, who had worked for the company since 1972. Among the Rouse Company higher-ups, the word was "Little Change Expected."[441]

Among the physical additions to the Columbia landscape in the 1980s were two new village centers. In 1986 Kings Contrivance opened as the city's sixth village center. Named after a 1730 land grant, the original property was owned by the Macgill family for more than two centuries. Macgill's Commons, one of the three village neighborhoods, is named after the family, and its street names were taken from a collection of American folk songs compiled by the noted folklorist Alan Lomax. Another village neighborhood (Huntington) drew its name from a historic home located there, and its street names come from the works of noted American poet Carl Sandburg. Dickinson, the third neighborhood, derives its name from Emily Dickinson, another famous American poet, and is the first Columbia neighborhood to be named for a woman. Amherst House, the village's community center, is named for Dickinson's hometown in Massachusetts. Dickinson's street names are also taken from her literary works.

Twenty-one merchants filled the center, along with an office complex, which housed medical and business clients. Anne Dodd, village manager for twenty-eight years, describes Kings Contrivance's best feature as its physical beauty, owing to the Little and Middle Patuxent Rivers coursing through it. Another is that its housing has withstood the tests of time and weather, giving the village an impression of newness that is deceptive. Also, politically speaking, it was the first village to apply the one-person, one-vote rule to village elections, a principle that spread to other villages.[442]

An interesting characteristic of the village's new residents was that 40 percent of the homes in Macgill's Common (a neighborhood composed solely of single-family detached houses) were bought by people already living in Columbia, some of whom were "pioneers" from Columbia's first year.[443] Outside Macgill's Common, the trend was toward multifamily housing units—apartments, town houses, condominiums—a reflection of the ever higher real estate prices. Howard Homes, one of Columbia's first major builders of town houses in Wilde Lake that were priced in the $12,000–$15,000 range in 1967, was now offering models costing $90,000–$100,000.[444]

The other new village, Dorsey's Search, was named for a 1696 colonial land grant. This village was not part of the original New Town zoning created by the county for Columbia in 1965. It was purchased by the Rouse Company in 1970 to prevent the creation of a regional shopping mall that would compete with its nearby Columbia mall.[445] The village has two neighborhoods, Dorsey Hall, consisting of single-family units, town houses and condominiums and Fairway Hills, with no single-family dwellings, making it the only neighborhood in Columbia without them. Fairway Hills was named for the former Allview Golf course, which the Rouse Company razed to build the neighborhood. The remaining open space was used to replace the old golf course with a new one.

There were zoning battles regarding Dorsey's Search, sparked by the Rouse Company's plan to make 80 percent of its domiciles apartments or town houses, almost 20 percent more than the Columbia village average.[446] Because all zoning changes had to be approved by the county council, such a request was made, and a compromise was eventually reached on this issue. Dorsey's Search Village Center opened in September 1989, with the village center located to the left of a long shopping complex, with a large parking lot that faces the nearby entrance road. It is quite different in shape and style from other village shopping centers.

Dorsey's Search village manager Jackie Felker sees the village center's 100-percent-occupied shopping plaza and the relative newness of the center's facilities as two positives. It also has a constituency that, when aroused, can become very active. When an adjacent outparcel was to be developed as a strip mall, the community fought against it and won. The residential units that will ultimately be built there suit the community's interest much better.[447]

Flexing Political Muscle

During the 1980s, Columbia continued to contribute political leadership to county government. The at-large councilmanic districts allowed the city to elect a high percentage of the council members, and people such as Ginny Thomas, Ruth Keeton and Lloyd Knowles continued to serve. When Dick Anderson resigned his seat and moved away, it was taken by Elizabeth Bobo, a countian with strong Columbia ties. Her appointment created a Maryland first: a county council with a female majority. This didn't last, as Bobo was elected as the county's first female executive, and Thomas embarked on a career as a member of the Maryland House of Delegates. But this council and its predecessor were responsible for enacting landmark legislation including farmland preservation, consumer protection, nonsmoking sections in public facilities and a human rights act that included gays and lesbians.[448] In 1984 Howard County voters approved a councilmanic district bill, which brought an end to Columbia's domination of the county council.

But this did not end Columbia's influence on council matters. When Ruth Keeton retired, her seat was filled first by Paul Farragut and then Mary Lorsung, all with close ties to each other. And consider the experience of C. Vernon Gray, a

Howard County Council, 1980. Liz Bobo, Lloyd Knowles, Ruth Keeton, Ginny Thomas and Tom Yeager (left to right) had the distinction of being the first lawmaking body in the state of Maryland to have a female majority. *Lloyd Knowles and Liz Bobo.*

Morgan State University professor and political aspirant, who was told that people outside Columbia wouldn't vote for him because he was African American.[449] He persevered and became the first African American to be elected to the county council—and ended up serving five terms. He gave support to health issues, affordable housing availability and employment and minority business assistance.[450] He was also elected president of the National Association of Counties in 1999. His success paved the way for other African Americans to follow, as witnessed by the election of David Rakes in 2002 and Calvin Ball, who won a council seat in November 2006.

County Services, Columbia Locations

From its inception, Columbia had been blessed with an informed and articulate citizenry who were willing to work hard to improve the quality of life. Two of the city's most important 1980s landmarks—the downtown public library and the city's first senior citizen center—primarily owe their existence to two people who were both Columbia "pioneers": Marvin Thomas and Florence Bain.

Howard County Library, main branch. Located in downtown Columbia, it anchors a nationally recognized library system. *Joseph Mitchell.*

Thomas was the one who led the county library system from the horse and buggy era to the modern technological one. The key to an improved system was a major branch in downtown Columbia. The Rouse Company had similar plans, and eventually agreed to donate the land for the library because "we want [it] located in downtown to help attract people to the area," said Mike Spear.[451] Once the project passed though the county approval system, construction began. On January 4, 1981, the downtown library opened its doors and became one of the nation's most heavily used libraries. Eventually, a second library was built in Owen Brown village, giving both east and west Columbia a branch to call their own. When Marvin Thomas retired in 1996, he left a library system that included six branches with 182 employees and 850,000 materials.[452] The library system continues to grow in both size and prestige and in 2005 was ranked first in the country (in circulation and percentage of residents with library cards) by Hennen's American Public Library Ratings.[453]

Florence Bain came to Columbia at the age of seventy, when the city was, in her words, "ninety families, a pharmacy, and a new Giant."[454] Her son Henry had been a member of Jim Rouse's Work Group, so she knew what Columbia was about and became one of its activist-oriented citizens. Her cause was the county's growing senior population and what they needed to continue leading productive lives. She had a chance to make her ideas known when she was appointed to the Howard County Commission on Aging in June 1969. She began to lobby for the creation of a senior center in the county, preferably in downtown Columbia. A 1972 proposal discussed by Florence Bain and Jim Rouse had the center located in or close to the mall, but by 1978 that idea was no longer feasible.[455]

Support for creating a center grew and in 1980 funding for it was obtained, but the site had not yet been determined. One idea was to place it next to the Wilde Lake Interfaith Center, but that too proved unworkable. Finally, the Rouse Company

The Bain Center. Florence Bain was a passionate advocate for senior citizen services. Columbia's first senior center was named in her honor. *Joseph Mitchell.*

Jim Rouse speaking to Howard Community College students, 1984. Rouse always valued education and welcomed any opportunity to meet and talk with students. *Howard Community College; photo by Quent Kardos.*

agreed to donate a parcel of land for the senior center in Harper's Choice, near the middle school. Construction began, and in 1983 the center finally became a reality. When Bain was told that the center would be named for her, she quipped, "I'm not dead yet!"[456] But she graciously accepted the honor, saying that if anything was due her, "I've received it in the good will and friendships I've found here." When she died in 1997, a newspaper editorial summed up her contributions to Howard County and its seniors with these words: "Countians young and old can be grateful that Mrs. Bain never believed that old age alone should halt a full and productive life."[457] In 2005 the center that bears her name was given a $2-million renovation, to enable it to better serve Howard County's seniors.

During the 1970s, Howard Community College grew in size and numbers, proving to be Columbia's major college success story. President Alfred Smith retired in 1981, and left a legacy that included an objectives-based learning program, a student-directed evaluation system and a nationally ranked nursing program. He was succeeded by Dwight Burrill, who would serve as HCC's president for seventeen years. Burrill is credited with bringing the college into the high technology era and strengthening ties with the business community, by tapping its expertise and encouraging its philanthropy. He also started a tradition that provided the college's students with a continuing source of scholarship money: the Columbia Classic Grand Prix, an equestrian competition that began in 1988 and is held annually on the college's front lawn. Pat and Ellen Kennedy's son Oliver, himself an equestrian events manager, suggested it to his father, who passed the idea on to Burrill, who brought it to fruition. Seventeen years later, many students have benefited from the almost $2 million it has raised.

Caring and Sharing

In 1980, while Doris and Claude Ligon were driving from Chevy Chase back to their Columbia home, Doris told her husband that she wanted to create a museum of African art. Soon, Claude started a process that resulted in the incorporation and eventually the birth of the African Art Museum of Maryland.[458] Claude provided the practical necessities such as organization and fundraising and Doris the artistic expertise, and together they put together an art collection, whose pieces came from private donors, that for a while had no permanent home. Its first audiences were Howard County schoolchildren, who were exposed to African art by way of a traveling exhibition arranged by the Ligons.[459] Howard Community College periodically served as a venue for their collections, until they settled in the Rockland Arts Center (now the Howard County Center for the Arts), located in a former elementary school in the Ellicott City area of the county. After five years there, in 1989 they moved to historic Oakland Manor in Columbia Town Center, where they found a permanent home.[460] In 2005 the museum celebrated its twenty-fifth anniversary, an event overshadowed by Claude's death earlier in the year. Doris continues to keep their dream alive, assisted by their son and daughter, enriching the lives of many visitors. Future plans could include branches of the museum in Annapolis and Baltimore.[461]

African Art Museum of Maryland, located in historic Oakland Manor. Founder Doris Ligon and docent Andy Edafiogho examine a piece from the museum's extensive collection. The museum was created by Doris and her late husband, Claude. *Joseph Mitchell.*

Howard County Center of African American Culture founder Wylene Burch has made Howard County's African American past accessible to all Howard Countians in the group's museum and research library. *Joseph Mitchell.*

Wylene Burch came to Columbia after years of accompanying her husband Olger, a career military officer, on his tours of duty around the world. Her interest in African American history had been piqued in the 1960s while in Germany, when she tried to teach her children about what was happening in the United States during that turbulent period.[462] When the family returned home, she began a teaching career and started to collect items related to the subject, "setting up displays...in schools, churches, and community centers,"[463] especially during Black History Month. She then decided that her collection needed a permanent home where all interested people could learn from it. Thus, the Howard County Center of African American Culture (HCCAAC) was born in 1981. Finding a permanent home proved to be difficult and over the years the center was located at Howard Community College, the Howard County Historical Society and the central branch of the Howard County Library. The Rouse Company and Donald Mannekin, a local builder and developer, also provided space for the center.[464] It finally found a permanent home in Columbia's Town Center, next to Oakland Manor, and also created a library and archives branch in Howard Community College's James Clark Library.[465] The experiences of Doris Ligon and Wylene Burch teach us first and foremost what is possible if minds, bodies and spirits are strong enough to make dreams become realities. Columbia's community-based environment and its supportive citizenry provided indispensable support.

Those same qualities and the community's commitment to philanthropy made possible the Columbia Foundation, which in 1989 celebrated its twentieth anniversary. Originally conceived and funded by Jim Rouse, it was designed to raise funds to assist civic and charitable groups that contributed to the well-being of Howard County and Columbia in charitable, scientific, educational, literary and religious domains.[466] The foundation's original trustees were Dick Anderson, Bill Finley, Mort Hoppenfeld, John Levering and Jim Rouse, all Rouse executives. Within two years, Jim Rouse, Dick Anderson and John Levering remained as trustees, and they were joined by seven people from the community. As intended, the Columbia Foundation eventually became a completely community-based group, with the power to raise and disburse funds.

At the beginning, Jim Rouse worked out an arrangement with the Columbia Bank, the city's first, that 10 percent of its net earnings would be contributed to the foundation, giving it a solid financial footing.[467] The Rouses responded with extra funds when a need arose, as it did in January 1972, when they donated 354 shares of Rouse Company stock (valued at approximately $10,000). In typical Rouse fashion, they asked that no publicity be attached to the donation.[468] It would not be the last Rouse contribution.

The Columbia Foundation has grown enormously over the years. In 1972 it gave $31,270 in grants to nine organizations; in 2004 that figure had grown to $476,501 in grants to fifty-two organizations, due to strong support from both the local business community and county citizens. To make giving more flexible, the organization allows people to set up endowments, scholarships and donor-advised funds, administered through the foundation. In 2004 these added $138,599 of donated monies, which brought the yearly total to $615,540. In that year, the foundation's net assets were close to $10 million, an increase of almost $1 million from the previous year.[469] The aforementioned African Art Museum and Howard County Center of African American Culture are but two of the countless groups and individuals that have benefited from the Columbia Foundation's support.

The Columbia Forum

It is interesting to note how many times in Columbia's history a conversation among friends turned into an important contribution to the city's existence. Columbia Forum was one such enterprise, which began in 1981 when Mary Lorsung, Marcia Harris and May Ruth Seidel met for lunch to discuss a common concern—that too many Columbians neither knew about nor appreciated Columbia's uniqueness as a model city, or as Harris called it, "a part of a noble experiment in living."[470] This luncheon led to other meetings attended by more like-minded citizens and dominated by questions regarding the Columbia concept: "What was it, how well was it working, and should it be changed?"[471] The forum earned a ringing endorsement from one Columbia resident named Jim Rouse, who would later refer to it as a "wonderful manifestation of the uniqueness of Columbia."[472] There were two 1982 meetings: one in February, which assessed Columbia's past, and another in June, which explored hopes for its next fifteen years.[473] When Jim Rouse was invited to speak to the group, his topic was "Columbia in the Year 2000." He praised the Columbia Forum for providing the leadership that Columbia needed as it looked ahead. He concluded with a challenge to Columbia's citizenry to become involved in planning for its future because "the only thing certain about Columbia in the year 2000 is that it will be whatever the people of Columbia make it."[474]

The forum participants took up Jim Rouse's challenge, and for almost fifteen years it was a vital force in identifying and shaping the issues important to Columbia's future. The forum employed a variety of mediums—large community events, small group discussions, ongoing work groups on a variety of subjects, including race relations and Town Center development. It held public forums and published its own quarterly newsletter.[475] For years, it represented the best of Columbia's active and informed electorate, constantly encouraging others to join them in their quest for a better city.

Columbia Turns Twenty

In 1987 Columbia left its teen years behind and headed into the world of young adulthood. In twenty years, it had experienced much growth, from no traffic signals and 1,000 residents in 1967, to twenty-seven traffic signals and 68,000 residents. During that period, the average price of a new Ryland home had risen from $30,000 to $150,000.[476] But amidst all the celebrations, including a city fair and a "Hail Columbia" patriotic music program at the pavilion, a moment of introspection crept in. Newspapers, magazines and journals compared the Columbia of 1987 to the 1967 goals that were set for it, and offered positive and negative comments on the outcome. Questions were raised regarding the city's present and future: Is Columbia a city, or just another suburb? Has it lived up to its goals and ideals? Should it be used as a model for other communities?

These questions were first raised by the Columbia Forum, which decided to use the city's twentieth anniversary to launch "Columbia Voyage," the creation of a symbolic ship to commemorate Columbia's trip into the future. By 1992, the five hundredth anniversary of Columbus's first voyage to the New World, the group hoped "to have identified goals for the city's next twenty-five years, much the way early planners set Columbia's first social, political, and economic agenda."[477] And as the city entered the last decade of the twentieth century, it could feel proud of its accomplishments, but a bit unsure about what the future would bring.

10

COLUMBIA IN THE 1990s

For all of us, Jim Rouse will always be Columbia's man for all seasons.
Pat Kennedy, 1982

As Columbia moved toward the twenty-first century, its parent company continued to prosper and the city looked toward completion with the development of its last village and the creation of final plans for its Town Center. Many longtime Columbians were deeply saddened in 1996 by the death of Jim Rouse; not only was he Columbia's founding father, but also—more than anyone else—he exemplified its spirit, heart and soul.

The Last Years of the Rouse Company

Tragedy hit the Rouse Company in 1990. On August 24, Mike Spear; his wife, Judy; and daughter, Jodi, were killed in a plane crash in Boston. A licensed pilot, Mike was bringing Jodi to Logan Airport for a flight to Japan, where she was going to study. Somewhere between Cape Cod and the airport, the plane went down and all aboard were lost. Three daughters, two of whom stayed behind on the Cape and another daughter already in school, survived.

Spear was the last link to Columbia's early history still working as a senior Rouse Company executive. He had started there in the mid-1960s as a summer intern. After graduate studies, he returned to Rouse in 1967 as assistant project director for Columbia, rising through the ranks and holding key top-level positions. Spear played an important role in guiding the company through the 1970s economic crisis. For most of that decade, he was Columbia's general manager, and to many he was the voice of and for Columbia. A lot of Columbians considered him a member of the family. Unlike

Anthony Deering, James Rouse and Matt DeVito (left to right). From 1939 to 2004, these men were the only CEOs of Rouse-named companies. Their leadership was crucial to the company's growth and development. *Enterprise Community Partners, Inc.*

many Rouse executives, he chose to live in the city, and so his loss for many residents was an extremely personal one.

The loss to the company was also serious. Warren Wilson, a thirty-year Rouse veteran, stated that he expected Spear, "a passionate believer and articulate advocate of planned community development," to succeed Matt DeVito as Rouse CEO.[478] DeVito himself said that he was grooming both Spear (the development man) and Tony Deering (the financial man) to run the company jointly.[479] With Spear's death, Deering began to exert more leadership. And when Matt DeVito retired, Deering was named company CEO, and the Rouse Company embarked on a more cautious and less developmental approach to business.[480]

A nationwide real estate recession negatively affected the company's bottom line from 1990 to 1996, resulting in net earnings losses for five of those years. During the latter half of the decade, the company rebounded spectacularly, and in 1999 reported earnings of $135,297,000. It also became a billion-dollar company, with revenues of $1,037,849,000. By 2003, which would be the company's last year, its net earnings totaled $260,589,000. Since 1999, its common stock share price had risen from $21.25 to $49.40.[481]

In September 1992, the Rouse Company announced that it was purchasing 9.5 million shares of the 11 million shares of its stock held by Trizek, the company that had presented a takeover threat to Rouse a few years earlier.[482] The price was $110 million, and the sale reflected both Trizek's weakened financial condition and Rouse's sounder status. The hunted had outlasted the hunter.

There were also major personnel changes at Rouse during the 1990s. On February 23, 1995, Matt DeVito retired after twenty-seven years, more than half of those as the company's boss. The firm had benefited from his acute business acumen and leadership, especially during times of economic instability. He was replaced by Anthony Deering, who came to the company in the early 1970s and rose to become president and chief operating officer. Having joined the company at the beginning of the 1970s recession as a director of corporate planning, Deering witnessed its slide toward bankruptcy. The lessons learned then were not lost on him; fiscal tightening and strong management strategies brought the company back from the brink. John Somers, an executive with Teachers Insurance and Annuity, stated that Tony "was the kind of guy you want running a big, public real estate company today…He understands the bottom line better than Jim [Rouse] or even Matt [DeVito]."[483] It was Deering who would ultimately engineer the sale of the company.

Retail and Industrial Development

In 1983 Dobbin Center became Columbia's first strip mall center. Built in east Columbia, it was designed to serve the east Columbia villages that surrounded it. After years of success, it became hobbled by tenant failures that left "For Lease" signs up for years and infected even the center's anchor stores. Compounding Dobbin Center's problems, a rival shopping center opened in 1997, directly across

Route 175. Columbia Crossing, as it was called, had more of the "big box" names that drew shoppers to it, making Dobbin Center seem like "it was caught in a time warp."[484]

Some began to question the Rouse Company's development strategy. Nicholas Mangraviti, chairman of the Town Center Village Board, saw the existence of these shopping centers in east Columbia as creating two Columbias—one, Town Center West (the Kittamaqundi area), and the other, Town Center East (the Route 175 shopping centers)—only a few miles away. Not only did this competition make Town Center development more difficult, it was also creating something that Columbia was built to avoid: suburban sprawl.[485]

In the late 1980s, the Rouse Company experienced both success and failure. In 1987 it announced the opening of Columbia Gateway, its most ambitious corporate park endeavor, located on a 584-acre site near the intersection of Interstate 95 and state route 175. The company used a proven strategy, selling parcels of land to developers to create their own office parks. When five companies quickly bought up almost one-fifth of the land, the venture was off to a flying start.[486] This stunning success, however, would have to counterbalance a major failure in 1989—the closing of the nearby General Electric appliance plant.

GE was supposed to be Columbia's greatest business coup—a prestigious corporation moving into the city with a promise of 12,000 jobs—that sounded almost too good to be true. Unfortunately, a slumping appliance market, combined with labor troubles, did in the company's Columbia venture. At its peak, the plant never employed more than 2,300 workers, and most of them did not live in Howard County, but instead commuted from Baltimore County.[487] At the time the closing was announced, only 900 people were employed at GE.

The real estate recession of the early 1990s did nothing to offset a dismal business outlook. The once-promising Columbia Gateway project took a tailspin, with vacant offices littering the landscape. Douglas McGregor, Columbia's general manager, responded that "short term profits are not what we're about," a statement some interpreted as confidence-building and others as arrogance.[488] Fortunately, when the recession ended, Columbia began to experience not only a recovery, but a construction boom, "which made it more of an 'edge city,' where suburbanites not only live, but work and shop."[489]

Residential Construction in Columbia

The 1990s real estate recession was felt in Columbia, as profits from land sales reached only $8.6 million in 1990, compared to $6.6 million the previous year, an increase but far below expectations. The year 1991 saw an increase to $9.8 million, a 14 percent rise. In 1992 earnings went up to $11.8 million, a 20 percent increase over 1991. These figures remained steady throughout the rest of the decade, declining somewhat due to the lack of saleable land. Except for Town Center, Columbia was almost completely residentially developed by the end of the 1990s.[490]

Hickory Ridge Shopping Center. Opened in 1992, it features The Avenue, whose tree-lined promenade divides the center. *Joseph Mitchell.*

In 1992 the Hickory Ridge Village Center opened. With development almost complete around it, this center was a conspicuous break from Rouse's earliest village centers, which had been built as a way to attract home buyers.[491] The village took its name from a 1753 land grant; its three villages were Hawthorn, taken from a work by American poet Amy Lowell, whose works are also used for its street names; Clemens Crossing, the neighborhood and its streets both named for Mark Twain and his works; and Clary's Forest, named after a 1734 land grant, whose street names can be found in the works of twentieth-century American poet William Carlos Williams. The shopping center, which was 97 percent leased at the opening, had a contemporary look to it, with a pedestrian mall called The Avenue splitting it in two and providing some visual interest. An unusual village feature is the location of the community center, the village's first, not near the shopping center, but in the Hawthorn neighborhood area.

Hickory Ridge village is permeated by so many outparcels (landowners who refused to sell to the Rouse Company) that it is referred to as the "swiss cheese" village. This situation is responsible for some confusion because these outparcels are not governed by Columbia covenant restrictions, and when village residents sometimes object to what is done next door to them, they discover that nothing can be done because of this.[492] According to Village Manager Jane Parrish, some of the village's most attractive features are its beautiful open space (part of it is located in the Middle Patuxent Environmental Area), its variety of natural beauty and the uniqueness of its commercial center's physical plant.[493]

Middle Patuxent Environmental Area. Environmentalist Al Geis convinced Jim Rouse not to develop this land. Today, its natural beauty, serenity and wildlife sanctuary prove the wisdom of that decision. *Joseph Mitchell.*

River Hill would be Columbia's ninth—and last—village, with a Clarksville postal address and disconnected from the city. Far from the center of Columbia's development, it had been used as an equestrian center and a game preserve. Because of its rural environs and the existence of large lot residential development on Trotter Road, it was decided that only single-family dwellings, two per acre, would compose River Hill's domiciles.[494] This was later modified through zoning changes brought about by the county council, which acts as the county zoning board.[495] But the village today still differs from its predecessors because almost 80 percent of its homes are single family detached, while the remaining 20 percent consists of town houses and condominiums.[496] There are no apartment rental properties in River Hill, which has made the village one of the county's wealthiest areas. River Hill Village manager Susan Smith describes her area's most prominent feature as having the most open space of all Columbia's villages. This is due to the presence of the Middle Patuxent Environmental Area, land originally slated for development, until Aldred Geis, an environmentalist and Trotter Road resident, convinced Jim Rouse to keep it as an open space wildlife sanctuary. This land is not only beneficial to River Hill, "but presents a tremendous resource for the entire county."[497]

The name River Hill had been used to describe the area for more than a century, and "dates back to an old plantation of that name, which was reputedly one of the first in the state to free its slaves."[498] It consists of two neighborhoods, Pheasant Ridge and Pointer's Run, the former named after a 1745 land grant. The neighborhoods' streets are named for noted American writers Walt Whitman and James Whitcomb Riley. Besides the requisite village shopping center, which has thrived since its opening, there is also an athletic club named Columbia Gym at River Hill. Unfortunately, this popular village and its center have generated a level of traffic congestion that has both residents and county officials concerned.

Town Center, Front and Center

It is often said that Columbia is a city of ten villages; but it is not. It is a city of nine villages and their Town Center, "a unique geographical form consisting of separate residential areas dispersed throughout the Downtown area,"[499] including Amesbury, Banneker, Creighton's Run, Lakefront, Vantage Point and Warfield Circle.

Town Center has many distinguishing features, including Oakland Manor, a historic mansion that now houses the Village Community Center, African Art Museum and Oliver's Carriage House, which was part of the manor and now serves the needs of the Kittamaqundi Community, a nondenominational religious group that counted Jim and Libby Rouse as founding members. Vantage House, Columbia's first continuing senior care facility, opened in 1990, and offers apartments, some penthouses and a nursing home component. Its thirteen-story building is thus far Columbia's tallest structure.

According to Town Center Manager Patricia Laidig, her constituency is different from that of the other villages; its residents are older and live more often in multifamily structures.[500] Its businesses also rely much more heavily on non-Columbia traffic for their well-being. Town Center board president Lee Richardson stated that less than 10 percent of those who attend concerts at the Merriweather Post Pavilion are from Howard County; the Mall in Columbia also attracts sizable regional traffic.[501] Both eagerly await new development in the Town Center, and hope such growth will favorably affect the area and its people.

With the completion of Columbia's village system due by 2000, the logical next step for the Rouse Company was to focus its attention on Town Center development. The mall in Columbia had attracted both Lord & Taylor and Nordstrom as anchor stores. Other recent additions to the mall's environs include a fourteen-screen movie complex, four restaurants and an L.L. Bean retail store. While not connected with the mall itself, their proximity to it makes them popular venues.

Close to these new additions, two luxury apartment and condominium complexes, the Gramercy and the Whitney at Town Center, have added more variety to the mall's landscape. And Evergreens, a fifty-five-and-over community, adds a different flavor to the residential mix. With more than half of Town Center's land still undeveloped, more construction must inevitably follow. What shape it will take has yet to be determined, but

some are already cautioning that the metamorphosis that Town Center is undergoing "should preserve the spirit and attitude that have made Columbia such an attractive place to live."[502] After years of neglect by the Rouse Company, Town Center is prepared to take center stage as Columbia's last major development project.

Village Center Woes

By the 1990s, Columbia's first four village centers (Wilde Lake, Oakland Mills, Harper's Choice and Long Reach) were beginning to show their age, and many believed the Rouse Company was doing little to stop the trend. "I think it's very clear that the village centers are no longer a priority of Rouse," former Howard County Executive and then–state delegate to Annapolis Liz Bobo said, going so far as to "wonder if Rouse doesn't want them to fail."[503] Vacancies in the village shops were slow to fill, and the closing of anchor-like supermarkets compounded an already serious situation. Some also expressed concern that the Rouse Company was more concerned with profitable ventures, such as Columbia Crossing in east Columbia. Frank Turner, a state delegate representing east Columbia, expressed dismay at Rouse's neglect of the village centers: "Personally, I'm very upset with the Rouse Company because I think they forgot who brought them to

Oakland Manor. Once owned by a slave owner and supporter of the Confederacy, it now houses the Town Center Community Association and, in a richly ironic twist, the African Art Museum of Maryland. *Joseph Mitchell.*

the dance. Their resources have been put into these mega-centers."[504] Fred Paine, who had once managed the village centers for Rouse, echoed these statements, saying that concerns regarding the centers "fell on deaf ears."[505]

Sarah Uphouse, Long Reach's village manager, and her board came up with an unusual way to get the Rouse Company's attention when it refused to provide badly needed renovations to the village center. They bought one hundred shares of company stock and announced their intention to attend the annual stockholders' meeting to publicly air their grievances. With that prod, renovation plans were announced before the stockholders' meeting occurred.[506]

A Rouse Company plan to renovate the four oldest village centers was soon announced, and Alton Scavo, Rouse Company vice-president, stated that "[we] are committed. The village centers are working. They work better when they have an anchor that meets consumers needs...To suggest that we're doing nothing is beyond belief."[507] Over the next four years, the oldest centers were renovated. While not a complete solution to the challenges facing them, this was an important and overdue first step.[508] However, in 2002 the Rouse Company announced the sale of its eight village shopping centers to Kimco, an out-of-state firm, for an estimated $120 million.[509]

Another Assessment

In 1992 the four-year Columbia Voyage came to an end. Sponsored by the Columbia Forum, it had featured three years of hard work by a dedicated group of citizens, who through committees had examined Columbia's twenty-five-year-old journey and offered suggestions for its future course. No aspect of Columbia's history escaped its analysis. Two of the most important areas of focus were governance and race.

The question of governance never seemed to go away. Every so often, some citizens advocated a change, either eliminating the Columbia Association or limiting its powers. These advocates all failed, but in 1992 Columbia Voyage offered them another opportunity. To obtain some data, the Columbia Forum commissioned a survey in 1991 entitled "Columbia Resident Knowledge & Attitudes on Local Governance." The results were interesting: when asked if Columbia needed a new form of government, 49 percent disagreed, while 39 percent agreed and 12 percent were not sure. Although the survey showed support for the status quo, only 31 percent judged the Columbia Association capable of serving the community well into the future, while 65 percent thought it would have to be changed at some point.[510] Not a ringing endorsement for CA, but neither was it a hue and cry for radical change.

When little of substance came from the forum debates on incorporation, some took matters into their own hands. The Columbia Municipal League was established, with Rabbi Martin Siegel of the Columbia Jewish Congregation as its spokesman. The group favored an elected mayor–council government system, a common form used in most American municipalities, and began circulating a petition to put the city's governance on the ballot as a referendum issue.[511] Soon another group, Columbians for Howard County, came forth to challenge the incorporation forces. They supported changes in the governance system without completely scuttling it. "Why use a cannon when you can use a pea shooter?" asked Henry Seidel.

With each group making strong, deeply felt arguments, fireworks were bound to erupt. They did in the form of a debate on incorporation between Rabbi Siegel and Jim Rouse on Diane Rehm's National Public Radio show, which spilled over into some off-air comments, where each accused the other of "not understanding Columbia."[512] When there appeared to be little public and institutional support for incorporation, the Columbia Municipal League disbanded. Like previous incorporation campaigns, this one failed due to lack of political insight by reform leaders and internal political divisions.[513]

As for race relations, the 1990s produced a new set of problems and some introspective discussions on how to deal with them. A January 1992 *Washington Post* article noted that Howard County's Office of Human Relations had reported forty-three recent incidents of racial, religious or ethnic affronts; about half of those incidents occurred in Columbia.[514] Some involved youths, reputedly associated with skinhead groups or the Ku Klux Klan, with white supremacist newspapers appearing unsolicited on the lawns of some Columbia residents. How to deal with these problems was debated by both county and Columbia officials. Some did not want to make too much of these incidents, lest that give hate groups the publicity they wanted. Others echoed the words of Roger Jones, chairman of the Howard County Human Rights Commission, who stated that "we can't play these incidents down. People are getting hurt and scarred by these things.[515]

One month later, an article appeared in the *Wall Street Journal* that examined another side of race relations: the social separation of blacks and whites. Some claimed it was caused by both white newcomers not having the same zeal for promoting integration, and by blacks who felt "more comfortable in their safety zone than in exploring new things." Also, this self-segregation was reported to be motivated by "black disillusionment and frustration with Columbia's unfulfilled promise." Citing lower test scores in student achievement tests, few black-owned businesses and the examples of bigotry recounted above, Reverend Bowyer Freeman of the First Baptist Church of [neighboring] Guilford stated, "In this context, you do some introspection. You come back to your own group and you strategize together as a source of strength."[516]

Contributing to this situation was the state of Columbia's older villages and their schools. In 1999 it was reported that African Americans were 16.7 percent of the county school population. Eight elementary schools in Wilde Lake, Harper's Choice, Owen Brown and Oakland Mills had student bodies that were 35.7 to 54.7 percent black—nearly double the range of nine years earlier.[517] Some school officials saw this as reflecting a natural process as blacks moved into what had been mainly white neighborhoods, replacing whites whose children had already passed through the schools and others who had moved to newer homes elsewhere. Others claimed that whites and affluent people of both races were rejecting communities with schools perceived as lower quality. Joan Heckman, a resident of Harper's Choice who helped run a nonprofit after-school program, describes the situation more seriously as "white flight, middle class flight. If we don't reverse this trend it will spread outward. People don't recognize that Columbia is following the pattern of a traditional urban area."[518]

Echoing these words was a three-part series that appeared in the *Baltimore Sun* on November 26–28, 2000, entitled "Columbia at a Crossroads." The lead article described the existence of two Columbias: one, "the affluent community with a diverse population, strong schools, escalating property values...and little crime; the other, a disparate collection of stagnating neighborhoods, struggling schools, and off-and-on trouble spots, that some refer to as 'Inner Columbia.'[519] The second article in this series concentrated on the increasingly segregated nature of some schools in Columbia's oldest neighborhoods, as more blacks moved in and whites began to leave Columbia, or made attempts to enroll their children in other county schools. Sherman Howell, a twenty-eight-year Columbia resident and veteran of the Southern civil rights struggles of the 1960s, stated that this trend "is a very serious threat to the future of Columbia. What happens there when you have drastic change throughout the community is first you have white flight, and then you have upper- and middle-class blacks following. They will leave, too, because they'll feel the schools are not doing well."[520] His sentiments were seconded by Gary Orfield, co-director of the Harvard Civil Rights Project, who said, "If you don't have policies to offset these trends, you end up with racial segregation and then economic segregation, and both of them together create classic inner-city-type school problems."[521]

The third article offered a variety of opinions as to the seriousness of the problem, and suggested possible solutions. Some proposed ameliorations were: end or curtail school transfers; devote more resources to the older schools; make racial integration a goal in subsidized housing; require builders to build affordable housing outside Columbia; tear down some older apartment houses; and find a visionary leader for Columbia who can bring such a program to fruition.[522]

The Rouse Company didn't defuse racial concerns. In fact, development of the new River Hill Village may have exacerbated them. In 2002 the village's high school's population was 78 percent white, 15 percent Asian, 6 percent black and 1 percent Hispanic.[523] One parent, whose family moved from Long Reach to River Hill in search of better schools, second-guessed the decision because it deprived their children of exposure to broad cultural and economic diversity and brought a sense of "social segregation" to their lives.[524]

Gays and Lesbians in Columbia

While on the county council, Virginia Thomas introduced an amendment to a human rights bill that would protect gays and lesbians from discrimination regarding employment and housing. After debate, the bill and its amendment were enacted and Howard County became one of the first Maryland jurisdictions to recognize the rights of gays and lesbians. It would be difficult to imagine this trailblazing in Howard County, if Columbia did not exist.

Like other groups, gays and lesbians made Columbia their home and quickly became a part of the new city in growing numbers. Linda Odum, a real estate agent, stated that by the late 1990s, gays and lesbians represented 5 percent of her real estate business. Columbia's reputation as a liberal, open community where "they will be able to lead a normal life"[525] makes it a very attractive place for them to live.

Although the actual number of gays and lesbians in Columbia is difficult to determine, the presence of Gay and Lesbian Community of Howard County (GLCHC) offers support and community recognition. A local chapter of PFLAG (Parents and Friends of Lesbians and Gays), founded as a support group, also became an advocacy group. Under the leadership of Colette Roberts, the group has lobbied for gay rights and worked with county government, the Columbia Association and the county school system on issues concerning benefits for domestic partners and anti-bullying policies.[526]

Unfortunately, problems do arise (hate crimes, vandalism) that make some gays and lesbians reticent to bring attention to themselves. But the general feeling is that Jim Rouse's open-door policy for Columbia has been extended to them as well.

Jim Rouse's Last Years

As the last decade of the century began, Jim Rouse was busy with the projects of the Enterprise Foundation. Patty Rouse had immediately become "a second pair of eyes and ears for her husband,"[527] and her graduate degree in urban studies and experiences in housing redevelopment in Norfolk made her a perfect partner for Jim in his last major endeavors.[528] She told a story that when Enterprise was created, she was assigned no formal role. Telling Jim, "I don't think you're using me the way you should," she suggested that her work in the nonprofit world could be useful in Enterprise's development. Within a week, she had an office and a full-time, non-paying job.[529] She was always by Jim's side then, accompanying him on trips, in fund solicitation meetings and in other important functions of Enterprise. But she was more than just her husband's companion. F. Barton (Bart) Harvey III, chairman and CEO of Enterprise, described Patty as "a woman consequential in her own right, who married a man and made his mission her own."[530]

Bart Harvey is another of Jim Rouse's occupational discoveries. A successful Wall Street investment banker for Dean Witter for ten years, his religious experiences with the Universal Unitarian Church motivated him to take a sabbatical from his job in order to rethink his future.[531] A corporate headhunter connected him with Jim Rouse, and Harvey's six-month sabbatical turned into another year. By then, Jim had convinced him that anyone could be a corporate banker for the rich; playing that role for the poor would be a much greater and more satisfying challenge.[532] Taking a 75 percent cut in pay, Harvey ran Enterprise while Rouse created projects and convinced investors they were worthy of their support. From 1982 to 2006, Enterprise had raised and invested about $7 billion for urban renewal projects, built more than 200,000 inner city homes and assisted 2,500 grass-roots, nonprofit organizations in 800 cities in making the urban landscape a better place to grow people.[533] A nice family touch to Enterprise's success story is the involvement, both as a financial contributor to Enterprise and trustee member, of noted actor-director-producer Edward Norton, who was raised in Columbia and is Jim Rouse's grandson.

In 1992 Jim Rouse experienced the first of the medical problems that would plague his later years. A chest pain resulted in a trip to Howard County General Hospital, where he was diagnosed by Dr. Michael Kelemen, a noted cardiologist and longtime Columbia resident, as not yet having had a heart attack, but as suffering from arterial blockage. A transfer to Johns Hopkins Medical Center resulted in quintuple bypass surgery. Afterward, in a thank you letter to friends who had extended good wishes to him, he described the surgery and his restored health in glowingly positive terms. He described his heart as "just pumping, all alone, each second of each day for 78 years—so far—providing and sustaining life and the human spirit—God's extraordinary invention."[534] One friend who received the letter commented to Mary Jo Cress, a secretary at Enterprise, that "Jim Rouse is the only damn man I know who could have a bypass and make it sound like you're really missing out if you don't have one."[535]

Because of his illness, Jim Rouse was not able to deliver the 1992 commencement address at the University of California, Berkeley. It would have been a special occasion

Jim Rouse and Bart Harvey. When Jim Rouse founded the Enterprise Foundation, he convinced Bart Harvey to leave a lucrative Wall Street job to manage his firm. Today, the company is at the forefront of modern urban renewal. *Enterprise Community Partners, Inc.*

because twenty-nine years earlier, he had delivered his "It Can Happen Here" speech, an urban reform manifesto, which hinted at the model city he was about to develop. But the come-full-circle event never took place; the speech he wrote was delivered instead by his son James. It had three sections, each devoted to an important phase of Rouse's public life: Columbia, the Enterprise Foundation and Sandtown-Winchester, his final project. The speech described that last place as "a representative neighborhood of persistent poverty, decline, loss of hope, fear, and violence—immediately adjacent to where the riots of '68 began in Baltimore.[536] He stated that the solution to this urban condition would require assistance from all parts of society: "The program will pull together the very best that can be done in the schools, in skill-training, in finding work, in healthcare, in drug and alcohol corrections and prevention, in training young parents, in child care and day care, in deterring adolescent pregnancy, in building family, in preventing crime and providing security, in helping the community build its sense of belonging, caring, self-respect, pride, and hope."[537] It would become Rouse's last crusade.

Sandtown-Winchester was a seventy-two-square-block neighborhood in south Baltimore. There, 12,000 people lived in 4,000 dwellings with a median income of $10,000 per household and an unemployment rate of almost 50 percent. Not surprisingly, it was one of the five highest crime areas in Baltimore. Martin Millspaugh, who got to know Rouse well while covering the Baltimore Plan story as a *Baltimore Sun* reporter in the 1950s and 1960s and then worked with him at Enterprise during the 1990s, recounted that the Sandtown-Winchester program's working model was a replica of the old Baltimore Plan, only larger in scope and intent.[538]

With the customary James Rouse optimism, he set out to change the course of a neighborhood that other outsiders had either ignored or forgotten. And there was a sense of greater urgency to his pace, as if he knew that he did not have a lot of time left. *Prime Time Live*, an ABC news show, featured Rouse and Sandtown-Winchester in its December 2, 1993 show. When the correspondent asked him about the motivation for his work and the urgency in his pace, Rouse replied, "I feel the hand of the Lord on my shoulder."[539]

While the Sandtown-Winchester project continued and Rouse's health deteriorated, several new honors came his way. In 1993 Howard Community College announced the creation of the James W. Rouse Scholars Program. Begun by college administrators Jerrold Casway and Barbara Greenfeld, it is an honors program that also facilitates transfer to four-year colleges that have agreements with Howard. Although this acknowledgement might appear small compared with the many awards that came Jim's way, he seemed deeply touched by it, especially since it gave some students an opportunity to earn a four-year education.[540] The program is now in its fourteenth year.

In 1995 James W. Rouse was presented with the Presidential Medal of Freedom, the highest civilian award a citizen can receive. In awarding the medal on September 29, President Bill Clinton said, "Every time I see James Rouse I think, if every developer had done what James Rouse has done with his life, we would have lower crime rates, fewer gangs, less drugs. Our children would have a better future. Our cities would be delightful places to live. We would not walk in fear, we would walk with pride down the

The nation's highest civilian honor. In 1995 James W. Rouse was awarded the Presidential Medal of Freedom by President Bill Clinton for his many urban reform endeavors. *Enterprise Community Partners, Inc.*

streets of our cities, just as we still can in small towns in America."[541] It was a frail Jim Rouse who accepted the award, having suffered a minor stroke and a broken shoulder from a fall. And if these weren't enough, a later diagnosis revealed lymphoma, which required chemotherapy, and the more devastating amyotrophic lateral sclerosis (Lou Gehrig's disease). By November 1995, his condition had worsened so much that going to work at Enterprise proved too difficult. He would continue to work at home, with papers brought to him regularly by company employees.

On April 9, 1996, the hand that Jim Rouse said he felt on his shoulder tapped him and said that it was time to go. The ravages of disease did something that nothing else could do—still the creative, compassionate mind that had worked so hard to make things better for an imperfect world. Fittingly, Rouse was on his way to his workplace in the kitchen of his Wilde Lake town house when he passed away. A memorial service at Brown Memorial Presbyterian Church on the morning of April 12 was followed by another in the afternoon at the Merriweather Post Pavilion. The attendance of Cabinet secretaries, U.S. senators, mayors, business leaders, ordinary Columbians, and community representatives from Sandtown-Winchester attested to the cross section of people whose lives Jim Rouse had touched.[542] The praise Rouse received for his life's achievements are too numerous to mention and probably would have embarrassed a man who often eschewed personal credit and gave it willingly to the people who worked for him. In a recent glowing tribute to his former boss and friend, Mel Levine ended his remarks with the most simple but moving testimony by stating, "He was a mensch."

11.

COLUMBIA AT FORTY

Columbia to a degree is a victim of its own success. Building a better place to live attracts ever more would-be residents who, in a market system like ours, bid the prices for homes up ever higher, which tends to undermine the goal of inclusiveness.

Kenneth T. Jackson

As Columbia approached its fortieth year of official existence, two major developments combined to form a major turning point in the city's history. First came the acquisition (in November 2004) of the Rouse Company by General Growth Properties (GGP), a Chicago-based shopping center firm. The leaders of the Rouse Company, most notably Anthony "Tony" Deering, had helped lay the groundwork for that transaction during the previous decade. By the mid-1990s the Rouse Company was the third largest real estate investment trust in the country, behind the Simon Property Group and GGP. Rouse "positioned itself [then] as an attractive takeover candidate, selling off its poorer-performing retail centers to concentrate on marquee properties."[543] And from 1999 to 2003, it trimmed its workforce by almost 25 percent.[544] Columbia was not exempt from this process, as Rouse sold off its village centers' commercial properties, and even offered to sell Merriweather Post Pavilion to Howard County.[545] All that remained was for someone to make the company an offer it couldn't refuse.

The Simon Group expressed interest, but finally backed out. General Growth Properties was actively encouraged by the Rouse Company in what was described as a "whirlwind courtship," which began in June 2004 and ended in August, when the deal was announced. The cost was $12.6 billion—$7.2 billion in cash and $5.4 billion in assumed debt. To assure stockholder approval, GGP offered 25 percent more than the stock's all-time high of $54 a share.[546]

There were mixed reactions, ranging from shock and dismay to resignation and acceptance. Columbians were particularly interested in how this sale would affect the city's future development. Former Columbia Association (CA) President Pat

Kennedy said that Columbia would continue its course, because it had grown into a strong and independent community. Columbia Council Chairman Joshua Feldmark wondered if GGP would take the community's spirit and ambition into account or "just think of us as another untapped strip mine."[547] Bob Tennenbaum, Columbia's chief planner, architect and city pioneer, expressed the opinion that GGP might be good for Columbia, especially its Town Center development because the Rouse Company had done little for the latter.[548] Time would tell which opinion would be closest to the truth.

A second major milestone came about two years later, when Columbia's official website announced that the town's population had finally reached the planned goal of 100,000 residents. Achieving it had taken much longer than expected (the original plan had called for Columbia to be fully populated by 1980), but there was no mistaking the significance of this development. Despite many unforeseen and serious setbacks, this leading new town born in the 1960s had reached maturity. The built environment of Columbia was not entirely finished by then, of course, but no city's built environment ever is.

And so as Columbia approached its fortieth official anniversary (June 21, 2007), the combination of the sale of the Rouse Company and the reaching of Columbia's target population seemed to mark the end of the city's formative stage. What, then, are we to make of Columbia at forty? Before proceeding to discuss specifics, a few general caveats are in order. First and foremost (as Rouse himself liked to remind Columbia's critics), heavy development of the Baltimore-Washington corridor was inevitable. There was no way, given the population growth pressures on that region, to preserve Howard County as a relatively pristine, agrarian place. Thus the question is not whether large-scale development ought to have occurred there, but whether Columbia marked a real improvement over other likely alternative forms of development. Second, Columbia's development necessarily took place within the constraints imposed by larger forces in society, economic, political, social and cultural. The question is not whether Rouse's vision for Columbia was compromised (which in some ways it obviously was), but whether other, better outcomes had been possible given those constraints. And third, Columbia was never meant to be a utopia; utopias don't get built. Rouse's venture was, from the very beginning, an exercise in the art of the possible. Keeping all of this in mind helps one to understand why Columbia has become what it now is, and how best to go about improving it.

The Natural Environment

Experts who have studied Columbia tend to give the town's creators a high mark for their approach to the natural environment. From the very beginning Rouse insisted, as he liked to say, that developers "respect the land" they were developing. What this meant in concrete terms was an effort to preserve as many mature trees as was practical and, more generally, to try to fit the city's structures into the existing waterways and land patterns rather than simply reshaping them with bulldozers. Nor did Rouse and his associates seek only to minimize what might be lost in terms of the natural environment; they also worked intentionally to enhance it. The attitude toward trees is especially revealing on this point. Rouse ordered the planting of many thousands of trees, which enhanced the natural beauty of eastern Howard County even as a new city arose in its midst. In this, as in other areas, what was done went far beyond what was necessary in order to attract residents (and vastly beyond what more conventional real estate development ventures undertook in terms of landscaping). The costly decision to create three new lakes (Kittamaqundi, Wilde and Elkhorn) for Columbia also enhanced the natural environment. The combination of these masses of greenery and bodies of water makes a strikingly positive impression on visitors and residents alike.[549]

Adding to that positive impression was the early farsighted decision to set aside almost 40 percent (5,360 acres) of the city's land as public open space, in such forms as waterways, woods, fields, pathways, playgrounds and a nature preserve (the Middle Patuxent Environmental Area). Perhaps the greatest achievement here was simply to resist the temptation to develop that land as property values rose greatly over the past forty years. This is not a hypothetical issue. On the contrary, it surfaced very early on in the planning process. Distinguished urban sociologist Herbert Gans, who belonged to the original Work Group that advised Rouse on Columbia's development, doubted from the start that the public open space could endure, given how valuable it would become as Columbia grew. Having studied suburban development carefully while writing a book about a Levittown development, where he actually lived while doing his research, Gans had been added to the Work Group as a "representative of reality." He believed strongly that as Columbia developed and property values there rose, the size of the potential profit to be made from selling off the open space would prove irresistible. When viewed from that perspective, Columbia's success (at least thus far) in keeping its public open space is noteworthy. With the demise of the Rouse Company, however, has come the possibility of a more profit-minded approach to running Columbia public facilities, most notably the open space. Whether the city's residents will become sufficiently engaged to restrain those pressures and guide them in constructive directions remains to be seen.[550]

In terms of air, noise and water pollution, Columbia's record is more mixed than its creators intended. The chief culprits here are the failure of vision with respect to transportation issues (about which more will be said below) and the overly successful effort to attract employers to the area. The result of the first has been a much greater dependence on cars to get around Columbia than Rouse intended, and, consequently, substantially more air and noise pollution stemming from them than he had hoped. The Rouse Company's spectacular success in attracting businesses to the Columbia area has made this air and noise pollution problem even worse, by making the region more congested than it could have been. Not everything about this has been bad. Concentrating so many employers near Columbia has doubtless diminished the commuting distances of many residents (who might otherwise have needed to drive to work in Baltimore or Washington), with positive environmental results. On the other hand, this has also meant much heavier traffic flows around Columbia, during rush hour especially, and thus increased air and noise pollution pressures on eastern Howard County. The impact on water quality of locating so many places of business in and around Columbia is less clear.[551]

The Built Environment

Columbia's buildings defy easy analysis. The city's planners deserve praise for insisting on much greater variety in housing types than can usually be found in suburbia. Instead of the numbing uniformity of house after house, there is a nice mixture—in the older villages especially—of detached houses, town houses and apartment buildings. The design of these dwellings has been faulted as too conventional, but the look of the places stemmed less from a lack of vision than from a hardheaded appreciation of buyers' tastes. No one was more blunt about that than James Rouse himself, who once famously remarked, "Unless Columbia is roundly criticized by the architectural critics of the country, it will be a failure." Rouse's refusal to aim overly high in terms of housing design enabled Columbia to succeed, in the sense that home sales moved quickly enough to enable the Rouse Company to keep control of the project. The obvious contrast here is to Reston, Virginia, whose founder's fondness for modernist architecture won praise from designers but put off too many would-be buyers, thereby causing the whole venture to go broke.[552]

What emerged instead in Columbia were a lot of houses that looked much like others being built at the same time elsewhere, such as colonials and split-levels. But that first impression is a bit deceptive. The Rouse Company established quality standards for housing construction that, with one exception early on, every contractor had to meet. The high quality of the public open-space landscaping and the costly decision to insist that power lines be buried also helped make Columbia's housing unusually attractive by suburban standards. A fair number of the detached houses in particular used more wood, glass and interesting angles than the more typical suburban box-style house. Elitists tended to dismiss Columbia's housing designs, but they usually won favor with middle-class and poorer residents and visitors.[553]

Columbia's public buildings drew similarly mixed reviews. James Rouse favored what he liked to call "forward looking architecture" for public buildings. The first village center (Wilde Lake) drew upon Rouse's earlier work at Cross Keys and had a nice, almost Western European feel to it, with offices located above the small shops, all of which surrounded an attractive public space with seating. The third village center (Harper's Choice) went even further in the direction of European models by including housing above the shops. The visual contrast with shopping centers and strip malls of the sort that filled America's suburban landscape was obvious and welcome. Critics noted correctly, however, that some of the later village centers lacked the attention to detail of the earlier ones, and that the shops often struggled to compete effectively against larger-scale merchants at the Mall in Columbia. With the coming of the so-called big box stores such as Lowe's and Target to strip malls located at Columbia's periphery, the village centers found themselves facing much more serious competition, and most began to have problems. Recent renovation of the older village centers has helped reduce (but not eliminate) those challenges.[554]

The Mall in Columbia, which first opened in 1971, has fared better. The design was very appealing, featuring lots of glass, greenery and fountains. In the early years, many residents used it literally as a kind of Main Street, just as Rouse had intended. It struggled then, however, because there were not enough people living nearby to support it. What enabled the mall to succeed was, above all else, the expertise of the Rouse Company. Rouse executives knew a lot more about how to make malls work than the trickier village centers, and so when some tenants left the mall, Rouse found new ones. When a further dose of new blood was required, the Rouse Company opted to expand the original mall in ways that attracted more customers.[555]

Columbia's other major buildings, such as the local community college, schools, the public library, the hospital and structures in the various office parks, were well built and functional, though not especially striking. The standout structures were ones designed in the early years by the now-famous architect Frank Gehry, such as the Rouse Company headquarters and Merriweather Post Pavilion.[556]

The decision to disperse Columbia's various public and office buildings can be faulted for having robbed it of a true downtown. The lack of vision for the Town Center is a real failing thus far of Columbia's built environment. The open space facing the lake at the Town Center is an appealing place. What is missing, however, are the other kinds of structures within easy walking distance that make for a truly urban center. Even the Mall in Columbia, which Columbia's planners envisioned as playing that role, is difficult to walk to because of the surrounding surface and structured parking. Most people drive to the Mall, bypassing the lakefront area in the process, which consequently often has a lifeless look to it. This need not be a permanent problem, of course; urban cores are constantly being developed and redeveloped. By 2006, in a very promising turn of events, county and Columbia planners had begun working together on a downtown planning process. As Columbia approaches forty, the Town Center appears to be the one part of the built environment still conspicuously unfinished.[557]

Education

Columbia's designers envisioned education as central to the life of their community, and not just for children either. Rouse and his colleagues saw education as a crucial part of Columbia's larger goal of enabling its residents to reach their full potential. In large measure, Columbia has lived up to its creators' hopes in this respect. The smaller sizes of the public schools when compared with those of suburbia in general have made learning more human-scale. Planning the schools' location in the midst of neighborhoods and villages concurrent with residential construction has allowed an extraordinarily high percentage of their pupils to walk to them, and encouraged participation in after-school extracurricular activities. While not without problems, Columbia's schools were of such high quality as to propel the

Howard County school system to the top in Maryland. Places of higher education in and around Columbia, most notably Howard Community College, have likewise fulfilled Rouse's vision of a city in which formal education is readily accessible and integral to the life of the community. The city still lacks a four-year-degree-granting college, but that will likely come someday. In the meantime, that need is met at least partly by satellite campuses of four-year institutions located elsewhere (Johns Hopkins, Loyola and the University of Phoenix), and nearby four-year schools, such as the University of Maryland campuses at Baltimore County and College Park, and Towson University. The centrality of formal education in Columbia has, not surprisingly, attracted a great many residents (including a lot of educators) for whom quality educational institutions are a high priority, thereby reinforcing that emphasis. Columbia has become distinctive as a result, by combining successfully a middle-middle-class ethos with an unusually strong emphasis on formal education. There have been highly practical benefits to this, as the fraction of good-paying jobs requiring a lot of formal education has risen steadily over the past generation. The less material benefits that Rouse envisioned from making education such a priority are harder to measure.[558]

There have been some drawbacks, of course. In the early years the biggest problems stemmed from some of the educational innovations of the mid-1960s, such as relaxed discipline, open-space design and continuous progress (the idea that failure is never final). Like so many ideas associated with sixties' liberals' efforts to improve public education, relaxed discipline, open-space design and continuous progress tended to work best for exceptional pupils and much less well for more ordinary ones. As these innovations were cut back or abandoned entirely, the Columbia schools achieved the kind of excellence intended for them. More recently, new problems have surfaced. In the early years, almost everyone moving to Columbia had school-age children, due in part to the larger family sizes prevalent then and the tendency of new communities to attract young families. Over time, as family sizes have declined and the overall population has aged, the percentage of residents with school-age children has dropped, in the older villages especially. This has understandably led to some decline in direct public connection to the schools, and to changes in the demographic makeup of student bodies. In some of the older villages, lower-income pupils have become a greater fraction of the schools' student bodies, at the elementary level in particular, because family size at the lower end of the income scale now tends to be significantly greater than for the upper reaches. There are racial implications to this as well. Some schools have consequently become much more attractive than others, to upper-middle-class parents in particular. In this, Columbia mirrors, albeit to a much lesser degree, patterns seen in cities and suburbs more generally. Addressing this issue successfully will require a great deal of community effort, and poses the most serious challenge for Columbia's schools in the years ahead.[559]

One other challenge deserving mention here is that of parental involvement in the learning process. Columbia's public schools, like most in the United States, were designed on the assumption that parents, and especially mothers, would actively supervise their children's learning, and reinforce teacher expectations in terms of behavior and work assignments. As workdays and workweeks have lengthened since the 1970s, that parental role has diminished. As ever more women with small children have moved into the paid labor force, that change has become even more pronounced. These national trends have been especially challenging for Columbia's school system. Columbia's high cost of living, many residents' high expectations for material comforts and an above-average divorce rate have combined to lead a high percentage of Columbia fathers to work longer hours and Columbia mothers with school-age children to take paying jobs. There is, to be sure, day care available, but its quality appears to vary significantly. Although one can overstate the importance of all this to learning in the public schools, parents who are more absent during the day and more tired in the evening and on weekends appear to be another challenge facing the Columbia school system to a greater degree than previously.[560]

Transportation

Columbia's transportation system has been rightly (and often) called the greatest failure of vision of the city's design. The low density of the housing and curvilinear roads worked fine in the early years, but as the volume of traffic steadily grew, the congestion on major arterial roads during rush hour began to replicate that of unplanned suburban sprawl. Attracting so many employers to the nearby office parks exacerbated that problem. Rouse and his associates had intended to address it by making the community so pedestrian-friendly as to diminish significantly the need for daily driving and, to a degree, that approach was successful. As the city grew in size, however, the need for effective mass transit increased, if the traffic volume were to be kept below suburban norms. The minibus system that Columbia's designers created to meet that need failed, however, to do so. Columbia's neighborhoods were simply not dense enough to support a conventional mass transit system. The volume of minibus ridership stayed too low to generate the income needed to support the system, despite a significant subsidy from the Columbia Association. During Columbia's first fifteen years or so, this longer term transportation issue was not very visible, but it became much more so over the next quarter century.[561]

Even though mass transit flopped in Columbia, driving there was still not as bad as such notorious low-density urban areas as Greater Los Angeles. Columbia's designers mostly sheltered its neighborhoods from the noisy arterial roads that often afflicted southern California communities. And Columbia did remain, even as it grew to its target population, much more pedestrian accessible than typical American suburbs, a fact that continues to keep down the number of daily short driving trips so common elsewhere. Columbia's strong commitment to community planning also gave it an edge over many other places because the city's leaders continue to study the transportation problem and look for solutions. Finding them, such as light-rail links to downtown Baltimore and Washington that would reduce the volume of auto commuters and revitalizing village center and downtown shopping and dining so as to cut down driving to outlying strip malls, is the single greatest challenge facing Columbia as a whole.[562]

Owen Brown Interfaith Center. This center once housed congregations of Protestants, Catholics, Jews, Muslims, Buddhists and Unitarians. It remains Columbia's most diverse Interfaith Center. *Joseph Mitchell.*

Family Life

Columbia from the beginning was intended primarily (though not exclusively) as a place for families raising children. Rouse himself was firmly committed to a vision of family life that can be thought of as a new and improved version of the fifties' social system. According to the Rouseian scheme, men and women would still get married (and stay that way), have children (who would typically be cared for when they were young mostly by a stay-at-home mother) and family interactions would be the central events of most people's daily lives. Unlike the fifties' version, however, mothers in Columbia would not become chauffeurs to their children, who could walk most places they needed to go. Nor would mothers suffer from the kind of isolation that postwar suburbs had usually brought, thanks to Columbia's more pedestrian-friendly design, the neighborliness and civic involvement it helped foster and the presence of restaurants, shops and recreational, educational and cultural institutions affordable to the vast majority of residents.[563]

Other major aspects of Columbia's design also aimed to address what Rouse and his associates perceived as the most glaring defects of 1950s-style suburban family life. The strong emphasis on readily available, high-quality educational institutions was intended in part to address the dullness of that life, by giving Columbia's residents the means to reach their full potential during childhood and keep growing as adults. The interfaith centers were meant to combine the benefits of mainstream organized religion (most notably values instruction for the young) without as much of the expense and social separation that denominational houses of worship tended to bring. Openness to African Americans, who were mostly excluded from 1950s suburbia, would gradually work to diminish racial prejudice as whites and blacks came to know each other as individuals rather than abstractions. Columbia's design tended to promote this kind of mid-1960s liberal social agenda for family life, especially in the city's early years. Although these reforms helped, they did not fully solve the problems created by suburban life, especially feelings of isolation among women.[564]

As family life began to change dramatically in Columbia and elsewhere during the 1970s, those problems became more intense and open. Rouse failed to anticipate both the revival of feminism, which challenged the notion of motherhood and homemaking as central to women's social role, and the backlash among many men against 1950s-style domestic life. Columbia's designers also failed to anticipate (like so many others) both the sharp rise in living costs and people's expectations (in a materialistic sense) then, which together pushed many women to take paying jobs, and both women and men to work longer at them than people usually did during the 1950s. The rise of the counterculture and a more polarized society in general also took Columbia's designers by surprise, as did the steep increase in the divorce rate. By the 1990s, these related changes had significantly increased the stress on families. So, too, had greater fears of crime. Although these were national trends, they affected Columbians more than many Americans, due to the high cost of living (and material expectations) in the Baltimore-Washington area, as well as the greater polarization of attitudes toward gender roles and embrace of the counterculture there than in the nation's heartland. Columbia's Family Life Center tried to address the challenges created by these developments, in particular by offering counseling to those in need, but that fell short of a complete solution. Whether all this signals a permanent change in the nature of family life in Columbia, or simply a phase from which it will emerge as economic, political, social and cultural conditions return to something more like the norms of the mid-1960s, is still unclear.[565]

Diversity

Greater diversity of population when compared with suburbia in general was from the start one of the Columbia's most noteworthy goals. At the heart of that commitment was a welcoming attitude early on to newcomers regardless of race, creed or income. With respect to the first two of those categories, Columbia has been a truly remarkable success. It is both diverse and stable in terms of race and religion especially, which is highly unusual for a sizable community in the United States.[566]

The most revolutionary aspect of Columbia's commitment to diversity had to with race, and the result there has been positive. Thanks largely to the Rouse Company's firmly expressed determination to open Columbia to black residents, the town early on achieved a substantial minority population. Blacks composed about 18 percent of Columbia's population by the mid-1970s and still do today. As the city approached its fortieth anniversary, roughly three-quarters of its residents were non-Hispanic whites and the rest were members of racial minority groups, most notably blacks, Asians and Latinos. And, crucially, Columbia's minority population was not concentrated into ghettos, but rather dispersed (although today poorer blacks are much more likely to live in the older villages, which have more apartments). The city's un-self-conscious racial mix is arguably its greatest triumph, and a source of much-deserved community pride. Columbia's mostly harmonious blend of people of different religious faiths (and no faith) similarly testifies to the city's success in promoting diversity in a positive way.[567]

There have been, to be sure, tensions and setbacks on the Columbia diversity front. The most basic stems not from race or creed, but rather from disappointments associated with trying to mix social classes. Although Rouse himself meant for Columbia to be open to people of all income levels, the sharp rise in housing costs since the early 1970s, and the reduction in federal government subsidies for low-income housing in Columbia's early years, have combined to produce a community populated mostly by households in the top fifth of the nation's income distribution. (This has also helped make Howard County one of the most affluent in the country.) But for Baltimore's and Washington's sizable numbers of upper-middle-class blacks, who moved to Columbia in great numbers, that setback on the class side would likely have meant a much smaller black presence there as well. There are some lower-middle-class and poor residents of Columbia, white and non-white, but as an overall fraction of its population, their numbers have become very small.[568]

Thus, in Columbia, mixing races and religions has mostly gone on within an increasingly upper-middle-class population sharing a middle-middle-class ethos. The greatest tensions stemming from Columbia's diversity commitment have been generated by middle-middle-class and upper-middle-class encounters with the poor living in subsidized rental apartments. There has been a certain amount of self-segregation, by race especially, even within the upper-middle-class population more recently, but what that means is debatable. It could signal a retreat from the earlier welcoming attitude, a more mature appreciation of the importance of commonalities in shaping family and social networks or, most likely, some of each.[569]

Civic Life

Rouse and his colleagues intended Columbians to participate more actively in the governance of their community than most Americans typically did. What Rouse seemed to have in mind here was an updated version of the New England town meeting approach, in which residents listened respectfully to civic leaders' ideas about needed policies, then debated those proposals and worked hard to develop broad agreement about the specifics of needed changes. In keeping with that model, Columbia's creators provided that each of the nine villages and the Town Center would have a governing body (the village boards), and that the city as a whole, though unincorporated, would feature a council. During Columbia's early years, these were all essentially advisory bodies; the real power remained in the hands of the developers, exercised through Howard Research and Development (HRD), the entity that directed Columbia's construction, and the Columbia Association (CA), which managed the various facilities and the public open space. Rouse and his financial backers felt obliged then to keep that control, due to Columbia's status as a privately financed venture in city-building. As Columbia matured and its investors were repaid, however, the city's governance bodies began to acquire genuine decision-making authority. The popularly elected Columbia Council, for example, acquired control in 1982 over the Columbia Association, which transformed it into a real homeowners' association.[570]

Columbia's civic life in its first four decades has passed through three distinct stages. The early years were marked by a flurry of meetings and discussions involving many early residents, who were enthusiastic about a more participatory kind of democracy. As the limits then on the authority of Columbia's governance bodies became clear, that early burst of civic activism died down. Next came a stage of much lower levels of participation and occasional unsuccessful efforts to incorporate Columbia in order to give it a more conventional urban government. More recently, the level of citizen participation in governance has grown somewhat, as Columbians have become aroused by such problems as some irregular business practices at the Columbia Association, the cost of the services CA provides and difficulty in finding a suitable successor to longtime CA President Padraic Kennedy when he retired in 1998. Troubled schools, traffic congestion and the unsatisfactory Town Center have also increased public engagement in recent years.[571]

Columbia's civic life thus far has usually lacked the high level of citizen engagement Rouse and his associates hoped for. The clearest sign of that has been the consistently low voter turnout in village board elections. Given the dominance of the developer during Columbia's formative stage, that does not seem so surprising. Whether Columbia can develop a more robust civic life now that power has passed to the local governing bodies remains to be seen.

One aspect of Columbia's civic life Rouse wanted that has materialized, though, is a much less adversarial approach to problem solving than can be found in many American cities. This appears, in part, to reflect Columbians' high levels of formal education, which inclines them toward practical solutions to concrete problems. The presence in Columbians' midst from the very beginning of socially responsible business leaders also seems to have contributed to that less adversarial approach. Columbia's more affluent residents in general tend to support a generous welfare state as well as charitable and philanthropic ventures, an outlook that seems also to have contributed to a Rouseian kind of civic life imbued much more with love than fear or anger.[572]

Cultural Life

Columbia's creators aspired from the start to create a place with a vibrant cultural life, in sharp contrast to what one could find in most of suburbia. Although there were some ambitious early efforts, Columbia's reach often exceeded its grasp then. That was due mostly to the small number of residents, their preoccupation with raising children and Columbia's distance from the major urban centers of Baltimore and Washington (which made trips there for cultural stimulus infrequent). Weeknights in Columbia, during the early years especially, were marked much more by television watching than concert- or theatergoing. To the extent there were cultural events, they were usually popular in nature, performed by the National Symphony (and later by rock bands) at Merriweather Post Pavilion.[573]

Columbia's reputation as a middle-class family town has continued to constrain its cultural horizons, but less so than a first impression might suggest. The heavy emphasis on education and first-rate public libraries has helped make Columbia a city of readers, as have the activities of the Howard County Poetry and Literature Society (HoCoPoLitSo). There is a vibrant musical world, too, thanks to Columbians' strong support for music education, through both private lessons and the public schools. Groups such as the Candlelight Concert Society have also brought in internationally known musicians to perform there. Local artists enjoy a lively subculture. A critical mass of viewers exists for artistically significant films, which have been shown regularly in Columbia (by the Columbia Film Society) from the very beginning. Lectures on a wide variety of subjects take place there. The Columbia Foundation has subsidized these kinds of activities, thereby providing the kind of supplementary private support required in a nation with relatively low levels of public funding for high culture.[574]

The most basic challenges to creating a more varied cultural life in Columbia are ones common to the United States in general: a very strong work ethic that leaves relatively little time or energy for high culture; a heavy emphasis on sports (watching more than playing, with soccer a conspicuous exception in Columbia) and popular culture in such forms as mass-market Hollywood movies and rock music; the much lower degree of attention to the arts in the public schools when compared with most other major industrialized countries; and the public's frustration with the high cost of such offerings as professional theater, the symphony and opera, which tends to make the world of high culture in America an unusually elite (and elitist) one.

Given those obstacles, Columbia has countervailed against them better than most of suburbia. Making high culture more central to the majority of Columbians' lives remains a long-term challenge, though, to which gradual forward progress seems the most that can be expected. There is reason for optimism, however, because Columbia more than most American communities encourages respect for cultural life, even among those residents with little interest in serious art, film or music. The unusually strong commitment to learning seems to be the reason. In that sense at least, Columbia's design has succeeded in encouraging the emergence of a significant cultural scene.[575]

Spiritual Life

Columbia's unusual approach to organized religious activity elicited a great deal of media attention during the early years. James and Libby Rouse were themselves deeply religious people, with a sort of nondenominational Christian worldview. That outlook informed Columbia's design, most notably with respect to the decision to create interfaith centers rather than encourage the construction of separate houses of worship. As noted earlier, there was a very practical side to that decision. The Rouses believed that putting every denomination into a separate building drove up the cost of organized religious activity so much as to depress participation. Interfaith centers promised economies of scale that would address that problem. Such places also would require the leaders of various denominations to work together, an experience the Rouses believed would diminish tensions and breed mutual respect.[576]

To a degree, the three interfaith centers have done that. In Columbia, Roman Catholics share the same baptistry with Baptists. Gentiles helped Jews in designing and constructing the ark (where the Torah scrolls are stored) for Temple Isaiah, one of the early Jewish congregations that joined one of the interfaith centers. Leaders of the various denominations located there appear to know and respect each other. Interfaith marriages are common.[577]

What the Rouses (and many others) failed to anticipate was the greater polarization of public attitudes toward spiritual life that developed in the 1970s and '80s especially. That trend tended to work against the interfaith concept and the closely related ecumenical movement then. Instead of ever-broader public participation in mainstream denominations that emphasized doctrinal commonalities rather than differences, more extreme attitudes toward spirituality grew and the moderate middle, theologically speaking, declined.

Signs of that change in Columbia began to appear during the 1980s. The most visible were the separate houses of worship that cropped up around Columbia then. The interfaith centers have not been abandoned, but they have not been as central to the spiritual life of Columbia as the Rouses intended. The first interfaith center (at Wilde Lake) in particular has lost most of its original member congregations. Another, less obvious, sign of change was tension in some of the schools between evangelical Christian groups, who sought to use school property for religious activity, and Jewish students, who objected to that. Whether these developments signal merely a dip in the road, or a more basic departure from the Rouses' vision for Columbia, remains to be seen.[578]

Commercial Life

"Columbia won't be a success unless it makes an outrageous profit," James Rouse often said, which captures succinctly the centrality of Columbia's commercial aspect to his vision for it. As a commercial venture, however, the city as a whole proved disappointing to all except long-term investors. In its first twenty years, Columbia made no money. At

Eighty years of Columbia Experiences. Tony Tringali opened Anthony Richard Barber
Shop in Wilde Lake Village in 1967 and is its only remaining tenant from that time. Bob
Tennenbaum was the planner-architect who helped design the village and still resides in it.
Joseph Mitchell.

the same time (and partly because Columbia generated no early profits), the amount
of investment capital needed to finance its creation steadily grew. Although Columbia
made a lot of money for investors during its second two decades, a record of slow
profitability and high upfront investment costs suggests that no more privately financed
new towns on the scale of Columbia would be built. Columbia's experience indicates
instead that public-private partnerships would be needed to do that.[579]

Rather than a model that could be replicated in toto, Columbia's experience as a
commercial venture suggests that it has more limited, though still significant, lessons
for community builders. The village centers and the downtown mall ultimately made
money. So too did the office parks (and much more quickly). And as the community
grew, the value of the land rose dramatically, which enriched the steadily growing
number of homeowners and not just the developers. Careful planning, public open
space, the village center concept and respect for the natural environment ultimately
proved profitable, for Rouse and many residents alike. In that more limited sense,
Columbia vindicated its creators' hopes for it as a business venture.[580]

Columbia: A City of Celebrations. Shown here is the Oakland Mills International Festival and some Celtic dancers, October 2006. *Joseph Mitchell.*

Columbia is also an economic success story in terms of job creation, to a degree unexpected even by Rouse himself. The office parks in particular are home to almost as many jobs as there are Columbia residents. That turn of events has enabled Howard County to keep its tax rates from rising very much even as the demand for social services greatly increased. To the extent there are problems with Columbia's success as a jobs magnet, they have to do with increased congestion and a weakening of the village centers, which might otherwise have housed some of these employers. Perhaps there was a kind of Faustian bargain at work here, in which the greater than expected success of the office parks helped generate enough income to keep the Rouse Company afloat during Columbia's lean years. If so, the results have been more than a little mixed.[581]

Conclusion

Columbia, like the other "new towns" of the 1960s, was intended to serve, above all else, as a kind of model for community development (and redevelopment). As a "city upon a hill," Columbia has met with mixed results. It is generally regarded as the most successful of the American new towns. That it was accomplished solely with private capital is truly remarkable, and sets Columbia apart from the leading Western European new towns of that era, such as Milton Keynes in Britain and Cergy-Pontoise in France, which relied on government subsidies.[582]

Columbia's problems as a business venture—and the predominantly upper-middle-class quality the city has acquired—suggest, however, that it has not succeeded in providing a model that can be copied in full. What has emerged, instead, is a sense that Columbia has useful lessons to teach to community builders, who can adapt various aspects of its design rather than try to create replicas. Columbia has become to American suburbia in particular what Frank Lloyd Wright's Fallingwater house has become to American home design. Both are essentially demonstration projects. Just as Wright's masterpiece of organic architecture encourages visitors to aim higher in the realm of house construction, so too does Columbia inspire those who see it to emulate its successes in such areas as comprehensive physical planning; promoting limited-size neighborhoods with pedestrian-oriented, mixed-use centers; respect for the natural environment; use of public open space; and commitment to racial and religious diversity.[583]

James Rouse also intended Columbia to demonstrate that if one improves a community's environment, people living there could achieve their potential more fully. The record in this respect is mixed, too, because Columbia emerged as structural problems in the American economy and society worsened, which led to higher levels of unemployment, crime and family breakdown than were prevalent when Rouse started working on Columbia in the early 1960s. Those increasing structural problems undermined to some degree what Columbia's design was intended to accomplish in terms of human development.

The example of the walking paths located throughout Columbia is instructive here. Rouse and his associates carefully planned these very well-landscaped and attractive walkways to make Columbia more like a campus than the typical American suburb. This would allow Columbia's children greater freedom to move about by themselves and give adults more opportunities to walk places rather than drive. Heavily used during the city's early years, they became less so as residents there, like Americans in general, became more apprehensive about walking alone, even during the day. This change illustrates clearly the limits to what can be done to bring about human growth by building better environments when underlying structural problems are getting worse.[584]

This kind of setback, like the inability to replicate Columbia as a whole, can seem more discouraging than it actually is. Just as partnerships between government and private developers could make replicating Columbia possible, so too could a greater attention to society's underlying structural problems help create conditions that allow the city's design to achieve more fully the results intended for its residents. As Columbia turns forty, it remains a place where optimism about the future seems justified.

12

INTO THE FUTURE

No one can doubt that thousands of families will come to live in the new houses. But whether they will come to sustain its [Columbia's] values and carry out its high moral purpose is quite another matter.
J.W. Anderson
Harper's Magazine, November 1964

Continuities and Discontinuities

Like every community's history, Columbia's reveals continuities and discontinuities. The commitment to planning, the unusually large range of urban amenities, racial and religious diversity and Columbia's status as an unincorporated urban area subject to county government have all remained the same over the past forty years. At the same time, though, there have been equally important changes. What was once a small town is now a genuinely urban place. The founding father (Rouse) and his company have departed through death and corporate merger. The goal of economic diversity has been overtaken by events beyond Columbia's control. The city's newspaper (the *Columbia Flier*), once a serious organ of investigative journalism, has evolved into a much more boosterish periodical. The Columbia Medical Plan, hailed at its inception as a pioneer in providing high-quality medical care to families at relatively low cost, has evolved into a more conventional health maintenance organization (HMO). Many more such examples could be listed here to illustrate the larger point that Columbia has both stayed the same and changed over its first forty years, and seems likely to continue doing so.

To the early settlers who came in the later 1960s and early 1970s, many of the changes tend to be seen as disappointing departures from the original vision, which have made Columbia more like other places. One suspects that pioneers often feel that way as their community evolves. That was certainly true for the Puritans living in the Massachusetts

Bay Colony, who saw later generations as less virtuous and more materialistic—more like the English—than they had once been.

Theirs is not the only perspective, however. Columbia, like colonial Massachusetts, has acquired settlers who came later, as well as new generations born and raised there. These newer inhabitants tend to have their own somewhat different views on how and why the city has evolved. They tend to be less wedded to (and sometimes actually unaware of) earlier conceptions of what their community ought to be, more practical about its purposes and problems and more hopeful about its future. Unburdened by the high expectations of the founding generation, to whom everything seemed possible because nothing had as yet been set in stone, the newer settlers and the children of the older ones tend to look forward rather than backward. These are the kinds of Columbians who are now moving into leadership roles.

The Next Generation

What are they likely to do? At a minimum, Columbia's next generation seems likely to make their city more livable for the elderly, whose numbers will surely rise substantially. More assisted-living communities, nursing homes and healthcare services tailored to their specific needs will likely appear, probably in or near the Town Center. This could also be a reason for mass transit there, and for more pedestrian-oriented areas in and around the Mall. Columbia's peculiar aversion to funeral homes and cemeteries will also likely diminish in the years ahead. More generally, the imagery of the city will become more inclusive of its older residents, which will make Columbia a more well-rounded place.

The next generation of Columbians also seems highly likely to do something about the still unsatisfactory Town Center. Among the most likely possibilities is a plan to turn Symphony Woods into a space more like New York's Central Park, which would make the Town Center more of a magnet for Columbians on weekends. Also desirable would be the kind of amenities one typically finds on the main streets of a college town, such as galleries, a movie house that shows foreign films, a locally owned bookstore and small eateries. Columbia's highly educated population seems likely to embrace that sort of vision for the Town Center. The steady expansion of Howard Community College and the presence of a four-year institution of higher learning would bring ever more college-age students to Columbia, and shore up support for that kind of new and improved Town Center.

Other changes in the years ahead are much more difficult to predict reliably. One can feel fairly confident, though, that Columbia's future will be shaped both by the actions of its residents and by larger forces in society beyond Columbians' control. One suspects, too, that Rouse's original vision for it will also continue to exert a meaningful, though subtle, influence as time goes by.

Rouseian Ideals

Jim Rouse set lofty goals for Columbia and was confident that its people would work hard to make them happen. This optimism is manifested today in the city's charitable heart, sense of political commitment and dedication to make Columbia the best city imaginable, as residents work hard to make a prophet out of their founder. Columbia's charitable side continues to be reflected in the workings of the Columbia Foundation. Here are only three examples. First is the Foreign-born Information and Referral Network (FIRN), founded in 1981 by Pat Hatch. Now celebrating its twenty-fifth anniversary, FIRN continues to assist the county's newest residents as they create new lives for themselves and their families. It has served Columbia's newest pioneers, who speak forty-nine different languages and come from ninety-three different countries. Executive Director Roy Appletree and his staff have developed a program in association with the county public school system to offer free assistance to students who do not speak fluent English, thus making their learning experiences more meaningful.

A second example is the Women's Giving Circle, founded by Jean Moon, Linda Odum and Yolanda Bruno in 2002 as a CF donor-advised fund. It has raised $400,000 to assist groups and individuals that provide help and services to women and girls. A particularly innovative and useful program of the circle, the Emergency Relief Fund, provides immediate financial assistance to those in need. A communications line advises members of those in need; funds are collected immediately and dispensed.

A third example is Grassroots, a hot line emergency care service and a frequent beneficiary of the foundation, which recently received a grant from the Women's Giving Circle. Founded as a volunteer-led hot line service, it has turned into a multi-service crisis intervention center. It now operates shelters to better serve some of its clients and is in the process of adding another facility.

The Horizon Foundation also continues to serve Columbia and Howard County's need for citizen services. A result of the merger of Howard County General Hospital and Johns Hopkins Medicine in 1998, the organization offers a variety of grant programs dedicated to promoting health and wellness. A major focus in Horizon's approach is its funding of programs that will ameliorate conditions before they become societal problems, a form of preventive medicine that Jim Rouse had in mind when the Columbia Medical Plan was first developed in Columbia's early years. Two recent examples of Horizon's work are Neighbor Ride, a program that provides transportation services for the county's fast-growing senior population, and Connections, a teen-based project, which helps students develop "a caring, supportive environment" in their own schools. With a fund that now exceeds $84 million, the foundation is poised to carry out philanthropic traditions already well established in Columbia and Howard County.

Both the Horizon and Columbia Foundations have actively supported programs to assist the county's fast-growing Hispanic population through grants to organizations providing services to them. FIRN's clientele is predominately Hispanic and the two foundations have been generous in their support for its programs. Two groups, Alianza de la Comunidad and Conexiones, have received similar grants that enabled them to start up and begin providing assistance to the Hispanic community, with a "by Hispanics

Ken Ulman. Ken became the first Columbia-born person to be elected to the Howard County Council. In November 2006, he was elected county executive. He symbolically represents a new generation of political leaders needed to carry out Jim Rouse's dream. *Ken Ulman.*

for Hispanics" philosophy. Thus far, programs ranging from community health issues and assistance to school-age students have been initiated.

Politically, Columbians still seek to improve their city through their exercise of the democratic process. Columbia is now old enough to witness a new generation of political leaders such as Ken Ulman, Jen Terrasa, Calvin Ball and Joshua Feldmark, all of whom grew up in Columbia's ideals-based environment. Hopefully they will carry on the traditions established by past leaders such as Ruth Keeton, Ginny Thomas, Lloyd Knowles and C. Vernon Gray, in keeping Columbia's ideals alive, especially in regard to the Town Center development plans. Liz Bobo, a former member of the county council, former county executive and now state delegate, represents a bridge between the generations, providing a positive role model of a dedicated public servant for the new political leaders to emulate.

Individual Dreams

And then there are individual Columbians who continue to try to make their city a better place. Bob Moon's goal is the creation of a Thunder Hill Nature Park, where students and families can be exposed to the wonders of nature through a variety of educational and recreational activities. The available land is the former Nancy Smith property, owned by a woman who refused to sell to Jim Rouse. Using her land for such purposes would fit in with her wishes not to have her land commercially developed.

Sherman Howell came to Columbia in 1971 after experiences in the civil rights movement in the South, which included sit-ins in Memphis, Tennessee restaurants, the 1965 Selma-to-Montgomery March and the Poor People's March in the nation's capital in 1968. Familiar with Martin Luther King's dream of racial equality and the sacrifices required to achieve it, he came to Columbia in 1971 to participate in Jim Rouse's version of that vision. Through the African American Council of Howard County, which he helped establish, and membership on the county's housing commission, Howell continues to challenge others to realize the King-Rouse dreams of racial harmony and decent housing for all.

Since 1968, Jean Toomer has worked hard to assure that Columbia's ideals were being achieved. And when they weren't, she spoke out and worked harder to see that they were. Early, it was the Rouse Company's lack of minority employment and the county school system's failure to meet the needs of black students that got her attention.

Later, she turned her attention to such subjects as the mental health needs of black families and black involvement in community development. While working for the Columbia Association, she helped initiate a before-and-after-school care program for elementary school children that still exists. As head of the Howard County Office of Human Rights, she initiated a number of programs, involving fair housing, community building and hate crime prevention. Even in retirement, she continues to work on the community's behalf, creating programs such as mediation and conflict resolution and community building in Howard County. In all that she has undertaken and accomplished, Toomer has managed to build bridges to create a

TAI Sophia Institute. Although no longer located in Columbia, this school is the only one of its kind in the country, offering graduate degrees in acupuncture, applied healing arts and herbal medicine. *Joseph Mitchell.*

better community. In a rational and persuasive way, she has contributed enormously to keeping Columbia's ideals alive.

Institutions and Leadership

Some of Columbia's older villages are creating plans to revitalize their communities. In Oakland Mills, manager Sandy Cederbaum and her village board have developed a long-range plan to recreate their village center and surrounding area—a revitalization model that could be used as a model to inspire other older villages. A recent town meeting held to unveil the plan drew a large enthusiastic crowd ready to tackle the problems. It was a moment that would have made Jim Rouse proud. In Wilde Lake, Columbia's oldest village, Bernice Kish and her board are pursuing a coordinated effort involving police, business, government and local forces to bring the village back to its prominent place in Columbia's story. Kish states that the vibrancy of the people in Columbia's oldest village will prevail, but worries that many newcomers know nothing about Columbia's ideals.

In the Columbia Archives, director Barbara Kellner makes sure that Columbia's story is alive and accessible, through her work there and her weekly cable television show *Columbia Matters.* Her greatest job satisfaction comes from being able to transmit Jim Rouse's vision to others and see them become enthusiastic about Columbia. She was motivated by his infectious optimism and has confidence that Columbia's future will be a bright one, regardless of what challenges the future may bring.

Some people work within their institutions to make Columbia a great city. Dianne Connelly and Robert Duggan have turned the Traditional Acupuncture Institute into the

Howard County General Hospital in the future. A 2007 addition will change the face of the hospital and allow it to better care for its patients. *Howard County General Hospital.*

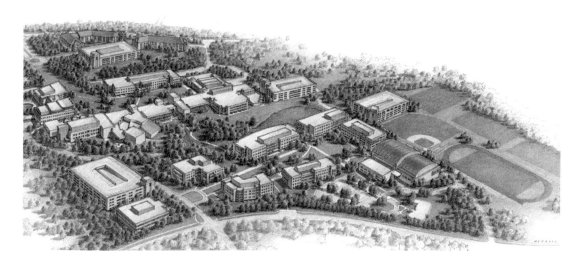

Howard Community College's future. The master plan shows additions to the campus that have been completed and those that will be in the future. It contains the type of planning that would have made Jim Rouse proud. *Design Collective; created by Luc Herbots.*

Into the Future

TAI Sophia Institute for the Healing Arts, the only institution of its kind in the country. Now located south of Columbia on a twelve-acre site, it offers master's degree programs in acupuncture, herbal medicine and applied healing arts. Throughout the years, the institution has brought nationally known healing arts experts such as Rollo May, Ivan Illich, Andrew Weil and Deepak Chopra to Howard County for speeches, seminars and meetings. Recent accreditation has confirmed the institute's accomplishments in the complementary healing arts.

Howard County General Hospital continues to develop as a first-rate medical institution. Involved in a continuous pattern of physical expansion and improved medical care, CEO Victor Broccolino and all who work at the hospital prepare for a future where healthcare for the county's rapidly increasing aging population will be a priority. A new expansion this year will provide another step in that never-ending process.

Mary Ellen Duncan was installed as Howard Community College's third president in 1998 and found a forward-looking community very supportive of education. When fifty-five people volunteered to serve on the college's Committee on the Future, Duncan knew this was a place "where things could get done." With total community support, the college embarked on a building campaign that included a Children's Learning Center, providing day-care services for students; an English, Foreign Language and Business Building; a Visual and Performing Arts Building; and the college's first parking garage. The new arts building testifies to the college's efforts to play a leadership role in the county's cultural life. Since 1993, HCC's Rep Stage has led the way in this process by bringing professional theater production to county audiences at reasonable prices. Seven Helen Hayes awards and thirty-seven nominations attest to the quality of the productions. HCC students who have the opportunity to work in these professional productions gain experiences that will enrich their theater-based education.

Using both state and local public funds and aggressive fundraising campaigns, Duncan has managed to create a small campus that would make some four-year colleges envious. And there's still more to come. A Student Services Building opened in spring 2007, and plans for another parking garage are in place. The future will bring a Health Sciences Building, dormitory rooms for three hundred students (and perhaps some faculty members), and more parking garages. An attractive architectural plan shows that open, green space will not be ignored, making HCC's campus a place where Columbians will feel comfortable. All of this, combined with many top-notch academic programs, has truly made HCC one of the county's leading institutions.

Maggie Brown arrived in Columbia in 1970 with her husband, Nesbitt, and three children. Coming from a racially segregated coal-mining town in West Virginia and conditioned by the turbulent events of the 1960s, she was attracted by the promise of a racially open city, but had doubts about whether it would really happen. From the beginning, Columbia became what she was hoping for. After a period of community volunteering, she worked part time for the Columbia Medical Plan. When she sought full-time employment, Pat Kennedy suggested that she apply for a job with the Columbia Association, selling package plan memberships in the Mall in Columbia. Eventually, she left the Columbia Association (CA) to work for the county government, only to return

Jim Rouse and Maggie Brown. Brown, now Columbia Association president, credits Jim Rouse's vision and spirit with inspiring her life and work. Here they participate in one of Columbia's birthday bashes. *Maggie Brown.*

to CA when the job of community services director opened up. She applied and was hired. When an out-of-town candidate was hired to take Pat Kennedy's place as CA president in 1998 and didn't work out, Brown was hired to replace her. She has been CA's president ever since.

Maggie Brown credits Jim Rouse and his plans for Columbia with making all of this possible, as she continues to serve the public with the same spirit and commitment that he would have wanted. She sees positive things in CA's future, as the new board of directors, with a new management system, works together with her to bring Jim Rouse's mission and vision to all Columbians. She also sees CA playing an important role in the city's Town Center development, Columbia's next major project.

The Future of the Dream

What happens to Town Center will be the next defining point in the city's short history. Three groups will determine its fate: General Growth Properties, Howard County government and Columbia's people. Nothing can occur without the three coming together to work for the common good. Such a process began with the creation of a charrette (public forum) to seek community input, a move promoted by County Councilman Ken Ulman and County Executive Jim Robey. Ulman had led the fight to save the Merriweather Post Pavilion from potential development, and through the charrette, opened the entire Town Center development process to public scrutiny. The county hired an architectural firm to direct the process that was run by the county office of planning and zoning. From it came a consensus of what the public wanted to see in downtown development. Then came the creation of a focus group that advised planning and zoning on various aspects of the county plan.

A preliminary county plan was presented to the public and the reception was mixed. While some liked it, a group of citizens, led by Lloyd Knowles and Liz Bobo, criticized it for ignoring some of the charrette's major points. Eventually, a group calling itself the Coalition for Columbia's Downtown was formed, which claimed that "much of the citizens' input was dismissed or ignored by County officials." Members have vowed to make sure that Jim Rouse's ideals are included in any Town Center development. How much public support this group will get remains to be seen.

General Growth Properties holds the key to downtown development. It owns the land and can use it for any purpose, as long as it obtains approval from county government. The company did not endear itself to the public when lakefront land it sold was slated to become a twenty-three-story condominium development. But it did garner public support when it hired Doug Godine to be Columbia's general manager. Godine worked for the Rouse Company from 1961 to 1978, and has strong ties to Rousean ideals. He was hired by Warren Wilson, GGP's senior vice-president for planned community development, to create a plan that would be "good for GGP and good for the community." Godine is preparing a long-range plan that will deal with sensitive subjects like density, transportation and affordable housing. Within ten years, he expects that 80 to 90 percent of the Town Center's retail and residential space will be completed; office

Columbia Town Center

Preliminary Town Center plan. The process has just begun; this represents the type of development that will ultimately take place. *Howard County Office of Planning and Zoning.*

The Kittamaqundi lakefront. What the future will bring to this scenic area and the entire Town Center expanse represents Columbia's last major development project. *Joseph Mitchell.*

space is more problematic. Regardless of what is done, noted architect Victor Swaback, who was brought in to advise GGP, gave a sobering assessment of the downtown situation: if it does not grow, it will die!

The Next Generation Takes Over

The November 2006 Howard County election results propelled younger Columbians to new heights. Councilman Ken Ulman was elected county executive, while the new county council will have three Columbia residents: Mary Kay Sigaty, Calvin Ball and Jen Terrasaa; another, Courtney Watson, has Columbia ties. What effect this will have on Town Center development remains to be seen, but during the campaign, Ulman expressed strong opposition to the new condominium project.

A majority of the people who spoke to us about Town Center development expressed varying degrees of confidence that a satisfactory plan will eventually be created and accepted. But it will take hard work and compromise to accomplish that goal, and it must include an active, diligent community to ensure that the founder's goals are part of the plan.

In the past, Columbia has faced challenges and managed to overcome them. It will happen again with Town Center development. But J.W. Anderson's words that opened this chapter provide a sobering reality check. With Columbia entering its second generation, will its residents still "sustain its [inherited] values and carry out its high moral purpose?" We are confident they will.

LIST OF ABBREVIATIONS

CA—Columbia Archives
CRD—Columbia Research and Development
HRD—Howard Research and Development
MC—Manuscript Collection
MHP—Mort Hoppenfeld Papers
RG—Rouse Group
TIAA—Teachers Insurance and Annuity Association
VFS—Vertical File Series

The following people agreed to be interviewed for this book. The initials listed in parentheses refer to their citations in the notes.

Bruce Alexander (BA), June 28, 2006
Richard L. Anderson (RLA), July 1, 2005
Roy Appletree (RA), October 9, 2006
William Becker (WHB), September 12, 2006
Douglas Berman (DB), June 26, 2006
Liz Bobo (LB), October 6, 2006
Ruth Bohse (RB), September 12, 2006
William Bolen (BB), December 10, 2006
Sol Bowling (SB), August 3, 2006
Jack Bridner (JB), September 26, 2006
Maggie Brown (MB), October 5, 2006
Wylene Burch (WB), August 16, 2006
Betty Caldwell (BC), February 16, 2006
Sandy Cederbaum (SC), August 23, 2006

Herman Charity (HC), September 29, 2006
Matt DeVito (MDV), May 23, 2006
M. Scott Ditch (MSD), May 31, 2006
Anne Dodd (AD), August 23, 2006
Cathy Drew (CD), June 6, 2006
Mary Ellen Duncan (MED), October 6, 2006
Jackie Felker (JF), August 15, 2006
William Finley (WF), March 8, 2006
Danielle Fosler Lussier (DFL), July 13, 2006
Warren Fuller (WDF), December 1, 2006
James E. Furniss (JEF), May 12, 2006
Herbert Gans (HG), January 27, 2006
Doug Godine (DG), October 18, 2006
Barney Goldberg (BG), August 20, 2005
C. Vernon Gray (CVG), October 25, 2006
Thomas Harris (TH), April 5, 2006
E. Barton Harvey (BH), August 9, 2006
Guy Hollyday (GH), March 29, 2006
Sherman Howell (SH), September 30, 2006
Kenneth T. Jackson (KTJ), August 28, 2006
Shep Jeffreys (SJ), July 12, 2006
John Martin Jones (JMJ), March 10, 2006
Mary Margaret Kamerman (MMK), August 7, 2006
Barbara Kellner (BGK), October 6, 2006
Ellen Conroy Kennedy (ECK), July 25, 2006
Padraic Kennedy (PK), July 25, 2006
Bernice Kish (BK), September 8, 2006
Lloyd Knowles (LK), October 6, 2006
Patricia Laidig (PL), September 1, 2006
Mel Levine (ML), March 4, 2006
Doris Ligon (DL), August 18, 2006
James Medwin (JM), September 8, 2006
Martin Millspaugh (MM), August 25, 2006
Robert Moon (RJM), September 7, 2006
Jean Flanagan Moon (JFM), July 25, 2006
Robert Morris (RM), February 28, 2006
Joshua Olsen (JO), March 13, 2006
Jane Parrish (JP), September 12, 2006
Randy Pausch (RP), July 27, 2006
Lee Richardson (LR), September 1, 2006
James Rouse Jr. (JR), October 5, 2006
Patty Rouse (PR), August 17, 2006
Winstead (Ted) Rouse (TR), October 5, 2006
Barbara Rudlin (BWR), November 2, 2006

LIST OF ABBREVIATIONS

Barbara Russell (BR), September 23, 2006
Charles Russell (CR), November 7, 2006
Helen Ruther (HR), June 28, 2006
Martin Ruther (MR), June 28, 2006
Malcolm Sherman (MS), August 8, 2006
Susan Smith (SS), August 15, 2006
Kenneth Stevens (KS), September 5, 2006
Robert Tennenbaum (RT), March 10, 2006
Ginny Thomas (GT), October 26, 2006
Donald Tobin (DT), June 26, 2006
Jean Toomer (JT), November 6, 2006
Daniel Carroll Toomey (DCT), August 1, 2006
David L. Tripp (DLT), June 29, 2006
Wendy Tzucker (WT), August 15, 2006
Kenneth Ulman (KU), September 21, 2006
Sarah Uphouse (SU), September 12, 2006
James Wannemacher (JW), May 10, 2006
Frederick Weaver (FW), May 20, 2006
Warren Wilson (WW), August 31, 2006
Wes Yamaka (WY), March 22, 2006

NOTES

1. Howard County Before Columbia

1. Joetta M. Cramm, *A Pictorial History of Howard County* (Virginia Beach, VA: The Donning Company, 1987), 25.
2. Barbara W. Feaga, *Howard's Roads to the Past* (Ellicott City, MD: Mays & Associates, 2004), 4.
3. Winthrop Jordan, *White over Black: American Attitudes Toward the Negro, 1550–1812* (New York: Penguin Books, 1969), ii.
4. Robert Brugger, *Maryland: A Middle Temperament, 1634–1980* (Baltimore: Johns Hopkins University Press, 1988), 44.
5. Alex Haley, *Roots: The Saga of an American Family* (New York: Doubleday, 1976), 682–83.
6. J.D. Warfield, *The Founders of Anne Arundel and Howard Counties, Maryland* (Baltimore: Regional Publishing Company, 1980), 337.
7. Celia Holland, *Landmarks of Howard County* (Privately printed, 1975), 16.
8. Gill Chamblin, "The Clarks of Clarksville and Columbia." CA: RGI; 2, b1, fClark Family.
9. Alison Ellicott Mylander, *The Ellicotts: Striving for a Holy Community* (Ellicott City: Historic Ellicott City, 1991), 40.
10. Cramm, *A Pictorial History*, 45.
11. Jan Fisher and Ann Dargis, "How Now, Howard County?" *Country*, December 1981, 4.
12. Brugger, *Maryland*, 128.
13. Scott Ditch, "The Naming Of Columbia," in *Creating a New City: Columbia, Maryland*, ed. Robert Tennenbaum (Columbia: Perry Press, 1994), 75.
14. "Original Land Grants of Howard County, Maryland" CA: RGV; Howard County History, fIndex to Caleb Dorsey Land Grant Map.
15. Cramm, *A Pictorial History*, 26.

16. Feaga, *Howard's Roads*, 34.

17. Henry K. Sharp, *The Patapsco River Valley: Cradle of the Industrial Revolution* (Baltimore: Maryland Historical Society, 2001), 25.

18. Courtney B. Wilson, *The Baltimore & Ohio Railroad: The Birthplace of American Railroading* (Baltimore: B&O Railroad Museum), 1.

19. "General Assembly Created Howard District in 1839." *Ellicott City Bicentennial Journal* (Summer–Fall 1972): 10-A.

20. Celia Holland, *Ellicott City, Maryland: Mill Town, U.S.A.* (Historic Ellicott City, 2003), 5.

21. Larry Madaras, "A Short History of Howard County through the Civil War, 1689–1868" (Columbia Archives, 1991): 16.

22. Ira Berlin, *Slaves Without Masters: The Free Negro in the Antebellum South* (New York: Oxford University Press, 1974), 136–37.

23. John Noble Wilford, "An Abolitionist Leads the Way in Uncovering of Slaves' Past," *New York Times*, September 6, 2006.

24. Barbara Jean Fields, *Slavery and Freedom on the Middle Ground: Maryland during the Nineteenth Century* (New Haven: Yale University Press, 1985), 24.

25. Paulina C. Moss and Livern Hill, eds., *Seeking Freedom: A History of the Underground Railroad in Howard County, Maryland* (Columbia: Howard County Center of African American Culture, 2002), 35.

26. Scott Sheads and Daniel Toomey, *Baltimore During the Civil War* (Glen Burnie, MD: Toomey Press, 1997), 136–37.

27. Wilson, *The Baltimore & Ohio Railroad*, 14.

28. DCT.

29. Ibid.

30. Ibid.

31. Paul Travers, *The Patapsco: Baltimore's River of History* (Centreville, MD: Tidewater Publishers, 1990), 163.

32. Daniel Toomey, *The Civil War in Maryland* (Glen Burnie, MD: Toomey Press, 1994), 124–29.

33. JB.

34. Charles Wagandt, *The Mighty Revolution: Negro Emancipation in Maryland, 1862–64* (Baltimore: Johns Hopkins University Press, 1964), 262–63.

35. Margaret Law Callcott, *The Negro in Maryland Politics, 1870–1912* (Baltimore: Johns Hopkins University Press, 1969), vii.

36. Alice Cornelison, Silas E. Craft Sr. and Lillie Price, *History of Blacks in Howard County, Maryland* (Howard County, Maryland: NAACP, 1986), 39.

37. M. Elaine Harding, "A History of Howard County" (unpublished manuscript, Howard County Library System, circa 1945).

38. Thomas Phillips, *The Orange Grove Story* (Washington, D.C.: Privately printed, 1972).

39. Sharp, *The Patapsco River Valley*, 99, 102.

40. JB.

41. Sharp, *The Patapsco River Valley*, 103.

42. Cramm, *A Pictorial History*, 167.

43. Geospatial & Statistical Data Center, University of Virginia Library, 2006.

44. B.H. Shipley Jr. and William K. Klingaman, *Remembrances of Passing Days: A Pictorial History of Ellicott City and its Fire Department* (Virginia Beach: The Donning Company, 1997), 100.

45. Travers, *The Patapsco*, 193–94.

46. JB.

47. Travers, *The Patapsco*, 83–84.

48. "Best Places to Live," *Money*, September 2006, 99.

2. James Rouse: Maryland Son, 1914–1945

49. J. Preston Dickson, *Talbot County: A History* (Centreville, MD: Tidewater Publishers, 1983), 280.

50. Gurney Breckenfeld, *Columbia and the New Cities* (New York: Ives Washburn, 1971), 195.

51. Joshua Olsen, *Better Places, Better Lives: A Biography of James Rouse* (Washington, D.C.: Urban Land Institute, 2003), 1.

52. James Rouse, interview by Patricia J. La Noue (1974), transcript, CA: Maryland Historical Society Oral History Collection, 2.

53. Ibid.

54. Breckenfeld, *Columbia*, 199.

55. TR.

56. Boyd Gibbons, *Wye Island: Outsiders, Insiders, and Resistance to Change* (Baltimore: Johns Hopkins University Press, 1977), 13.

57. Louise Hawkins, "Jim Rouse's Boyhood Days Recalled by Old Friends," *Howard County News*, January 17, 1980.

58. "Easton High School Transcript," May 25, 1931, CA: RGI: 7.4; f10.

59. Rouse, interview, 11.

60. *Belfrey Bat*, April 1929, CA: RGI; 7.4, f10.

61. Olsen, *Better Places*, 5.

62. Ibid.

63. Adam Sachs, "More Is at Stake Then Just Sandtown, Rouse Says," *Baltimore Sun*, July 23, 1995.

64. James Rouse, "Essay on Selfishness/Unselfishness," ca. 1931, CA: RGI; 7.4, fTome School.

65. Correspondence between Murray P. Busch and Willard J. Rouse Jr., May 27, 1931, CA: I; 7.4, fTome School.

66. Bill Rouse to Jim Rouse, May 31, 1931. CA: I: 7.4, fTome School.

67. Olsen, *Better Places*, 8.

68. Correspondence between Murray P. Busch and Willard G. Rouse Jr., May 27, 1931, CA.

69. Rouse, interview, 13.

70. University of Hawaii Yearbook, 1932, CA.

71. Jim Rouse, "Notes on Hawaii," March 24, 1932, CA: RGI; 7.4, fUniversity of Hawaii.

72. James Rouse to Margaret Rouse Balch, June 20, 1932, CA: RGI; 7.4, fUniversity of Hawaii.

73. Stanley Hallett, "Columbia Book" (Unpublished manuscript, ca. 1969) CA: RGI: 3; b38, f12.

74. Olsen, *Better Places*, 8.

75. James Rouse to Margaret Rouse Balch, June 20, 1932, CA.

76. Bill Rouse to Assistant Secretary of the Navy Ernest Leo Jachnke, July 21, 1932, CA: RGI, 7.4, fUniversity of Hawaii.

77. University of Virginia Transcript, 1932–33, CA: RGI; 7.4, fUniversity of Virginia.

78. Bill Rouse to Jim Rouse, March 4, 1933. CA: RGI, 7.4, fUniversity of Virginia.

79. Rouse, interview, 29.

80. Ibid., 30.

81. Ibid., 32–33.

82. Barbara Palmer, "Dollars and Dreams: The Jim Rouse Story," *Baltimore Magazine*, May 1979, 78.

83. James Rouse to U.S. Senator Millard Tydings, April 29, 1935; James Rouse to U.S. Representative T. Alan Goldsborough, September 11, 1936, CA: RGI; 8.4, f1936–1950.

84. Guy T.O. Hollyday to James Rouse, May 27, 1936.

85. GH.

86. James Rouse to Herman Moser, June 2, 1936, CA: RGI; 8.4, f1936–1950.

87. Ibid., "Mortgage Agreement Between Title Guarantee and Trust Company," December 25, 1937.

88. Margaret Barksdale Nuttle, *Beginnings, et cetera: A Short History of The Rouse Company* (Unpublished manuscript, 1968) CA: Manuscripts, 11.

89. Rouse, interview, 28–29.

90. Ibid., 31.

91. William Welling to James W. Rouse, CA: RGI; 7.4, fBrown Memorial Church.

92. James W. Rouse, "A Young Man Votes," 1936, CA: RGI; 8.4, fPolitics.

93. Libby Rouse, "The Spiritual Dream Behind Columbia and the Vision Still Openly Ahead for It," March 1977, CA: Manuscripts; f20.

94. Olsen, *Better Places*, 23.

95. Jim Rouse to Brothers and Sisters, August 1942, CA: RGI; 7.2; fNavy-1942.

96. Mark Cohen, "Captain Enterprise," *Baltimore Magazine*, April 1987, 114.

3. James Rouse: Urban Visionary, 1945–1960

97. Hunter Moss to Jim Rouse, November 2, 1945, CA: RGI; 1.1, b402, f25.

98. James W. Rouse, "The Mortgage Man's Role in G.I. Financing," *Appraiser's Journal* (June 1946): 299.

99. Ibid., 303.

100. MM.

101. Ann Ogden, "First Installment of a Blighted Area by Private Industry is Planned Here," *Baltimore American*, September 15, 1946.

102. "The All-American Cities," *Look Magazine*, February 10, 1953, 42.

103. William A. Andrews, "The Fight Blight Fund, Inc.: Six Years of Experience," CA: RGII; b107, fFight Blight Fund.

104. James W. Rouse, "The Baltimore Plan," *Baltimore Evening Sun*, April 8, 1953.

105. "Set Backs for Rehabilitation," *House and Home*, April 1953, 128.

106. Olsen, *Better Places*, 36.

107. Martin Millspaugh, "Baltimore Pilot Area" (Unpublished manuscript, 1954) CA: RGII; b107, Baltimore Plan Manuscript.

108. James Rouse to Harry Hollins, October 24, 1952, CA: RGI; 7.2, f17b.

109. Ibid., October 28, 1952.

110. "United World Federalists Resolution," June 19, 1951, CA: RGI; 7.5; fFederalists.

111. Dwight D. Eisenhower to James W. Rouse, September 22, 1953, CA: RGI, 7.5, fCorrespondence.

112. James Rouse to Aksel Neilsen, December 12, 1952. Taken from Arnold R. Hirsch, "The Last and Most Difficult Barrier: Segregation and Federal Housing Policy in the Eisenhower Administration, 1953–1960," *Report Submitted to the Poverty & Race Research Action Council*, March 22, 2005, 6.

113. James W. Rouse and Nathaniel S. Keith, "No Slums in Ten Years: A Workable Program," CA: Vertical File Section; 1, f1, 3.

114. "The New Washington," *Washington Post*, January 15, 1955, 6.

115. "Neighborhood Conservation to be Pushed," *Baltimore Sun*, November 16, 1954, 26.

116. James W. Rouse, "Address Before the Newark Conference on the ACTION Program for the American City," May 5, 1959, CA: RGV; b1, f17, 14.

117. James Rouse, interview with Howard Cable 8, 1992, CA: Tape 547.

118. Greater Baltimore Committee, http://www.gbc.org.

119. MM.

120. James W. Rouse, "Charles Center Project," September 9, 1959, CA: RGIV; b1, f3.

121. Hunter Moss and Jim Rouse, "What do We Want?" ca. 1948, CA: RGI; 1.1, b401, f14.

122. Hunter Moss to Claude L. Benner, June 8, 1951, CA: RGI; 1.1, b401, f1.

123. Hunter Moss to Jim Rouse, May 4, 1961, CA: RGVIII; Personal Correspondence (1961).

124. Harry Bart to Margaret Barksdale Nutter, June 1968, CA: RGI; 1.5, b37, f6.

125. "Shopping Strip," *House and Home*, May 1953, 148–49.

126. Breckenfeld, *Columbia*, 211.

127. Seward H. Mott, "Report to the Moss-Rouse Company on the Development of Mondawmin," February 8, 1950, CA: RGI; 1.1, b402, f12b, 1–2.

128. Harry Bart to Margaret Barksdale Nutter, June 8, 1968, CA: RGI; 1.5, b37, f6.

129. "News Release," December 21, 1956, CA: RGI; 2.3.

130. Gibbons, *Wye Island*, 17–18.

131. Dickson, *Talbot County*, 339–40.

132. James Rouse to S. Page Nelson, July 1960, CA: RGI; 1.1, b4, f1.

133. Olsen, *Better Places*, 80–81.

134. James Rouse to Staff, October 24, 1961, CA: RGI; 1.4, b421, f5.

4. Columbia's Genesis, 1960–1965

135. David Rockefeller, *Memoirs* (New York: Random House, 2002), 348.

136. "Telephone Conversation with Lindquist Regarding Tarrytown," April 4, 1961, CA: RGI; 5, b54.

137. James W. Rouse, untitled, undated document, CA: RGI; 5, b.54.

138. Olsen, *Better Places*, 121.

139. Rockefeller, *Memoirs*, 348–49.

140. Ned Daniels, interview with Joshua Olsen, July 5, 2000, CA: Guide to Joshua Olsen's Interview Transcripts, 13.

141. Breckenfeld, *Columbia*, 263–64.

142. Nutter, *A Short History*, 46.

143. John Martin Jones Jr., e-mail correspondence, March 12, 2006.

144. TH.

145. "The Howard County General Plan for 1960," *Howard County Planning Commission*, 1960.

146. KS.

147. HC.

148. Ibid.

149. Breckenfeld, *Columbia*, 168–69.

150. Ellison Moss, "Secret 'Land Grab' On in Howard," *Baltimore News-Post*, March 25, 1963.

151. Wallace Hamilton, "Columbia History: Chapter on Land Acquisition," CA: RGII; 1. Work Group Papers, f1.

152. Breckenfeld, *Columbia*, 224.

153. Edward P. Eichler and Marshall Kaplan, *The Community Builders* (Berkeley: University of California Press, 1967), 61.

154. JMJ.

155. Robert Moxley, "Land Acquisition: The Realtor's Perspective," in *Creating a New City* (see note 13), 26.

156. Hamilton, "Columbia History," 7.

157. Olsen, *Better Places*, 142.

158. Anthony Bailey, *Through the Great City* (New York: Macmillan Company, 1967), 93, 96.

159. James W. Rouse to Irving G. Bjork, October 15, 1962, CA: RGI; 5, b24.

160. Peter Alexander Michel, "The Public Official and the New Town Developer: A Study of the Initial Negotiations Between the Rouse Company and Howard County, Maryland" (Unpublished Manuscript) CA: Studies (1971), 55.

161. Ibid., 136–37.

162. Bob Tennenbaum, conversation, July 21, 2006.

163. Moxley, "Land Acquisition," 28.
164. "Land Acquisition a 'Masterful' Job," *Central Maryland News*, September 21, 1972.
165. James W. Rouse, "It Can Happen Here," speech given at the Conference on the Metropolitan Future, University of California, Berkeley, September 23, 1963, CA: JWR Speeches.
166. Tom Harris, "Fitting Columbia into Howard County: The Planner's View, " in *Creating A New City* (see note 13), 85.
167. "Howard's Planned Community," *Central Maryland News*, November 7, 1963.
168. "Baltimore Firm Acquires 14,100 Acres in Howard County for Planned New Community," James W. Rouse & Company, October 30, 1963, 2.
169. Edward G. Pickett, "Howard Project Stirs Wariness," *Baltimore Sun*, October 31, 1963.
170. MSD.
171. "'Thrilling Gamble': Rouse Labels Land Plans," *Central Maryland News*, December 12, 1963.
172. MSD.
173. Ditch, "The Naming of Columbia," in *Creating a New City*, 78.
174. "Columbia: A Presentation to the Officials and Citizens of Howard County, Maryland," Community Research and Development, Distribution to County Leaders and Citizens, November 11, 1964, 2.
175. "Reaction of Howard County Residents to the Columbia Plan," January 1965, CA: RGI; 1, 1965; f12.
176. "Poll Runs 75% in Favor of Columbia," *Howard County Times*, April 4, 1965.
177. For the Howard County Citizens Association, see Olsen, *Better Places*, 179; for the Howard County League of Women Voters, see "League Finds Columbia Would Benefit County," *Howard County Times*, May 12, 1965.
178. Hamilton, "Columbia History," 6.
179. "Growth Is Inevitable: An Interview with Members of the Howard County Delegation to the State Legislature," *Columbia: A Quarterly Publication of the Rouse Company* (Summer 1966), 14.
180. Ibid., 15.
181. Harris, "Fitting Columbia into Howard County," 87.
182. Breckenfeld, *Columbia*, 269.
183. Doris Thompson, "Wanted—Leadership," *Howard County Times*, January 25, 1965.
184. Breckenfeld, *Columbia*, 272.
185. BG.

5. Columbia: The Next America, 1965–1967

186. J.W. Anderson, "A Brand New City for Maryland," *Harper's Magazine*, November 1964, 100.
187. Donald Canty, "A New Town Approach to New-Town Planning," *Architectural Forum*, August 9, 1964.

188. Benjamin Ruhe, "Columbia: City in the Country," *Washington Star Sunday Magazine*, March 14, 1965.

189. RT.

190. WF.

191. Ibid.

192. Ibid.

193. "Jim Rouse to Company Directors," October 25, 1962, CA: RGI; 4, b2, f5.

194. WF.

195. Mort Hoppenfeld, foreword to "Columbia History" (Unpublished manuscript), 5. CA: MHP; RGXL, b1, f1.

196. Mort Hoppenfeld, "Planning for Today: A Redevelopment Project for Neighborhood Number 7: Cambridge, Massachusetts," September 1952, 1. CA: MHP; RGXL, b1, f1.

197. RT.

198. James W. Rouse to Irwin Miller, September 8, 1972, CA: RGI; 4, b14, f2.

199. Olsen, *Better Places*, 151.

200. Robert L. Siegel, "Can These Thinkers Help Put Across a Vast New Town?" *House and Home*, December 1963, 83.

201. Breckenfeld, *Columbia*, 51.

202. Hallett, "Columbia Book," CA: RGI; 3, b38, f12.

203. Jim Rouse, "Opening Remarks to the Work Group," October 14, 1963, CA: Speeches; b4, f6.

204. "The Messianic Master Builder: Jim Rouse and His City," *Life Magazine*, January 24, 1967.

205. Breckenfeld, *Columbia*, 253.

206. James W. Rouse, foreword to *Creating a New City* (see note 13), x.

207. Breckenfeld, *Columbia*, 255.

208. Howard Gillette Jr., "Assessing James Rouse's Role in American City Planning," *Journal of the American Planning Association* (Spring 1999), 160.

209. Rouse, interview with LaNoue, 22.

210. Ibid., 23.

211. Olsen, *Better Places*, 172.

212. RT.

213. Hallett, "Columbia Book."

214. Ditch, "The Naming of Columbia," 75–76.

215. James Rouse to William Finley, June 23, 1963, CA: RGII; 2 Outgoing Correspondence (1963–1969), b2, f2.

216. Wallace Hamilton, "The Evolution of the Physical Plan." *HRD History*, September 17, 1964, CA: RGI; 1, f3.

217. Hallett, "Columbia Book."

218. Ibid.

219. RA.

220. James Wannemacher, "Early Buildings: People and Projects," in *Creating a New City* (see note 13), 107.

221. "Columbia's Construction Team of Fifty Headed by Robert Cameron," *Columbia: A Rouse Company Publication*, Spring 1967, 22.

222. "Bob Cameron, 80, Pioneer," *Columbia Flier*, September 3, 2005.

223. JEF.

224. Robert Cameron, "Early Land Development Construction," in *Creating a New City* (see note 13), 104.

225. RM.

226. Mel Levine, personal correspondence, March 28, 2006, 1.

227. JMJ.

228. "William Finley," *Columbia: A Rouse Company Publication*, Winter 1967, 14.

229. Mahlon Apgar IV, *Managing Community Development: The Systems Approach in Columbia, Maryland* (McKinsey & Company, 1971), 24–26.

230. Wallace Hamilton, "Financial Projections," *HRD History*, September 3, 1964, 1. CA: RGI.1; f3.

231. Ibid., 2–3.

232. Robert Tennenbaum, "Planning Determinants for Columbia: A New Town in Maryland," *Urban Land*, April 1965, 4.

233. Mort Hoppenfeld, "A Sketch of the Planning-Building Process for Columbia, Maryland," *Journal of the American Institute of Planners* (November 1967): 398.

234. William Finley, "The General Planning and Development Process," in *Creating a New City* (see note 13), 3.

235. Wallace Hamilton, quoted in Peter Hanrahan, "In the Beginning," *Columbia Flier Special Birthday Edition*, June 19, 1975, 22.

236. Hallett, "Columbia Book."

237. Wallace Hamilton, quoted in Hanrahan, "In the Beginning," 22.

238. Ibid.

239. Breckenfeld, *Columbia*, 276.

240. RT.

241. "Plan Approved for Village of Wilde Lake," *Columbia Newsletter* (Spring 1966), 1–3.

6. Columbia's First Year, 1967

242. Morton Hoppenfeld, "The Columbia Association: A Unique Partnership" (Unpublished manuscript) CA: MHP; RGXL, b6, f65.

243. Ibid.

244. JMJ.

245. Teachers Insurance and Annuity Association to HRD, January 4, 1968, CA: CPRA Deeds, Incorporation, Bylaws, Etc.

246. Wallace Hamilton, "Buildings I," Interim Memo, July 6, 1964, CA: RGI; 1; f3.

247. "Homebuilder Bucks Ebbing Sales Tide," *Business Week*, August 20, 1966, 106.

248. Fran Fanshel, "Ryland: 20 Years and 63,220 Houses Later," *Columbia Flier*, April 2, 1987, 26.

249. Malcolm Sherman, "Early Homebuilding," in *Creating a New City* (see note 13), 119–20.

250. James Clark Jr., *Jim Clark: Soldier, Farmer, Legislator* (Baltimore: Gateway Press, 1999), 115.

251. James W. Rouse, "Equality of Opportunity in Housing Policy," August 22, 1967, CA: RGI; 3, f3/4/65-8/22/67.

252. MS.

253. Ibid.

254. Sherman, "Early Homebuilding," 121.

255. Missy Zane, "No Blacks Allowed: The Weavers Found the Doors Opened Here," *Times of Ellicott City*, June 19, 1977, 1B.

256. Larry Carson, "Howard First: Negro Named to County Board," *Baltimore Evening Sun*, March 19, 1969, C5.

257. BR.

258. Ibid.

259. Richard Corrigan, "Columbia Pioneer Families Move In," *Washington Post*, July 4, 1967.

260. WY.

261. Ibid.

262. BC.

263. Kim Remesch-Allnutt, "The Call to Serve: Peace Corps Celebrates 25 Years," *Columbia Magazine*, November 1985, 18.

264. JM.

265. Myra MacPherson, "Symphony Gala Ends as Okefenokee of the Arts," *New York Times*, July 18, 1967.

266. JEF.

267. MacPherson, "Symphony Gala."

268. Carolyn Kelemen, conversation, November 7, 2006.

269. James Wannemacher, "Early Buildings: People and Projects," in *Creating a New City* (see note 13), 108.

270. "Minibus to Have Separate Road System," *Columbia: A CRD Newsletter*, Spring 1966, 13.

271. "Hittman Associates: First Columbia Industry," *Columbia: A CRD Newsletter*, Spring 1966, 9.

272. *Columbia Flier*, April 11, 1991.

273. "Columbia Construction Starts," *Columbia: A Rouse Company Publication*, Winter 1967, 8.

274. Ibid., 14.

275. Ibid., 13–14.

276. Ibid.

277. James Furniss, e-mail message, March 25, 2006.

278. CR.

279. MR.

280. HR.

281. FW.

282. "Planned City Celebrates Its First Birthday," *Columbia Information Press Release*, June 19, 1968.

283. John B. Willmann, "Columbia 'Walking' for First Birthday," *Washington Post*, June 22, 1968.

7. Columbia: Making its Mark, 1968–1972

284. "CRD Annual Reports, 1960–1964." CA: CRD Annual Reports; f1.

285. "The Rouse Company Annual Reports, 1966–1970." CA: RGI; 5, b13.

286. Olsen, *Better Places*, 182.

287. "The Rouse Company, 1969 Annual Report," 4. CA: RGI; 5, b13.

288. JW.

289. FW.

290. James Rouse to Everyone in the Company, June 26, 1968, CA: RGI; 3, b61, fPolitical Candidates and Politics, 11/1/65–9/20/74.

291. David Barkley, "Fear Knocked; Faith Answered," *Columbia Times*, July 1, 1968.

292. James W. Rouse, "We Have a Dream–One America," June 27, 1968, in *A Larger Vision: Jim Rouse and the American City*, Patty Rouse and M. Scott Ditch, eds. (private printing, 1994), 38.

293. Barkley, "Fear Knocked, Faith Answered."

294. JR.

295. Edward M. Norton Jr. to James W. Rouse, February 4, 1968, CA: RGVII; 1 (1942–1973), f18.

296. James W. Rouse, "Wage Peace, Mr President," in *A Larger Vision* (see note 292), 40–41.

297. "WAGE PEACE, MR. PRESIDENT," *Washington Post*, May 7, 1970.

298. "Columbia: Ecumenical Adventure," *The Communicator: News of the Episcopal Church in Maryland*, November 1966.

299. Ibid.

300. Wallace Hamilton, "Church Planning for Columbia," *HRD History*, October 5, 1964, CA: RGI; 1, b2, f20.

301. Stanley Hallett, "Working Papers in Church Planning: Columbia, Maryland," 20–26. CA: MHP; RGXL, b1, f7.

302. "Articles of Incorporation," *Columbia Religious Facilities Corporation*, May 31, 1966, 2. CA: RGXXIV; fOrganization.

303. "Religious Facilities Corporation Formed," *Columbia: A Newsletter Published by Community Research & Development* (Spring 1966), 12.

304. Jewish Council of Howard County, "Articles of Incorporation," March 1967, CA: Phyllis and Meyer Kuritzky Papers; b2, f1.

305. SJ.

306. "Unpublished Notes," CA: Phyllis and Meyer Kuritzky Papers; b2, f8.

307. Wallace Hamilton to James Rouse, William Finley and Mal Sherman, November 15, 1967, CA: RGI; 3, b12, f1.

308. Wes Yamaka, "Low-Middle Income Housing," *Columbia Today*, May–June 1969, 4.

309. James W. Rouse, "It Can Happen Here," *Conference on the Metropolitan Future*, September 26, 1963, 5. CA: Speeches; b4, f3.

310. Wallace Hamilton, "Health and Medical Facilities," *HRD History*, CA: RGII; 1, Work Group Papers, f2.

311. "Dr. Joseph Sadusk Appointed to Johns Hopkins Medical Faculty, Will Study Columbia Satellite Hospital," Press Release, May 27, 1966.

312. Ned Daniels to James Rouse, William Finley and Wallace Hamilton, March 8, 1967, CA: RGI; 3, b54, f2.

313. Connecticut General Life Insurance Company, "Columbia Medical Plan: Summary," February 19, 1968, 1. CA: RGI; 3, b54, f3.

314. Elizabeth W. Rouse, "'Trial Balloon' Concept of a Family Life Center in Columbia, and Its Possible Initial Form in the Village of Wilde Lake," CA: RGXXVII; b1, f1.

315. Geoffrey Himes, "Family Life Center Must Raise $36,000 by December," *Columbia Flier*, ca. 1976.

316. Alisa Samuels, "Family Life Center Now Placing More Emphasis on Serving Young," *Baltimore Sun*, September 5, 1976.

317. Ibid.

318. Mary Hovet, "Innovations in Education," in *Creating a New City* (see note 13), 129.

319. Christopher Jencks, "Alternative Educational Programs for a New Community" (unpublished manuscript), March 1, 1964, 42–45. CA: RGI; 1, b2, f17.

320. BWR.

321. Wallace Hamilton, "The University of the City," February 1966, 1. CA: RGI; 3, b12, f8.

322. James Rouse, "Potentials for a College in Columbia," May 28, 1965, CA: RGI; 3, b12, f7.

323. Wes Yamaka, "Interview with Robert McCan," *Columbia Today*, August/September 1969, 10.

324. "A Gift for Mr. Rouse," ca. November 1968, 3. CA: RGI; 3, b1, f18.

325. James Rouse to Morris Keeton, December 9, 1968, 3. CA: RGI; 3, b1, f13.

326. "Establishment of a Field Studies Center in Columbia," August 8, 1968, CA: RGI; 3; b1, f13.

327. David Lightman, "Antioch Giving Up On Columbia," *Baltimore Evening Sun*, June 21, 1971.

328. "Harper's Choice," *Columbia Flier*, May 9, 1991.

329. Susan Thornton Hobby, "Longfellow Fourth of July Parade Will Never Grow Up," *Columbia Flier*, July 8, 1999.

330. James Rouse to William E. Finley, December 20, 1965, CA: RGI; 3, b37, f2.

331. G.L. Greenslit, Bendix Field Engineering Corporation, "Why Relocate," *Columbian*, May 13, 1969, CA: RGI; 3, b5, f6.

332. "T.C. Wolff to W.G. Rouse," February 11, 1969, CA: RGI; 3, b5, f5.

333. "Bendix and the Men on the Moon," *Columbia Today*, October–November 1969, 26.

334. "Willard Rouse, Active Leader, Dies," *Ellicott City Times*, October 1970.

335. Olsen, *Better Places*, 217–18.

336. "Bill Rouse Speech at General Electric Dinner," CA: RGI; 3, b37, f4.

337. Jim Ryan to Jim Rouse, July 10, 1969, CA: RGI; 3; b37; f4.

338. Jim Rouse to Jim Ryan, August 25, 1969, CA: RGI, 3; b37, f4.

339. PK.

8. Columbia in the 1970s

340. Mel Levine, personal correspondence, March 28, 2006, 1.

341. Olsen, *Better Places*, 203–04.

342. Gibbons, *Wye Island*, 12.

343. Jim Rouse, "Jobs, Spirit, People's Impact on Restructuring," *Rouse Company Profile*, June 1, 1971, 2.

344. Ibid., 3.

345. Mark Cohen, "Captain Enterprise," *Baltimore Magazine*, April 1987, 115.

346. MDV.

347. Richard Maine to Michael Spear, June 18, 1976, CA: RGI; 3, b22, f6.

348. Olsen, *Better Places*, 236.

349. WDF.

350. Ibid.

351. Hope Landauer, "Quadrupled Rouse Company Cuts Back," *Baltimore Sun*, February 9, 1975.

352. Rudolph A. Pyatt Jr., "Firm Feels Stronger After Recession Cutback," *Washington Star*, September 14, 1976.

353. MSD.

354. Wilhemina Kelly, quoted in Larry Carson, "Columbia's Residents Question 'New America' Concept," *Baltimore Evening Sun*, April 17, 1970.

355. Ibid.

356. "Hopkins Survey Shows Support for Columbia," *Central Maryland News*, July 20, 1972.

357. Ibid.

358. Tom Graham, "The Balkanization of Columbia?" *Columbia Flier*, February 26, 1976.

359. "A Brief History of *The Columbia Flier*," CA: RGV; Miscellaneous, Columbia Flier, b5.

360. All statistics listed here were taken from the *Rouse Company Annual Reports*, 1972–1979, CA: RGI; 12, Reports Labeled By Year.

361. Hope Landauer, "Columbia Is Now Home to 40,000, Now Site of 140 Industries," *Baltimore News American*, June 24, 1976.

362. Larry Light, "Catching Up Takes Time," *Columbia Flier*, n.d.

363. SU.

364. RB.

365. Ibid.

366. Fran Fanshel, "Hospital Leaders Pull off the Deal of a Lifetime," *Columbia Flier*, March 26, 1998, 22.

367. Conversation with Diane Connelly, February 22, 2006.

368. "Mrs. Z's—The People Place," CA: RGV; Miscellaneous, Mrs. Z's, b20.

369. James W. Rouse to Richard L. Anderson, June 9, 1971, CA: RGI; 3, b1, f10.

370. Jill Hudson Neat, "Masterpiece Theater," *Sun in Howard County*, August 19, 1999.

371. ECK.

372. Mike Giuliano, "Ellen Gets Award for 'Excellence,'" *Columbia Flier*, October 23, 1997, 47.

373. RJM.

374. "The Columbia Pro Cantare Chorus," CA: RGV; Miscellaneous, Columbia Pro Cantare Chorus, b7.

375. Columbia Orchestra Letter, August 31, 1979, CA: RGV; Miscellaneous, Columbia Orchestra, b7.

376. JT.

377. Douglas B. Sands, undated 1971 letter, CA: RGI; 3, b56, f9.

378. "Rouse Policy Change on Minority Employment," *Baltimore News American*, October 21, 1971.

379. "Rouse Asks His Firm to Hire More Negroes," *Baltimore Sun*, November 2, 1971.

380. Karen DeWitt, "Black Business in a New Town," *Black Enterprise*, November 1974, 41.

381. James W. Rouse, Video Interview, 1986. CA: Video Tape, AV545.

382. HC.

383. Tom Graham, "Lake Kittamaqundi: A Crime Scene as Well as an Entertainment Scene," *Columbia Flier*, September 13, 1973, 2.

384. Jean Strohl, "Racism in Columbia Stirs Concern," *Baltimore News American*, ca. 1973.

385. Ellen Theologius, "Black Groups: A Chance for Leadership and an Opportunity to Meet Minority Needs," *Columbia Flier*, December 18, 1975, 19–21.

386. Jean W. Toomer, "Bridging the Gaps: Report of the Black Family Life Project," March–June 1976, 29.

387. Ginny Manuel, "Survival of Black and White in the Next America," *Columbia Flier*, May 12, 1977, 36.

388. Betty Friedan, *The Feminine Mystique* (New York: Dell, 1963), 27.

389. Antonia H. Chayes, Draft Memorandum, January 24–25, 1964, CA: RGI; 3, b76, fWomen.

390. Olsen, *Better Places*, 161.

391. Louise Yolton Eberhardt, "Developing a Support Base for Women," in *Psychology of the Planned Community: The New Town Experience*, ed. Donald C. Klein (New York: Human Sciences Press, 1978).

392. "Women's Center of Howard County Proposal," September 1974, 2. CA: RGV; Miscellaneous, Women's Center; b26.

393. "Announcing the Birth of The Women's Resource Center," March 2, 1973, CA: RGV; Miscellaneous, Women's Center, b26.

394. MMK.

395. "Women's Grants Given," *Columbia Times*, March 5, 1975.

396. Missy Zane, "Center Closes," *Columbia Times*, April 9, 1981.

397. "Telling Our Story: The Women's Center, 1969–1980," Reunion newsletter, May 19, 1990, document provided by Mary Margaret Kamerman.

398. Paul Tadashi Kaneko, "Citizen Participation in Government in New Towns—With Particular Focus on Columbia, Maryland" (unpublished manuscript, 1972), 148. CA: Studies Collection.

399. RA.

400. Maryanne Gallagher, "Columbia's Mini-Constitutional Convention," *Columbia Villager*, March 23, 1972.

401. Columbia Roles Study Committee, "Citizen Participation in Columbia: A Study of Roles, Relationships, and Processes in New Town Governance," September 1972, CA: RG; 3, b20, f3.

402. Michael J. Clark, "Plan to Incorporate Columbia Faces Defeat," *Baltimore Sun*, February 21, 1979.

403. Len Lazarick, "Where Are We Now? The People of Columbia: A Commemorative Magazine," *Columbia Flier*, June 16, 1977, 19.

404. Diane Brown, "Pioneers Throw Their Own Party," *Times of Ellicott City*, September 3, 1977.

405. Rouse, interview with La Noue, 38.

406. Libby Rouse, "The Spiritual Dream Behind Columbia and the Vision Still Hopefully Ahead for It," March 1977, CA: RGV; Miscellaneous, b17, fKittamaqundi Community.

407. Joshua Olsen, conversation with Libby Rouse, January 1, 2003, quoted in Olsen, *Better Places*, 232.

408. Rouse, interview with La Noue, 40.

409. Ibid.

410. *A Larger Vision*, 45.

9. Columbia in the 1980s

411. Walter Herman, "Rouse Shifts Its Development Emphasis," *Baltimore News American*, May 28, 1981.

412. MM.

413. TR.

414. MM.

415. Edward Gunts, "Possibility of Takeover Cloud's Rouse's Future," *Baltimore Sun*, May 20, 1985.

416. Ibid.

417. Herman, "Rouse Shifts Its Development Emphasis."

418. All information here is taken from the Rouse Company Annual Reports, 1980–1989. CA: RGII; 12.

419. BA; DT.

420. Veronica T. Jennings, "Growing Up Brings Painful Changes to Columbia," *Washington Post*, January 15, 1989.

421. BA.

422. MDV.

423. "Is HRD Arrogant, Inflexible?" *Columbia Flier*, October 3, 1985, 24–25.

424. Ibid.

425. Jennings, "Growing Up Brings Painful Changes."

549. Nicholas Bloom, *Suburban Alchemy: 1960s New Towns and the Transformation of the American Dream* (Columbus: Ohio State University Press, 2001), 40–41, 48; Ann Forsyth, *Reforming Suburbia: The Planned Communities of Irvine, Columbia, and the Woodlands* (Berkeley: University of California Press, 2005), 130–32, 224–26, 257–60, 266.

550. Forsyth, *Reforming Suburbia*, 256; HG.

551. BA; Bloom, *Suburban Alchemy*, 49–50.

552. Carrie Brown, "Twin Cities," *Columbia Magazine* (Winter 1992), 31–37.

553. Bloom, *Suburban Alchemy*, 42–43; Forsyth, *Reforming Suburbia*, 131–32, 148–52; DFL.

554. "Town's Health Connected to Village Centers," *Baltimore Sun*, November 28, 2000; Bloom, *Suburban Alchemy*, 41–43, 51–52; Forsyth, *Reforming Suburbia*, 132.

555. "Columbia, Md: Waiting for Godot," *Clothes*, April 1, 1974, 30–37; Bloom, *Suburban Alchemy*, 46, 51–52; Forsyth, *Reforming Suburbia*, 124–29.

556. Bloom, *Suburban Alchemy*, 43–44.

557. BA; WHB; KU; Bloom, *Suburban Alchemy*, 50–51.

558. Bloom, *Suburban Alchemy*, 38–39; Forsyth, *Reforming Suburbia*, 121–22, 156–58.

559. RP; "Drooping Test Scores Spur School Exodus," *Baltimore Sun*, November 25, 2000; "Debate over Decay in Rouse's Columbia," *Baltimore Sun*, November 28, 2000; "Facing Reality in Columbia," *Baltimore Sun*, December 24, 2000.

560. Bloom, *Suburban Alchemy*, 214–19; Forsyth, *Reforming Suburbia*, 238–43; HG.

561. BA; WHB; Bloom, *Suburban Alchemy*, 49–50; Forsyth, *Reforming Suburbia*, 267-69.

562. KTJ; BA; Forsyth, *Reforming Suburbia*, 267–69.

563. Olsen, *Better Places*, 139–41; Forsyth, *Reforming Suburbia*, 111–12.

564. Bloom, *Suburban Alchemy*, 38–39, 48; Forsyth, *Reforming Suburbia*, 142–52, 155–56.

565. Olsen, *Better Places*, 195–203, 223–24, 231–33, 237–39; Forsyth, *Reforming Suburbia*, 238–243; Bloom, *Suburban Alchemy*, 48–50; "Is the Dream Dead?" *Columbia Flier*, December 30, 1999.

566. Olsen, *Better Places*, 195–98; Bloom, *Suburban Alchemy*, 192–93; BA.

567. Bloom, *Suburban Alchemy*, 193–205; BA; WHB.

568. Forsyth, *Reforming Suburbia*, 260–62; Bloom, *Suburban Alchemy*, 195; "Rouse's New Town Now an Adolescent," *Baltimore Sun*, June 15, 1992; BA.

569. Lynne C. Burkhart, *Old Values in a New Town: The Politics of Race and Class in Columbia, Maryland* (Westport, CT: Praeger, 1981); CD; RP; "30 Years and Counting," *Columbia Flier*, June 19, 1997; "Debate over Decay in Rouse's Columbia," *Columbia Flier*, November 28, 2000.

570. Bloom, *Suburban Alchemy*, 99–105; Forsyth, *Reforming Suburbia*, 152–55.

571. "The Settlers Settle Down," *Columbia Flier*, June 17, 1982; "Columbia Falls Short of Rouse's 60s Vision," *Baltimore Sun*, October 10, 1995; "Power to the People in Columbia?" *Baltimore Sun*, January 31, 2000; Forsyth, *Reforming Suburbia*, 152–55.

572. Bloom, *Suburban Alchemy*, 100–08; and Forsyth, *Reforming Suburbia*, 152–55.

573. "Columbia, Md.: Waiting for Godot," *Clothes*, April 1, 1974, 32.

574. Bloom, *Suburban Alchemy*, 247–53; DFL; WHB.

575. Bloom, *Suburban Alchemy*, 247–53.

576. Olsen, *Better Places*, 139–41; Forsyth, *Reforming Suburbia*, 155–56.

577."Columbia's First 15 Years," *Washington Post*, February 27, 1982; DT; Forsyth, *Reforming Suburbia*, 155–56.

578. DT; DB; WHB; Forsyth, *Reforming Suburbia*, 155–56.

579. DLT; "New Towns: Realities Dim Dreams," *Washington Post*, January 12, 1975; "Columbia at 15: Unfinished Business," *Columbia Flier*, June 17, 1982.

580. DLT.

581. Bloom, *Suburban Alchemy*, 49–50.

582. HG; KTJ.

583. Gretchen Elizabeth Schneider, "Re:New(ed) Urbanism," MA thesis, Harvard University, 1997.

584. SB.

Visit us at
www.historypress.net